# THE HISTORY OF THE
# GOSPEL STANDARD
# MAGAZINE

*Edited by B.A. Ramsbottom*

GOSPEL STANDARD SOCIETIES
1985
50 Wales Avenue, Carshalton,
Surrey, SM5 3QU, England

ISBN 0 9510796 0 3

Published by the Gospel Standard Societies
Printed in Great Britain by J. W. Arrowsmith, Bristol BS3 2NT.

# CONTENTS

The Editors (1835–1985)     v
Preface     vi

## Part 1
## THE HISTORY OF THE MAGAZINE

1. The Beginning     3
2. Early Days     7
3. God's Provision     10
4. A Remarkable Editorship     15
5. The Wrapper     22
6. John Gadsby Returns     32
7. Changes and Difficulties     36
8. The Jubilee 1885     40
9. Memories     47
10. The End of an Era     53
11. A Long, Gracious Editorship     58
12. The Centenary 1935     65
13. The Last Years     71

## Part II
## THE LIVES OF THE EDITORS

William Gadsby     79
John M'Kenzie     93
Joseph Charles Philpot     102
John Gadsby     114
Grey Hazlerigg     130
Charles Hemington     144
Joseph Hatton     153
James Dennett     168
Alfred Coughtrey     180
Enoch Feazey     185
James Kidwell Popham     191
John Hervey Gosden     205
Sydney Frank Paul     223

# THE EDITORS (1835–1985)

The early issues from 1835 were edited by William Gadsby and his son John. From 1836 John M'Kenzie and J.C. Philpot helped in the editorial work.

1840–1849    John M'Kenzie and Joseph Charles Philpot (joint Editors)

1849–1869    Joseph Charles Philpot

1870–1877    John Gadsby

1878–1880    Grey Hazlerigg (except June 1879, John Gadsby)

1881 January to June    Charles Hemington

1881 July to 1882 January    Joseph Hatton

1882 February and March    Charles Hemington

1882 April–1884 April    Joseph Hatton

1884 May to July    Charles Hemington

1884 August–1890    James Dennett

1891 January    Alfred Coughtrey (only able to write the Annual Address)

1891 January to June    James Dennett

1891 July–1898    Alfred Coughtrey

1899–1905 May    Enoch Feazey

1905 June–1935 June    James Kidwell Popham

1935 July–1964 June    John Hervey Gosden

1964 July–1970    Sydney Frank Paul

1971–present    Benjamin Ashworth Ramsbottom

# PREFACE

It is said that when Oliver Cromwell was having his portrait painted, he gave strict instructions to the artist to paint him "warts and all." It is in that spirit we have attempted this history of the *Gospel Standard*. We have tried to leave nothing out, to cover nothing over, to give the bad as well as the good. Is not this the way that the Word of God relates its histories?

The book consists of two sections. The first is the story of the *Gospel Standard* from 1835 to the present day. We would emphasize that it is a history of the *magazine*, not the churches or the societies; that is why certain things, even of importance, are only referred to and not thoroughly covered.

The second section contains the lives of thirteen Editors. (The present Editor thought it unwise to include any account of himself.) We have tried, as far as possible, to make these of equal length. But how different the sources! With J.K. Popham we had a book of 350 pages; with Enoch Feazey a mere two or three pages. Some left accounts of their own writing; others nothing. Some accounts were mainly spiritual; others mainly providential. And in some cases we had to glean a little here and a little there.

Apart from the old *Gospel Standards* (especially 1871 where John Gadsby gives a little history), we found Volume 2 of the *The Seceders* invaluable, and also S.F. Paul's *Further Histories of the Gospel Standard Baptists*. Apart from these sources, we have stated at the end of each account if there is any biography of the Editor concerned.

To us this has been a labour of love. We trust we have written in the

vi

spirit of the word: "That in all things He might have the preeminence," and believe we have received special help. We are conscious of
many shortcomings in the work. It was desirable that the history
should be available at least by the end of the year and so, sorely pressed
for time, we feel that in many ways it has been "thrown together" (as
John Gadsby said of the memoir of his father). Yet like him "we hope
that criticism will deal gently with them (these pages); and that it
may please God to make them a blessing to His chosen, redeemed and
sanctified family."

In many ways it is a wonderful story, and we have been compelled
to think of the opening verses of Psalm 44:

"We have heard with our ears, O God, our fathers have told us,
what work Thou didst in their days, in the times of old. How Thou
didst drive out the heathen with Thy hand, and plantedst them; how
Thou didst afflict the people, and cast them out. For they got not the
land in possession by their own sword, neither did their own arm save
them: but Thy right hand, and Thine arm, and the light of Thy
countenance, because Thou hadst a favour unto them."

Our prayerful desire for the future can be expressed in no better
words than those of the apostle: "That the truth of the gospel might
continue with us."

1985                                        B.A. Ramsbottom
                                          Editor, *Gospel Standard*


Special thanks are due to Mr. J.A. Hart for help and advice.

# PART I

# *The History of the Magazine*

# 1

# THE BEGINNING

It was in an England vastly different from our own that the *Gospel Standard* first appeared. The Reform Bill had but recently been passed. Penny postage had not yet been introduced. Most travel was still by horse (or on foot) though the Manchester-Liverpool railway had just been opened. Victoria had not yet become Queen; her Uncle William IV was still on the throne.

The originator (he was always careful to use that term) was a young, energetic Manchester printer, John Gadsby, who described himself as "then in the full enjoyment of gospel liberty and equally full of zeal."

Quite graphic is the way John Gadsby tells of how the first mention of a new magazine was made by him to his honoured father, William, who had not only been pastor for thirty years at the Particular Baptist chapel in St. George's Road, Manchester, but was also well-known and loved throughout the country:

> "I suggested to my father that we ought to have a magazine of our own. He was quite startled, and said, 'Jack!' (he mostly called me Jack), 'you cannot afford it. You will lose money by it.'
>
> " 'I quite expect so,' I replied, 'but that is of no consequence for the Lord has given me a good business, as you know. We ought to have a magazine.'
>
> "He took time prayerfully to consider, and then said, 'Well, if you begin, I will try and help you, and I hope our labours will not be in vain.'

"Now, without his help, I could not have commenced. He, therefore, was the founder. I was only the originator."

So on August 1st, 1835, a new little magazine of twenty-four
pages, costing twopence, issued from an obscure printing works in
Newall's Buildings, Market Street, Manchester.

The question was: "What name should be given to it?" and
eventually the *Gospel Standard* was fixed upon, "not because it was
ever intended to be set up as a standard to measure by, but as a
standard, or banner, unfurled for the gospel." At first it carried the
sub-title, "The Feeble Christian's Support," but after some time this
was dropped, seemingly just by being overlooked.

William Gadsby himself wrote the opening address to the new
readers in which in uncompromising language he declares the sacred
truths on which the magazine had been founded:

"In our labours, we hope ever to keep in view the following things,
and to vindicate them, in all their bearings, whether men will hear, or
whether they will forbear:

"That there are Three Persons in the One-Undivided Jehovah — the
Father, the Son, and the Holy Ghost: that each Person in this blessed
Three-One God are equal — equal in power, and in glory, and in love
to the church; the love of the Father being displayed in Election, the
love of the Son in Redemption, and the love of the Holy Ghost in
Regeneration and the glorious things arising therefrom, and connected
therewith:

"That in eternity Jehovah, foreseeing even the most minute circumstance and event, chose to Himself, in Christ, a people whom He is
determined to save with an everlasting salvation, and who shall show
forth His praise; while the rest, being left to the hardness of their
hearts, must inevitably perish in their sins:

"That nothing short of the divine power and energy of God the Holy
Ghost in the heart of a sinner will make him spiritually repent — all
other repentance being, like Judas', fleshly:

"That wherever the blessed Spirit begins His work of grace in a
sinner's heart, He will perfect it, it being not in the power of Satan or
men to wrest one soul from His hands:

"That His blessed Majesty will daily lead His quickened children
into the mystery of the iniquity of their carnal nature, and into the
glorious mystery of God in Christ, as suited to and designed for them,

thus glorifying Christ in their hearts as all and in all, teaching them the deep things of God, and inspiring their hearts to bless the Lord Jesus Christ, that because He lives, they shall live also:

"That the imputed righteousness of Christ is absolutely necessary for the justification of a sinner, and His holiness for sanctification — fallen, ruined, guilty man, by nature as well as by practice, being utterly incapacitated from doing anything towards the salvation of his soul:

"That the gospel, which contains all the glory of all the laws that ever were promulgated from the throne of God, and in which harmonize all the glorious doctrines, promises, and precepts of the grace of God, is the only perfect rule of the believer's life and conduct, everything else leaving him destitute of hope:

"That the ordinance of the Lord's Supper can only be scripturally administered to those who have been made to feel their lost and ruined state as sinners, and who, having been enabled to give a reason of the hope that is in them, and the answer of a good conscience toward God, have been solemnly immersed in the name of the Father, and of the Son, and of the Holy Ghost: and, finally,

"That the Scripture, being the absolute, infallible, revealed word and will of God, is the only standard by which the faith of man can rightly be tried."

At the very beginning the following texts were given in full (later being replaced by the Scripture references) as being a summary of the Editors' position:

"Blessed are they which do hunger and thirst after righteousness; for they shall be filled" (Matthew 5.6).
"Who hath saved us, and called us with an holy calling, not according to our works, but according to His own purpose and grace, which was given us in Christ Jesus before the world began" (2 Timothy 1.9).
"The election hath obtained it, and the rest were blinded" (Romans 11.7).
"If thou believest with all thine heart, thou mayest." — "And they went down both into the water, both Philip and the eunuch; and he baptized him." — "In the name of the Father, and of the Son, and of the Holy Ghost" (Acts 8.37,38; Matthew 28.19)."

William Gadsby included an article written by himself on the first of the texts, signing it "A Soldier." A letter by William Tiptaft appeared; a letter written some years ago to William Gadsby by Ann Sturton; a piece of poetry "On the Gospel Standard"; another poem; various "gleanings" (among others, from Luther, Newton and Burder); and another article "God is Love" from William Gadsby's pen, signed this time "A Lover of Zion."

Initially only 500 were printed, intended for the Manchester congregation and other friends of William Gadsby in Lancashire and Yorkshire. However, the Manchester congregation took almost the lot! So 500 more were printed. Then a demand came from the London chapels, Gower Street and Zoar, Great Alie Street, and other places — so a further 1,000 were printed.

It may be asked: what lay behind the thought of a new magazine? What need was there for yet another? Were there no free grace magazines? John Gadsby's own answer is:

> "There was at that time no periodical to advocate the sentiments which had been for years dear to my father, and which were becoming increasingly dear to me. . . . Dr. Owen's works were lying dormant; Bishop Hall's were known to few; and even Newton's seemed forgotten. . . . It is true there was the *Gospel Magazine*, but that was Church of England, and the editor sometimes not very select in his remarks on baptism. There was also the *Gospel Herald*, but that magazine was a most erroneous one . . . originated by Mr. John Stevens, who was a pre-existarian, and who wrote so violently against my father on the law."

So, as the opening words of the new *Standard* put it, "the little vessel was launched into the wide ocean" — with many fears yet trusting in the Lord and with sincere desires for His honour and glory and the good of His people, those who "sigh and groan and cry for mercy, pardoning mercy, justifying mercy, in the Person, blood and obedience of Christ, for nothing short of this will satisfy their hungry souls."

## 2

## EARLY DAYS

The new magazine was received with much interest and affection by God's people and soon was circulating, with increased sales, throughout England. A people had been prepared and, like good ground, were ready to receive the good seed.

William Gadsby himself had been preaching to large congregations wherever he went, both in country districts and also in London, where a warm welcome always awaited him. Likewise the sinner-abasing, Christ-exalting ministry of the two Lancashire weavers that Gadsby had baptized, John Warburton and John Kershaw, had had a marked effect. Since 1810 John Warburton had been pastor at Trowbridge, Wiltshire, and since 1817 John Kershaw at Rochdale in Lancashire. These two men, likewise, could fill the large London chapels on their periodic visits. Under such preaching a people had been raised up by God who could not be satisfied with light or formal things. They wanted divine realities. Burdened under a sense of guilt, they longed for Christ as their only salvation and, deeply tried and exercised, often in much poverty, they cried out for a ministry that entered their pathway and fed their souls.

It would appear that the general run of Baptist preachers had become dry and formal with a strong touch of legality. Though still, at least outwardly, adhering to a Calvinistic creed, their preaching did not satisfy the needs of these living souls. The strong insistence on duty was little help to those who mourned over their helplessness.

"True religion," wrote John Gadsby, "had so greatly fallen that, though there might be some who preached the doctrines, there were few who preached them in an experimental way, with the dew and savour of the Holy Spirit. There was little or no distinction made between those who held the doctrines in their judgment merely and those who, having been condemned in their consciences as breakers of God's holy law in thought, word and deed, lost and ruined apparently beyond hope, felt their need of those doctrines, and realized the soul-humbling and Christ-glorifying power of them in their hearts."

The power, value and savour of the ministry of Gadsby, Warburton and Kershaw (and their friends), and the reason why it was so attractive, was well summed up by an old, esteemed Baptist church member when he heard William Gadsby for the first time:

"I really must say he is the best preacher I ever heard in my life. I was never so blest in my soul under any minister before. *He does not preach a new gospel*; it is the old gospel brought forward in a way so blessedly calculated to meet the cases of the Lord's tried family that I would have you to go and hear him for yourself."

As on William Gadsby's first visit to Manchester thirty years or more before, there were few present in the morning, a fair number in the afternoon (as word spread of the nature of the ministry) and a packed chapel at night.

This, then, was the way in which the ground had been prepared for the reception of the new magazine.

But there was opposition. Fifty years later John Gadsby was to recall:

"I think I may fearlessly say there never was in the whole world another magazine started which met with so much opposition as did the *Gospel Standard*. Arminians and Mongrel Calvinists of all grades were most furious against it, and the children of Ashdod were foremost in their assaults.

"But," he continued, "God was on our side, and it was in vain they tried to swallow us up. 'Fear not; I will be with thee,' was our encouragement, and I for one was never left to have the slightest doubt of our success."

But the new magazine was also made profitable to some who had never heard the truth preached.

Out in Cheshire lived two sisters who were dairy farmers. They had never attended anywhere but the local parish church where the vicar was a stranger to the truth. Yet under the power of the Holy Spirit's work these two ladies had been brought to feel the burden of their sin so that though they found no profit under the preaching, they could heartily join in the prayer book confession, "Lord, have mercy upon us, miserable sinners."

The vicar often called at their little farm to talk to them, telling them they should not be so serious or their minds would be affected. They knew he was wrong somewhere, but how and where they did not know.

Well, one Saturday they had been as usual to the Manchester market selling their butter and eggs when, as they went along Shudehill, they happened to pick up on a bookstall some magazines that said on them: "The Gospel Standard; or, Feeble Christian's Support." They looked at each other. Both wondered what "Gospel Standard" could mean.

However, they bought the lot and eagerly began to read them as soon as they reached home. They could not understand the "address" in the first issue; but when they came to William Gadsby's "The Blessedness of the Hungry," their hearts and eyes were opened. Their hearts leapt for joy at the wonderful things they read. How they thought their vicar would rejoice with them!

But no! When he saw the name of Gadsby he solemnly warned them against him. They could not argue, but they knew they had found what their souls had longed for.

The following Saturday they called at John Gadsby's offices in Newall's Buildings and told him their own story.

This, then, was one of the first encouragements. But soon it was to be followed by another. At Wilmslow, about twelve miles from Manchester, lived a tall, striking-looking man with only one eye. The only people he knew were the Methodists, but feeling his great need, as they explained various points and told him what to do, he would exclaim, "If you're right, then I'm wrong!"

This man also week by week came to the Manchester market and, again, in the mysterious providence of God, a *Gospel Standard* came into his hands. He, too, called at John Gadsby's office telling him that the new magazine had made things plain to him. Taking a few copies home with him he caused quite a stir by putting them up for sale in the window of his house.

"So mightily grew the Word of God and prevailed."

# 3

# GOD'S PROVISION

God's timing is always perfect. It was August 1835 when the *Gospel Standard* was launched. The following month saw two events take place, seemingly unconnected, about two hundred miles apart, which in the divine purpose had an intimate part in the history of the new magazine.

On Lord's day, September 6th, at Blackburn, Lancashire, a young Scotsman was baptized. His name was John M'Kenzie and he had been excommunicated by the Independents in Preston for believing and teaching the doctrines of grace. He had been a travelling pack-man, and the following year was appointed pastor over a Particular Baptist church in Preston.

Then, on September 13th, a young clergyman, who had just seceded from the Church of England, was baptized in the little chapel at Allington, Wiltshire, by John Warburton of Trowbridge. His name was Joseph Charles Philpot and he was to have probably more influence for good on the *Gospel Standard* than anyone else. An Oxford M.A., Fellow of Worcester College, he had ended his ministry in the established church at Stadhampton the previous March. "Have I not made a good exchange?" he said, "an easy conscience for a galled one, liberty for bondage, worship in the spirit for worship in the form, and a living people for dead formalists."

The two had never heard of each other, but for the next decade and more, until M'Kenzie's early death in 1849, they were destined to work together as joint Editors of the *Gospel Standard* and never had a single difference.

John Gadsby himself wrote of this:

"Some persons may call all this chance; but I view it as a most remarkable providence that, just at the very time that it was put into my heart to arrange for commencing this magazine, two men who were subsequently to take so invaluable a part in its management should be called out, simultaneously as I may say, from the people with whom they had so long stood connected. Of Mr. M'Kenzie I had never heard, and I had only heard of Mr. Philpot in an indirect way. Mr. Tiptaft was supplying for my father in the autumn of 1834, and often visited me at my office. One morning I gave him a letter which was addressed to my care for him. 'O!' he exclaimed, 'it is from my friend Philpot! I have no doubt the Lord will ere long bring him out [of the Church of England]; and I shall be glad to see his Reasons for coming out, as he says my Fifteen Reasons are very poor.' When Mr. Philpot had come out, I wrote to him, asking him if he would lend a helping hand in the publishing of the magazine. He replied he was too much engaged to think of it; but if he did help, it would be writing the Reviews. He, however, wrote several short pieces before he wrote a Review. I believe the first Review that he wrote was of *Warburton's Mercies*, in April, 1838."

Of Mr. M'Kenzie's connection he continued:

"I do not know the exact time when I was first introduced to Mr. M'Kenzie, and when he enlisted in the *Gospel Standard* service; but I believe it was early in 1836. In the church books at my father's chapel at Manchester there is an entry, July 1st, 1836, that he (Mr. M'Kenzie) should be asked to supply on August 28th; but he preached there on a Tuesday evening some weeks prior to this, and slept at my house. From that time a union existed between us that was never ruffled, and which I humbly trust will never be dissolved."

So we find these two eminently godly men assisting with the editorship of the magazine. J.C. Philpot at first wrote reviews and later the Annual Address. Other reviews were written by William Gadsby and John M'Kenzie. By 1840 Mr. M'Kenzie and Mr. Philpot had become sole joint Editors and in that year found themselves constrained to relieve John Gadsby of all editorial responsibilities except "the wrapper." (This title "the wrapper" has always been used for the outside pages of the *Gospel Standard*, largely consisting of the list of chapels and ministers, advertisements, and at times even spiritual pieces and poems.) For the next thirty years John Gadsby had no control over the "body" of the magazine.

But things were not always smooth in the early years. William Gadsby reviewed Philpot's famous sermon *The Heir of Heaven Walking in Darkness* in May 1837, and though approving of it, added:

"Nevertheless, we do frankly confess that we think a little more expression of the glory of Christ; of what God, in His rich grace, has made His people in Christ, and what they derive from Christ; and of the way in which the Holy Spirit draws them from self to Christ, would have been an additional glory to the discourse. Still, we consider the work well calculated for much good in this day of blasphemy and rebuke."

This hurt Mr. Philpot, and who would have expected a statement like this from him (of all people): "You will find I can hit the *Standard* as hard as I have hit —?" In after years he more than once told John Gadsby, "I have often thought your father was right."

In 1838 Mr. Philpot severely criticised a sermon by William Nunn, minister of St. Clement's Church, Manchester. He said, "A man who talks in this way knows nothing experimentally of either law or gospel, and can never spiritually have felt either the one or the other."

This grieved the Gadsbys, for Mr. Nunn was a dear friend of theirs. (John's sister, Phoebe, when quite young, had been brought into gospel liberty under his preaching.) John Gadsby wrote:

"My father did not approve of this. I can, as it were, see him now, sitting in his rush-bottomed wooden armchair, attentively listening while I read the piece, now and then smiling, and at last exclaiming, 'Poor, dear man! If Nunn had not been in the Church, this would never have been written.' And at first he objected to the insertion of the article, as he highly esteemed Mr. Nunn; but at last he said, 'Let it go. It will do for him (Mr. Philpot) to reflect upon by and by.' And most assuredly he (Mr. Philpot) did reflect upon it, and more than once referred to it with regret."

It was in 1838 that Mr. Philpot's celebrated reply to the question,

"What is it that saves a soul?" was published. Many times has it been republished in pamphlet form, only the last year or so in the U.S.A.

After J.C. Philpot and John M'Kenzie were established as joint Editors, John Gadsby used to send the pieces he received to Mr. M'Kenzie who marked them: 1. Good; 2. Moderate; 3. Rejected; and then returned them. This continued till his death when Mr. Philpot undertook the task. He, however, only selected "number ones," and these were very sparing.

In 1840 Mr. Philpot summarized the first years of the new magazine:

"If spiritual hearers in bondage to a letter-preacher have, through us, seen his leanness, good has been done. If men and works of truth have become wider known, profit has been communicated. If a bond of union amongst experimental people throughout England has been originated or continued through us, good has been effected. If secret encouragement has been given, through us, to champions of truth, if we have ever blown the coals or turned the grindstone so as to give their spiritual weapons a better temper or a keener edge, our publication has not been issued in vain. And if truth in our pages has stirred up and made manifest enemies, if that which has been crushed has broken out into a viper, and if experimental and heaven-sent ambassadors have been more widely separated from doctrinal preachers of the letter, our correspondents have not written, nor we published in vain. But we need every encouragement to keep our heads above water, and in the strength and name of the Triune God of Israel do we hope still to continue our publication."

Thus under the blessing of God, the curiously contrasting gifts of three such different men, as John Gadsby, John M'Kenzie and J.C. Philpot were used for the establishing of the new magazine and, as beautifully expressed in *The Seceders*, to make it "a rich storehouse of that divine teaching usually known as the doctrines of grace, and of authentic spiritual experience." Yet all were, in varying degree, consumptive invalids.

In less than six years the *Gospel Standard* had attained a monthly circulation of 7,400 copies; in another six years it had reached 9,000. Because of this, and the prosperity of John Gadsby's business, it was decided in 1845 to move both printing and publishing offices to Bouverie Street, London, E.C.

But in 1844 the honoured founder, William Gadsby, had passed to his eternal rest. For some time he had had no editorial responsibilities himself. On August 12th, 1849, John M'Kenzie followed, choked to death by the bursting of a big blood vessel in one of his lungs. His thirteen years of conscientious service had helped to tide the *Gospel Standard* over the dangers of its beginning. John Gadsby, showing signs of a lung infection and beginning to spit blood, had been driven to winter abroad in 1846. Henceforth there were numerous journeyings to the Middle East and even to the U.S.A. While still superintending its commercial needs, the spiritual part of the magazine was to be left to "men more deeply taught and better educated than himself." Yet *The Seceders* confesses: "One cannot rate too highly his services to the *Gospel Standard* during the first critical years of its existence." But it continues: "It almost looks as if providence having endowed John Gadsby with the wonderful instinct for choosing the right men to act for him, had then thought well to fill him with that 'wanderlust' that craze for travel, which kept him elsewhere."

And the care of the *Gospel Standard* from 1849 to 1869 was left in the hands of J.C. Philpot.

# 4

# A REMARKABLE EDITORSHIP

It was during the editorship of J.C. Philpot that the *Gospel Standard* really became established — established in two ways.

First of all, the pattern (which has generally been followed ever since) developed: a monthly sermon; spiritual letters; doctrinal and experimental articles; book reviews; hymns and poems; and obituaries. What a feature these obituaries have been over the years — accounts of men, women and young people who have lived and died in the faith; their hopes and fears, their sinkings and risings, and in many cases their triumphant deaths! Rich and poor, well-known and unknown, from all parts of the country — it has been said that no other magazine has ever had a feature like this.

It will be noted that news items, reports of anniversaries, religious "tit-bits" have always been jealously excluded.

But, secondly, the *Gospel Standard* was established as a magazine of character and value. (How many even today with delight pick up the bound volumes dating from J.C. Philpot's editorship!) Here was a most remarkable thing. A highly learned man, an Oxford M.A., writing for a readership for the most part poor and unlearned, those able to read having received only the bare rudiments of education. But the deepest truths, the most profound doctrines were, by him, opened up in such a sweet and simple way that month by month the magazine was looked forward to by those who, perhaps, never read anything else apart from their Bibles.

J.C. Philpot's reviews are rather unusual. They are not reviews in the strictest sense of the word. Rather does he take a book as "a peg to hang his thoughts on." It is the *subject* rather than the *book* which is his concern. So his readers were introduced to a multitude of subjects which otherwise would have been entirely unknown to them. It is not surprising that after his death these reviews were published in two volumes, along with his answers to the various enquiries which from time to time were sent to him.

Perhaps, especially, his "meditations" were the most profitable (apart from his well edited, carefully revised sermons, which are still being published today — ten volumes in the past twenty years). Such themes as the sacred humanity of Christ, the Person, offices and work of the Holy Ghost, the first chapter of the Epistle to the Ephesians, provided a field for his remarks.

And the magazine became known and loved throughout the world. Settlers in Australia, soldiers in the Crimean War, emigrants to the United States, alike looked forward to its publication month by month.

There was also controversy. (J.C. Philpot on one occasion referred to about twenty pamphlets being written against him in the course of a single year.) The great controversy came to a head in the 1860's. A number of Strict Baptists had begun to deny that Christ is eternally the Son of God. They contended that the term "Son" refers to the office which He undertook in the covenant of grace, and that He is not the Son in His divine nature.

J.C. Philpot saw the tremendous danger of this — that not only was it a departure from truth and a dishonouring of the Son of God, but that also it was an assault on the whole doctrine of the Trinity. There had been rumblings of this controversy as far back as 1844 when Mr. Philpot had written: "To my feelings, the real, true and proper Sonship of Christ shines with such a ray of light through the New Testament that I could no more give it up than I could His blood and righteousness. Nay, I consider the denial of it to be a serious and dangerous error and not very far removed from that passage, 'Whosoever denieth the Son, the same hath not the Father.' "

This controversy continued till 1860 when it was accentuated by a sermon preached by William Crowther at Mount Zion Chapel, Hitchin, on March 7th. Mr. Philpot, in reviewing this sermon, and afterward extending his review, most graciously, ably and scripturally defended the eternal Sonship of the Lord Jesus. He also made it plain that this was the orthodox view which the church of God had always held.

A magazine named the *Earthen Vessel* took up the controversy, publishing articles and letters in defence of Mr. Crowther's position denying the eternal Sonship.

It was as a result of this controversy that those Strict Baptist churches which adhered to the doctrine of the eternal Sonship separated from all other Strict Baptists who either denied or in any way deemed unimportant this vital doctrine. This is the reason why our churches have been known as Gospel Standard Strict Baptists.[1]

J.H. Gosden, speaking at the centenary of the *Gospel Standard* in 1935, said of this:

> "Early in Mr Philpot's editorship, he was led by the Holy Ghost very clearly to enunciate the one great doctrine which identifies us and separates us from all other Strict Baptists. I refer to the doctrine of Christ's proper, natural, unbegun, eternal Sonship."

J.C. Philpot's own comments on his editorial work were:

> "Let men think or say what they will, editorial work is no ordinary work, especially when some measure at least of grace and gifts, as in the case of the *Gospel Standard*, is required. It is not for me to speak of myself or of my qualifications, even were I called upon to magnify my office; but this I think must be plain to most minds, that as all private Christians are not fit to be ministers, so all ministers are not fit to be Editors. There are men in the church of God of deeper and richer experience than myself, and more able ministers of the New Testament, who are no more fit to be Editors than I am fit to drive an express train on the Great Western. Some measure of literary ability and of the use of the pen, which can only be acquired by practice, is necessary; and as some men are good for six sermons who might not be good for six months, so a man might be good for six months' editorship who might not be good for six or sixteen years. There must not only be a gift, but, as in the case of the ministry, a living spring to feed the gift, if a man is to go on year after year without drying up. Judgment also and discretion are required, and a willingness and ability to work month after month with undeviating regularity; for the press, like the two daughters of the horseleech (Prov.30.15), is ever crying, 'Give,

---

[1] The whole subject is thoroughly dealt with in S. F. Paul's *Historical Sketch of the Gospel Standard Baptists*.

give', and must be fed almost to a day. But I forbear. As no man knows the cares, toils and anxieties of the ministry but those who are in it, so no one but an Editor knows the cares, toils and anxieties of editorship."

And again:

"None but Editors know what is required to conduct a periodical with any degree of success; and none but a spiritual man can know how these difficulties are increased when there is a desire to carry it on for the glory of God and the good of His people. Many may read my reviews, addresses, or meditations, and think, perhaps, that all I have to do is to sit down some evening, and knock them off in an hour or two. If I could so knock them off, they would not be worth reading. I do not mean to say that the Lord might not pour in a blessed stream of divine thought and feeling into my soul, and supply me with a similar flow of words to give them utterance. Bless His holy name, I am not an utter stranger to this, and perhaps some of my best pieces have been written in this way and under this influence. But these are rare seasons, and I am not looking for what I may call miracles every month. No.

"As also of late years my mind has been directed to some of the deepest and most important points of our most holy faith, I have proportionally shrunk from hasty, superficial writing, not only as knowing how easily a slip may be made with the pen unless carefully watched, but as feeling that for the sake of the glory of God and the good of His people I was bound to set before them only such provender as had been winnowed with the shovel and the fan.

"But apart from this, I am for the most part but a slow composer; and as upon such subjects as have lately occupied my pen want of clearness of thought and expression would be a serious defect, what I write has to be well thought out, and very carefully read and re-read, and revised both in manuscript and proof. I generally give to my work my best hours in the day, that is, when my mind is most clear, my heart most warm, my soul most alive, and my spirit most prayerful. Often and often do I lay down my pen for want of the right thoughts, the right feeling, and the right flow. But, taking one month with another, I generally consider that my editorial work takes up the primest and best hours of the first fortnight.

"I say nothing about what comes from my pen. Let others judge. But I may say this, that, bad or good, worthless or profitable, it costs me a great deal of labour, care and anxious revision, with prayer and supplication before and after, that what I write may be made a blessing to the church of God.

"But when that part of my work is done, other remains almost as difficult. Pieces have to be selected for insertion for a future number, ill-written manuscripts to be read, and those only chosen which seem to have some life and power, savour and dew upon them. Then comes the reading what is called 'proof,' that is, printed matter, which has to be most carefully gone over, not only that no printer's errors may escape correction, but that no erroneous, inconsistent, unbecoming expression may creep in.

"But it is not worth while to go through all this work, or do more than allude to the anxiety, responsibility, and constant stretch of mind which all this entails. Most of our literary men, and especially Editors, die in the prime of life, worn out with what is called 'brain-work'; and I look upon myself as a miracle that I have gone on for so many years with a very weak body and doing so much work, both ministerial and editorial, and yet retain my mental faculties so far unimpaired."

At times there were difficulties with John Gadsby, though for the most part the two worked harmoniously together. One disagreement was concerning which ministers' names should appear on the wrapper, Mr. Philpot thinking the list should be confined to well-known men, Mr. Gadsby thinking that they should refuse none who were accepted by the churches of truth. Another was that Mr. Gadsby wished to throw the magazine open to the writings of many good men still alive while Mr. Philpot preferred to confine it to just a few living men along with the writings of those who were now dead.

But the chief disagreement came through a misunderstanding. In 1864, when J.C. Philpot resigned his joint pastorate at Stamford and Oakham, John Gadsby opened a testimonial fund in the pages of the *Gospel Standard* for the Editor. This deeply grieved Mr. Philpot, who never wanted to benefit financially, and especially at the expense of the poor.

John Gadsby said, "Without consulting him, I advertised for subscriptions for a testimonial to him. I am sure I had the purest of motives; but O how deeply I had to regret it!" Later Mr. Philpot wrote to him: "I believe your motive was good."

However, from this latter difficulty, two things emerge. We learn a little of the Editor's salary. Up till 1855 he received nothing at all, except an occasional £10 to give to the poor. In 1855, because of increasing family expenses and a reduction in his income, he received £30 a year, increasing to £50 in 1860, £55 in 1863, and £60 in 1864, and finally £100.

But also, J.C. Philpot at this time gives his own little account of how and why he became associated with the *Gospel Standard*:

The *Gospel Standard* was started by Mr. John Gadsby, then resident in Manchester, in August, 1835. I had withdrawn myself from the Church of England in the March of the same year, and had, I believe, become known by report to him through my Letter to the Provost of Worcester College, Oxford, which had been already somewhat widely circulated. But I was not consulted by him about the new periodical, or asked to write or take any part in it, though, if I remember aright, a proof of the opening 'Address' was sent to me to read, which I returned without doing anything to it beyond suggesting one or two insignificant verbal alterations. At the foot of the Address occur the words 'The Editors'; but who they were I never enquired and do not to this day know. I certainly was not present at the birth, nor did I dress the child, or rock the cradle of the infant now grown into a sturdy man. The first volume is now before me; but on cursorily running through its pages I cannot trace any mark of my pen as having contributed any communication to them. Looking in the same way over several subsequent volumes, those for instance for 1836, 1837, 1838, I find that I must have contributed various pieces, some signed by my name, others by my initials, and some Addresses and Reviews, of course anonymous. But at that time I had nothing whatever to do, as an Editor, with the work.

"But the question may be naturally now asked, 'How came you to write Addresses and Reviews when you were not an Editor?' I can hardly answer the question, except that it arose mainly from two reasons, partly from what is commonly called 'good-nature,' and partly from my own activity of mind and pen. Mr. J. Gadsby, for instance, would drop me a few lines asking me to write the New Year's Address, or would send me a book requesting my thoughts upon it. At first I complied with his requests chiefly to oblige him, but when my hand was in, on it ran in those days with a zeal which sometimes, I freely acknowledge, outran discretion. But, as my dear friend Tiptaft used to say, 'If a man has not zeal when he is young, what will he be when he is old?' Do you, therefore, who remember those days forgive me this wrong which I am not now likely to repeat.

"But this occasional writing, and I believe I may add the way in which it was received, combined with the really improved pieces in the *Gospel Standard* from the pens of J.K. and J. M'K, Letters of Warburton, Congreve, etc., increasing the circulation and influence of the magazine, my hands became more and more fastened to the plough stilts; for I became an Editor much as many good men become ministers — by degrees, one step leading to another, till there is no turning back. Still, though thus doing much editorial work, I was not one of the Editors till, I think, about the year 1840, when some circumstances unnecessary to mention convinced M'Kenzie and myself, for both of us had somehow or other got into editorial harness, that it was desirable for us, as we had been for some time the real Editors of it, to assume the name and office, and with it the whole control, he taking the part of reading and selecting pieces for insertion, and I for the most part writing the Reviews, Addresses, etc. Thus much for my being installed into office, which I can only say was not of my desiring or seeking, and to take which I should not have consented, but for a desire, I hope, to carry it on profitably for the living family of God."

It can truly be said that J.C. Philpot's death in 1869 marked the end of an epoch.

# 5

# THE WRAPPER

A very interesting feature of the old *Gospel Standards* was what was known as "the wrapper" — that is, the outside pages.

Month by month a list of chapels and ministers appeared — only five in the first issue (Manchester, Rochdale, Blackburn, Allington and Macclesfield) — but later a long list. The emphasis tended to be on the *minister* rather than the place; perhaps it was even a chapel where the truth was not preached, which had been borrowed for the occasion — sometimes a house or a mill. But over the years this grew into an accredited list of chapels and ministers who signified their agreement with the *Gospel Standard* Articles of Faith.

At first John Gadsby used his own discretion, sometimes challenged by J.C. Philpot; but later the responsibility of the list of chapels and ministers fell upon the Committee of the Societies — though we find James Dennett insisting that the Editor should have the last say.

And then there were the advertisements — fascinating, quaint advertisements of an age now for ever gone. No history of the *Gospel Standard* would be complete without a passing look at these. What an insight they give into life in England in the middle of the last century!

Many were of goods for sale or situations vacant:

Bailiff. — Wanted, a Working Bailiff, a good Ploughman, and one that will take the lead in all things. Not under 38, nor over 50. The wife to attend the poultry and dairy. No family. One that can read and write. None need apply without three years' reference. A house to live in, 16s. per week, £2 extra for harvest. Apply to W. Webster, jun., Waltham Abbey, Essex.

**Winter Boots** — Gentlemen's Extra Strong Clamp Sole Boots, either Balmorals or Side Springs, 16s.6d. Capital Short Wellingtons, 12s.6d., and 14s.6d. Ladies' Excellent Kid Boots, stout double soles, with military heels, 9s.6d. per pair. John J. Rusk,* Family Bootmaker, 53, High Holborn, near Brownlow Street, London, W.C.

*Son of the late John Rusk, whose writings are published in the *Gospel Standard*.

**To Cheesemongers**, &c. — Wanted, an active young man, from 17 to 20 years of age, in a Cheesemonger, Pork, and Poulterer's Shop; who can make himself useful in carrying out, sausage making, or trussing poultry. Apply, personally, any morning before Ten o'clock, at 32, High Holborn.

**General Servant**, — Wanted, in a quiet private family, an experienced General Servant, as good Plain Cook. Wages, £10 [a year], with tea, sugar, &c.&c. Also an active young Housemaid. Wages, £7, with tea and sugar. It is requested that none will answer this advertisement but such as are accustomed to rise early and be punctual. The privilege of attending a Gospel Ministry. Address, stating age and full particulars, to Mrs. B., 10 Regent's Park Terrace. N.W.

## HORNIMAN'S PURE TEA
### SOLD IN PACKETS BY 2280 AGENTS

The Chief Commissioner of the Sanitary Report visited the Docks to inspect the PURE TEA imported by HORNIMAN & CO., LONDON, from having on investigation found that many teas in general use are covered by the Chinese with an objectionable powdered colour which is drank when the tea is made. Horniman's Green is a natural dull olive, — not bluish, — the Black is not intensely dark; by importing the leaf *uncolored*, the Chinese cannot disguise and pass off as the best, brown flavourless sorts, consequently, Horniman's Pure Tea is strong, delicious, and wholesome. Price 3s.8d., 4s.0d., & 4s.4d. per pound.

There were medical books for sale:

Price 3d.,

**Homoeopathy and Sir Benjamin Brodie.** By C.H. Marston, M.D., London: Turner & Co., 77, Fleet Street. Two copies sent free for six stamps, by Dr. Marston, Devizes.

"Dr. Marston has given the best treatise which has yet appeared." — Notes of a New Truth.


Now ready, limp cloth, lettered, price One Shilling, post free, "Man and His Many Changes" or 7 times 7. A popular Treatise on the domestic management of certain disease incidental to us during our Sevenfold State; with advice to Mothers on the treatment of themselves and their Offspring. By George Corfe, M.D., M.R.C.P., (Lond.,) M. & L.A.C., (Lond.,) Physician to the Western General Dispensary, and late Senior Resident Medical Officer at the Middlesex Hospital.

London: Houlston & Wright, Paternoster Row.


For some years included with the wrapper, was a "supplement" (often pink in colour) where at times a choice poem or a gracious obituary would appear.

And then there were John Gadsby's little pieces to the readers:


A friend says "people complain of our spelling the names of their friends wrong in the 'Standard' and on the wrapper. Dunk was called Duck, Howitt was called Howe, and so on." This is not the fault either of the compositor or of the corrector of the press. If our correspondents wish names to be spelt correctly, they should write every letter in the names carefully. A compositor can often read words when badly written, as he can make them out from their connexion; but this cannot be done with names. Dunk badly written might easily be mistaken for Duck. In looking over MSS. before giving them out to the compositor, J. Gadsby has sometimes to cast a piece aside altogether, as he could more easily decipher the hieroglyphics of ancient Egypt than he could the writing of such piece. It is said of Dr. Johnson that his writing was sometimes so bad that he could not read it himself. A compositor once asked him what certain words were which were in some of the Dr.'s copy, when the Dr., finding he could not make them out, exclaimed, "It is my business to write, *yours* to read." And really some of our correspondents seem to think the same. However poor a hand a person may write, he should always make his letters distinct, especially in names of persons or places. Some, when writing names, will imitate print; and this is a very good plan: D u n k.

Owing to the illness of the compositor who for some years has superintended the making up of the *Gospel Standard*, and the unavoidable absence of the publisher, an advertisement crept into our last No. which the publisher would not have admitted on any terms whatever, had it come under his eye, as he is averse to quackery in every shape. The advertisement referred to is headed, "To the Afflicted," and purports to be from a Mr. Stockwell, who asks, "the afflicted" to send him a stamped envelope for advice. J. Gadsby advises them to do no such thing, though he fears the advice will be a month too late, some persons having probably, ere this, been silly enough to comply with Mr. S.'s request.

Now follows an advert for a girls' school:

**Claremont House, Robertsbridge.** — Mrs. and Miss Elliott's Seminary for Young Ladies (little boys taken under 10 years). Terms, board and general tuition, comprising instruction in English Grammar, History, Geography, Writing, Arithmetic, plain and ornamental Needlework.

|  | £ s. d. |  | £ s. d. |
|---|---|---|---|
| Boarders, per quarter . | 4 10 0 | Under 6 years . . . . . . . | 3  0 0 |
| Under 10 years . . . . . . | 4  0 0 | per quarter |  |
| Weekly Boarders  . . . . | 3 10 0 | Music . . . . . . . . . . . . . | 0 10 0 |
|  |  | Laundress . . . . . . . . . . | 0 10 0 |

The duties will recommence on the 20th January, when they will be happy to meet with two or three more boarders. A quarter's notice required before the removal of a pupil.

Month by month there were details of John Gadsby's lectures on his travels in the east:

**Eastern Life**. — Mr. J. Gadsby's Illustrations of Biblical and Oriental Life will (D.V.) be given as follows: STOCKWELL (National Schools, Chapel Street, Stockwell) — Feb.3,4,7; PECKHAM (Rosemary Branch) — Feb.11,12,14; ST.LUKE'S LUNATIC ASYLUM, City Road, Special Lecture to the Lunatics — Feb.13; CANTERBURY — Feb.17,18,20; SYDENHAM (New Lecture Hall) — Feb.24,26,28; SALISBURY — Mar.4; WILTON, Mar.5; GLOUCESTER — March 6; STROUD — March 11,12,13; TEWKESBURY — March 18,19,20; READING — March 25,26,27.

The Lecture announced last month for Feb.14th to the Aged Pilgrims will not be given, one having been given last month in lieu thereof.

And how strange today does the sale of little souvenirs from the east seem!

Olive Leaves, mounted on a neatly engraved Card, with miniature representation of Jerusalem, embellished with Palm Trees, and Olive Branches with Fruit, for framing, or for the Portfolio, One Shilling each, post free. These leaves were taken by Mr. and Mrs. John Gadsby from Trees on the Mount of Olives, on March 12th, 1860. Every leaf will be authenticated. WATER from the RIVER NILE and WATER from the RED SEA, in small Bottles. One Shilling each. SAND from the ARABIAN DESERT, that "great and terrible, howling wilderness;" (Deut.i.19; xxxii.10;) SAND (fine as Charcoal Powder) from the TEMPLE of ABOU SIMBEL: (See "Wanderings," Vol.I.,371, and Vol.II.,269;) Small SHELLS from the RED SEA; and SHELLS from the TOMBS of BENI HASSAN. (See "Wanderings," Vol.I.,382, and Vol.II.,342.)

Any of the above may be had in small bottles or packets, Sixpence each, except the Shells from the tombs of Beni Hassan, which can only be had in packets. Every bottle and packet will be authenticated, having J. Gadsby's initials on the label. The packets, both of Sand and Shells, may be sent by post, free; but the bottles can only go in parcels.

The whole proceeds will be given to the Aged Pilgrims' Friend Society.

Orders to be sent to J. Gadsby, George Yard, Bouverie Street, London. E.C.

But best remembered of all are the adverts that almost seemed to "belong" to the *Gospel Standard* — Mazawattee tea and Congreve's Elixir!

Possibly of more interest than anything else are the details of the "cotton famine" in Lancashire in the 1860's and the attempts to raise money to help in the acute distress. Altogether £2,000 (a vast sum in those days) was raised, a wonderful witness to the practical effect of the truths of the magazine in the hearts of the readers:


**Distress in Lancashire.**

"My dear Friend, You have set me a task that I cannot perform, that is, to send you a list of our poor. We have so many either entirely out of work or employed only two or three days a week that I cannot tell the number. Besides those who reside in the town, there are many at Heywood, Whitworth, Milnrow, Small Bridge, &c. I am astonished at the patience of the poor sufferers. The Lord has been good in sending me help for the poor. Our Middleton friends say that had it not been for what I have been able to send them, they would have been quite fast. I have now got into the *third* £100. Whatever you may send me shall be faithfully given. The friends at Charlesworth and Blackburn are also in great distress.

"In love to you and yours,

"Rochdale, June 12th."                                  "John Kershaw."


Clothes have been received from Miss Hunt, Croydon; Mr. Fox, Reading (new); Miss Laurie; Mr. Hankey, Upper Street, Islington; Miss Bullivant, Birmingham.

Contributions in money may be sent to Mr. Philpot, Stamford, and Mr. J. Gadsby, Bouverie Street, and Cowley, near Uxbridge. Clothes and linen will also be very acceptable, which may be sent to Mr. Gadsby's Office in Bouverie Street, London.

| By J. Gadsby – | | | | By Mr. Philpot – | | | |
|---|---|---|---|---|---|---|---|
| A Friend | 0 | 3 | 0 | H. M. Leicester | 5 | 0 | 0 |
| Miss Hunt, Croydon | 0 | 13 | 0 | W.C. | 5 | 0 | 0 |
| Mr. S. Adams, Dudley | 0 | 5 | 0 | J.C. | 5 | 0 | 0 |
| Mr. J. Smith, Strand | 1 | 1 | 0 | Mr. Healey, Ashwell | 1 | 0 | 0 |
| Mrs. Sutton, Judd Street | 0 | 5 | 0 | Mr. Turner, Shurdington | 1 | 0 | 0 |
| Clarissa | 5 | 0 | 0 | F.G., Oakham | 0 | 2 | 6 |
| A Servant | 0 | 5 | 0 | P.J., Do. | 0 | 1 | 0 |
| T.B.M. | 0 | 10 | 0 | Friend, Barking | 0 | 10 | 0 |
| A Well-wisher | 2 | 10 | 0 | Mrs. T., Leamington | 0 | 10 | 0 |
| Two Friends, Worcestershire | 0 | 9 | 0 | Friends, Brighton | 0 | 10 | 0 |
| A Real Friend and Lover of the | | | | Do., Stamford | 0 | 10 | 0 |
| Lord's Poor | 0 | 5 | 0 | Anonymous, by P.O. Order | 1 | 0 | 0 |
| Miss Corney | 2 | 0 | 0 | Friends, near Stamford | 0 | 10 | 0 |
| Mr. Tyrrell, 55, Edgware Road | 1 | 1 | 0 | Do., Oakham | 1 | 0 | 0 |
| H. Clayton, Esq., Reading | 0 | 5 | 0 | Do., do | 0 | 2 | 0 |
| Mrs. Cook, Mortlake | 0 | 5 | 0 | Do., Gower Street | 0 | 10 | 0 |
| Mr. D. Forman | 0 | 10 | 0 | Miss Newbury and Pupils, Oxford | 1 | 0 | 0 |
| Collected by Mr. Wickham | 0 | 18 | 0 | Miss Aikin and Pupils, Billesdon | 0 | 11 | 6 |
| One to whom the Lord has lent a | | | | Friend, Whissendine | 0 | 2 | 6 |
| little | 0 | 5 | 0 | Friend, Oakham | 0 | 5 | 0 |
| | | | | George W. | 0 | 10 | 0 |

**Haslingden.** — "I divided the money last night. Some of them were without clogs, others without coals, and others short of food. May the Lord bless the givers. I do think, brother, if you had been with us, you would have been glad to see with what thankfulness they received it." — R. Hargreaves.

**Charlesworth** — "The money has been divided among our poor members, who firmly believe the Lord put it into your heart to remember them at this trying time, which it has been for about eight months. One large factory (Sidebotham's) has been stopped altogether during that time. Wood's has been working only three days a week, and they usually employ between 3,000 and 4,000 hands; and Summers's, with about 2,000 hands, only two days a week. The greater part of our members are factory operatives, and have been greatly tried in temporal affairs. Many of them have scarcely food enough for the support of their bodies. Our clergyman has had £100 sent to him from the General Fund; but it has been chiefly given to those who attend Church" – G. Drake.

**Preston** — (The late Mr. M'Kenzie's Chapel) "I began to give the money to the friends at the chapel today, and most thankful they were for it, both to you and the kind donors and to Him who influenced you. One old man said it was 'just in the nick of time.' 'But,' said he, 'He that orders all things knows best when to send it.' Yet this old man, and such as he, do not make known their troubles, but are real honest, striving Chrisitians." — T. Howarth.

**Bury** — After describing a most distressing case of a family, Mr. Kay writes: "Most of the others had saved a little money (out of their earnings), say from £5 to £20; but through work falling off the last year, it is all becoming exhausted, and several of the mills are stopping altogether."

**Rochdale**. — "Your letter came to hand, informing me that you had £10 for the poor, and that you hoped to have a little more and some clothes. This was good tidings, as my poor-fund had got down to £3. While I was at Blackburn attending the funeral of our friend Horbury, there came to my house at Rochdale a cheque for £5 14s. 6d.; and I have been to the bank and got silver for it; so that I can begin to give it where it is so much needed. The distress increases. I met John Bright, M.P., this morning, as I was coming from the bank. He asked me what was to be done for the poor as there was no prospect of any change in America [the source of the cotton supply]. I told him my friends in the South were sending me help for my poor friends, and that I had been to get a cheque cashed and had the money in my pocket. He seemed pleased, and gave me two sovereigns towards the collections for our school, which are to be next Monday."—J. Kershaw.

**Great Boughton, Nr. Chester**. — "It gives me great pleasure, on the behalf of a small Particular Baptist church meeting here, to forward to you, for the relief of the distressed Christians in Lancashire, £5. Two years ago, one of the friends proposed for each to contribute at the table of the Lord as we should be enabled with a view of opening a more public place (we now meet in the house of one of the friends) for the worship of God; but we are willing to leave that matter now in the Lord's hands, trusting that in due time He will provide for our wants in that particular, and we devote our little stock to the more pressing wants of His own dear people in distress.

"Yours in Christian love, Signed on behalf of the Church,

July 15th, 1862.                              "Samuel Ledsham."

When some twenty years ago a book was being published on social conditions in Lancashire in the 1860's, the author found the *Gospel Standard* wrappers a mine of information. In fact, so highly were the wrappers (and supplements) esteemed that not only were bound volumes of the *Gospel Standard* issued year by year, but sometimes a volume of just the supplements and wrappers!

# 6

# JOHN GADSBY RETURNS

The death of J.C. Philpot at the end of 1869 meant that all those connected with the *Gospel Standard* in its early days were now gone — except for one, John Gadsby. John Gadsby now took up the reins of the editorship himself for the next eight years.

Generally speaking he left the writing of articles to others. Thus the New Year Addresses were written by such men as Charles Hemington of Devizes while Grey Hazlerigg of Leicester contributed some beautiful pieces on the Song of Solomon. The one difficult time was when Mr. Gadsby's wife and daughter died in 1872, and he almost filled the *Gospel Standard* with the letters of condolence he received.

When J.C. Philpot died the circulation of the *Gospel Standard* was 14,000. When John Gadsby laid down the editorship this had risen to 17,500.

It was in the early years of his editorship that a society was formed in connection with the *Gospel Standard*, a society to help aged or infirm ministers or ministers' widows. It has been recorded of the founder of the *Gospel Standard*, William Gadsby, that "benevolence was his element. He felt that it was more blessed to give than to receive, and he acted up to what he felt." This same spirit seems to have prevailed among the ministers concerned with the *Gospel Standard* in the generation after his death.

However, in 1872 a few friends became concerned that something in the way of regular help should be given to aged and infirm ministers, and to minister's widows. The first step seems to have been when Joseph Hatton, pastor at Smallfields and Redhill, wrote to Mr

John Gadsby, enquiring if something positive could be done. Mr. Hatton's letter read:

> "It has been suggested to me that at present the widows of deceased ministers are so unequally provided for, it would be a good thing to raise a general fund and invest it, and grant allowances therefrom. . . . Now, my dear friend, will you aid, or, I mean rather, will you take the lead in this thing? I do not know anyone who could better set it going and keep it so."

John Gadsby's delight in organising being equalled by his generosity, he gladly lent his support. Further encouragement was given by the beloved Francis Covell of Croydon with the result that a meeting was arranged for 11 o'clock on 17th May, 1872, at the Lecture Hall of the Sunday School Union, 56 Old Bailey. 64 persons were present and a committee of 25 was set up. Eleven committee meetings were held during the first year, another General Meeting held at which the Articles of Faith and Rules were introduced, and the Committee was increased to 34 members. At the end of the year it was reported that grants amounting to £75.7s. had been made. (During the centenary year, Aid Society grants were £3,354.)

Five years later on October 12th, 1877, another Society, united to the first, was formed at a meeting held at the Hall of the Sunday School Union once again, specially to help those in need who were not ministers.

Years later, speaking of these two Gospel Standard Societies, the Aid Society and the Poor Relief Society, Mr. Calcott of Coventry stated:

> "One cannot but believe that the founders of them were moved by the Lord to lay their foundations. Their growth has been steady, but strong; their branches have spread themselves more or less over the whole denomination; their fruit has been always seasonable and copious. It reaches to the valleys where many poor widows spend lonely hours; it enters the sick room where the infirm and afflicted lie lingering out their few last days on earth; it comes as a refreshing breath to the aged, who are bowed beneath a weight of years. Many praises and much gratitude have ascended to the Lord for the providential springs that have flowed from these two Societies."

A little magazine, the *Friendly Companion*, had been commenced by John Gadsby in 1857, intended to be taken alongside the *Gospel Standard* as a magazine for younger readers. After two or three years this had ceased to exist. However, in 1875 Mr. Gadsby revived the *Friendly Companion*, which has continued till now (1985).

Up till 1878 both the new magazine and the *Gospel Standard* were personally owned by John Gadsby. In that year by a most generous Deed of Gift he handed them and all profits arising to the Committee of the recently formed Societies. So they continue till today.

In the December issue of 1877 John Gadsby's farewell appeared. Part of it reads:

"Dear Brethren and Sisters in the Hope, I trust the sure and certain Hope, of Eternal Life — As stated on our last wrapper, my connection with the *Gospel Standard*, so far as any responsibility as to its contents goes, ceases with the present month. It is upwards of forty-two years since, in the providence of God, I was led to originate the work; and I have never ceased, I believe, to give it my best attention as the proprietor and publisher.

"But though, from the first, my labour has not been small, yet it has only been during the last eight years that I have felt to have any peculiar responsibility. I have had much to contend *for*, much to contend *with*. Of anything I have said, when contending *for* what I believe is the truth of God, if I except one little word, which got in a wrong place on the wrapper for Feb., 1875, I have nothing to retract; when contending *with* those who were opposed to me, I have used some harsh expressions, which I regret. When contending *for* the purity of our pulpits, especially for the Gower Street one, which was erected mainly through the instrumentality of my never-to-be-forgotten father, I have felt incompetent to express myself in terms sufficiently strong, without stepping over the bounds of prudence; when contending *with* those who seemed determined to introduce error into those pulpits, though in a new and white dress, I feel that 1 Cor.4.7 had not its due weight upon my mind. But, when I have found some publishing discourses, as different in character to those previously issued as light is from darkness, and which had the effect of misleading, I have felt it hard to restrain myself.

"When I look at the piles of encouraging letters I have received for years, I am half inclined to think I am committing a sin in resigning my trust; but when I look at those who are to succeed me, my fears vanish; for I believe, with God's blessing, the magazine, in their hands, will lose none of its usefulness.

"To my dear friends, Hatton, Hazlerigg, Hemington, and Taylor, I owe a deep debt of gratitude for the kind aid they have rendered me; to you, my brethren and sisters, who have supported me and indulgently passed over my infirmities, I am no less indebted; nor must I pass over my many kind correspondents; to my enemies, who have written and spoken against me, I tender my thanks, for they have been the means of making me more watchful and prayerful than, perhaps, I should have otherwise been; but, above all, the God of all my mercies, I would if I could, every moment of my life, bless and praise His holy name for all His goodness and mercy vouchsafed unto me. Goodness and mercy have followed me, and still follow me, all the days of my life. Praise the Lord!

"I had no thought of writing this until we were preparing to go to press and, therefore, have written in haste; but in true accordance with the feelings of my heart.

"Yours in Love, for the Truth's sake,

"Nov. 15th, 1877.                                                    J.Gadsby."


Two things specially gratified John Gadsby as he contemplated these years.

One was the thousands of pounds he had been able to raise for the Aged Pilgrims' Friend Society (founded in 1807 to provide homes for the Lord's aged people) by his strong advocacy of its claims in the *Gospel Standard*.

The other was the selection of hymns first published by his father in 1814. When the copyright fell into his hands, he reduced the price, added a supplement and advertised in the *Gospel Standard*. Later, at J.C. Philpot's suggestion, Hart's hymns were added, then another supplement of hymns selected by Mr. Philpot, and again the price was reduced. This was kept before the readers of the *Gospel Standard* in the advertisements. Who can say what an inestimable blessing Gadsby's Hymnbook has been to the church of God?

# 7

## CHANGES AND DIFFICULTIES

Following John Gadsby's Deed of Gift there came a difficult time in the history of the *Gospel Standard*. There was now to be the first *elected* Editor, chosen by the Committee of the Societies. Their choice fell on Grey Hazlerigg, an eminent minister for whose large congregation Zion Chapel, Leicester, had been built.

Concerning his appointment (January 1878) Mr. Hazlerigg wrote:

> "There is one who can bear witness that for some years we declined the post of an Editor when offered to us, feeling perfectly satisfied with a less prominent position, and the liberty we had to communicate our writings from time to time to the churches. We long shrank from the post of Editor feeling our insufficiency for it."

For some time Mr. Hazlerigg had written with acceptance, and this continued during his editorship. However, in 1879 John Gadsby objected to something Mr. Hazlerigg had said, done or written and took the magazine back into his own hands, editing the June number himself, revoking his Deed of Gift. This he claimed authority to do.

It would appear that almost all (if not all) the godly ministers on the Committee sympathized with Mr. Hazlerigg. In fact, there was talk of them establishing a new magazine of their own.

Dr. Doudney, as Editor of the *Gospel Magazine*, published a letter from Mr. Hazlerigg to the readers of the *Gospel Standard*. It is a gracious letter, in which he asserts his one desire to seek the glory of God and the good of His people.

Mercifully the breach was healed, at least outwardly, and Mr. Hazlerigg continued, the *Gospel Magazine* publishing a second letter which made it clear that "those contentions which so threatened the peace and prosperity of a part of Zion have been happily and properly ended". Mr. Hazlerigg stated that his helpers, Joseph Hatton and Charles Hemington, would really now be Co-Editors.

Of these sad happenings Mr. J.K. Popham wrote over fifty years later (he was a Committee member at the time):

> "After the death of our God-given teacher and leader J.C. Philpot, the magazine was carried on by its owner, John Gadsby, and various helpers, until he very generously gave it to the Societies then formed, and managed by a Committee chosen by himself; an Editor was elected, and for a time things went on smoothly. But the cause of God and truth has never prospered without arousing the enemy of God and man to some distinct effort to interrupt and, if possible, destroy it. Exalt Christ, and you provoke the devil. It is grievous when professors are instruments. So it was in regard to the first elected Editor of the magazine. Soon a cry was raised, and charges of teaching error were brought against him. Then commenced unseemly disputes, quarrels, wars of words, separation of friends, and grievous wounding of the simple godly in the churches. The charges were proved to be groundless, but bitterness continued. True it was found to be that 'a brother offended is harder to be won than a strong city'. So malignant were the disputants on one side that a new magazine was contemplated on the other side. To all this I, then in my spiritual youth, was a witness; in fact, against my earnest wish and protest, I was made a party. But Mr. Covell and other ministers were constrained to come to the front and support the falsely-accused Editor. All this grieved and vexed the Holy Spirit, and tender sheep and lambs were scattered. With the first elected Editor to the last immediately preceding myself, I was acquainted, and some of them honoured me with their friendship and correspondence; thus I had knowledge of some things which will die with me. However, the *Gospel Standard* lived."

So John Gadsby did *not* revoke his Deed of Gift after all.

However, at the end of 1880 Mr. Hazlerigg, who had taken up his office again, resigned on account of ill health. He wrote:

> "We have now for many years written for this magazine. During the

last three we have edited the periodical as responsible Editor. We are now through illness quite unequal to the work of writing. The grasshopper has indeed become a burden. That which was a pleasure has become a pain. We find it therefore imperatively necessary for a season to lay aside the responsibility and labour connected with editing the *Gospel Standard*. We hope we have not been unduly influenced by any wish to improperly spare ourself either trouble or anxiety. We would not shrink from either labour or suffering in the cause of Christ and our service to the churches. No! It is from necessity that we act as we are doing. At the present time we feel *physically* quite unfitted for the labour and anxiety which conducting the magazine would bring upon us."

The gracious Charles Hemington of Devizes temporarily stepped into the gap for the first six months of 1881. In fact, on three such occasions altogether was he willing to do this — perhaps *made* willing is more correct as, though a man of much grace and ability, he begged to be relieved, feeling his insufficiency. Nonetheless he is not the least of the Editors.

Joseph Hatton of Smallfield, Surrey, was then appointed. He was a preacher and pastor much used and much loved and, though a man of no formal education, had taught himself a measure of Greek. Few of those who followed J.C. Philpot were men of learning. Their education had been but small yet, with God's blessing, they had improved themselves. One of Mr. Hatton's outstanding pieces was a review on the dangers of the new Revised Version of the Bible.

Mr. Hatton's editorship was terminated by his death on April 16th, 1884 (Mr. Hemington having helped out for the months of February and March in 1882 when Mr. Hatton was ill). Only a few months before, he had written in his New Year Address:

"With some of us it is certain that our days are growing few; and with every one of us, in the end, the course of life will be arrested; and we must pass away to be gathered to our fathers. But there is a solemn question left unanswered by vast numbers, which attaches itself to the action of exchanging worlds: 'But man dieth, and wasteth away; yea, man giveth up the ghost, and where is he?' (Job 14.10). Yes, *where is he*? Where is it he has gone when he has entered eternity? Momentous question, both to our readers and ourselves; for 'where the tree falleth, there it shall be' (Ecclesiastes 11.3)."

Following his death a poem was published, "A Great Man Fallen in Israel," which commenced:

"A great man's fallen in Israel, —
Let Zion put her mourning on, —
A man made wise to handle well
Truth's weapons 'gainst the "wicked one";
Whom gracious doctrines, held by grace,
Made strong to labour, suffer, bear;
Whose Master's image saints may trace,
Throughout his life of faith and prayer."

Again Mr. Hemington was prevailed on to stand in the gap — for May, June and July — until an Editor could be appointed. This was James Dennett, minister of Frederick Street Chapel, Birmingham, where his ministry was instrumental in gathering a large congregation. Indeed, one of Mr. Dennett's problems during his editorship seemed to be the difficulty of his large pastorate *and* his editorial work. Mr. Dennett continued till the end of 1890, when he resigned through ill-health. (Almost immediately he resumed the office for a period of six months when his successor was taken ill.)

Mr. Dennett's sermons are still valued today — their beginning invariably the same: little or no introduction; a three or fourfold division of the text set out; and then straight into the subject.

During his editorship he contributed a most profitable series of "Thoughts on the Book of Ruth," afterwards published in book form.

It was also during his editorship that a very happy and notable event took place, the Jubilee of the *Gospel Standard* in 1885.

# 8

## THE JUBILEE 1885

"If, in 1835, the human founder of the *Gospel Standard* had been told that, in 1885, there would be a gathering three times in one day of from 1,500 to 2,000 people, from all parts of the country, east, west, north and south, to express their love for the truths that magazine advocated and their gratitude to God for putting it into the hearts of any to establish it, he (the said founder) would have had a more than usual smile upon his countenance; but it would have been a smile of incredulity. We say 'more than a usual smile'; for the dear man always had a smile upon his face; so much so that with the printers he went by the name of 'Old Smiler.' " So wrote John Gadsby of one of the happiest days in his life.

Wednesday, September 23rd, 1885, was a remarkable day. It is estimated that over 3,000 different persons altogether attended the Jubilee Services of the *Gospel Standard*, visitors coming from every part of the country, and even a few from America. (There were about 1,700 present at each service.) The meetings were held in the Memorial Hall, Farringdon Street, London, built on the site of the old Fleet Prison where many of the godly martyrs had been imprisoned before their martydom. Emphasis was made that it was for the same truths that the day's gatherings were taking place.

The November *Gospel Standard* reported: "It was a pleasing, almost overwhelming sight, to behold the vast assembly which congregated together." The large congregation "had assembled on this extraordinary occasion to celebrate the Jubilee of a magazine which, during the fifty years of its existence, has been the means of spreading the truths of the gospel almost all over the world. We never before attended so large a meeting where such quietness and becoming order were maintained."

The venerable A.B. Taylor, over 80 years of age, William Gadsby's successor as pastor, journeyed down from Manchester to take the morning service. Hymns 610 ("Precious Jesus! Friend of sinners"), 536 ("Behold a scene of matchless grace") and 720 ("Endless blessings on the Lamb") — all Christ-exalting hymns — were sung.

Mr. Taylor preached ("with extraordinary vigour") from the words: "He must increase" (John 3.30). He mentioned that the year he began to preach was the year the *Gospel Standard* was commenced so it was his Jubilee also.

At the afternoon meeting John Gadsby himself took the chair. It seemed a remarkable thing that the originator of a magazine should be present fifty years later at its Jubilee. The Secretary of the Gospel Standard Societies read Isaiah 41.10-16 and Psalm 124, after which Mr. William Knight, of Haywards Heath, prayed.

John Gadsby, who had not been well, did not give the Chairman's address himself, but a paper that he had written was read. In it he gave a brief history of the magazine up to that time. He concluded:

"The Lord has, I believe, kept me firm to the truths He has taught me and made dear to me, caring for no man or any set of men, false and slanderous as their tongues may have been. May He still keep me, and may the Blessed Spirit influence you at all times to reject all compromises and admit only of the Shibboleth upon which the magazine was founded. And also to pray for me that, so long as He has a work for me to do, He will give me will and power to do it, and at last, in the sweet enjoyment of the peace of God which passeth all understanding, give me an abundant entrance into that kingdom where the wicked cease from troubling and the weary are for ever at rest."

Several addresses followed. The first was by James Dennett, pastor at Birmingham, and Editor of the *Gospel Standard*. His emphasis was on the truths for which the magazine contended: 1. God's everlasting, free, unmerited love. 2. Predestination. 3. The work of the Lord Jesus Christ. 4. The work of the blessed Spirit. 5. God's pardoning mercy in the soul. He concluded by stating that though the gathering was so large, there were only two classes of people present, the righteous and the wicked, closing with a solemn warning.

The next speaker, Charles Hemington of Devizes, was introduced as one who was always willing to help the *Gospel Standard* in time of need. He said:

"It is now more than thirty years since I first took the *Gospel Standard* in. I was then a young man and a young minister, and I can say with all good conscience that God frequently in those days made the *Gospel Standard* a blessing to my soul. The more I read it the more eagerly I looked forward to every forthcoming number, hoping I might find something for the good of my soul in it. I did not take up my religion, faith, or experience from the *G.S.* I trust that God, our covenant God, had given to me, through the teaching of the blessed Spirit, a little religion, a little faith, and a little experience, and that little often made me say, when I read the *G.S.*, 'I hope, by the grace of God, to live and die by the truths advocated in this periodical.' "

He, too, went on to emphasize the truths for which the magazine stood, and so did the speaker who followed, Eli Ashdown, pastor at Zoar Chapel, Great Alie Street, London. Among other things also, he said:

"The *Gospel Standard* has been edited by some of the most honourable and honoured men that have lived in our day. The late dear Mr. Gadsby's writings have been blessed to many. John Rusk, how discriminating, searching, and yet savoury are his pieces! Dear Mr. Warburton's sermons, and Mr. Philpot's meditations on different branches of our most holy faith, together with his meditations on the humanity of our blessed Lord and Redeemer, also concerning the eternal Sonship. God blessedly helped that dear man. Some may say, 'We might have had his writings without the *G.S.*' Perhaps we might, but most likely we should not. God works by means: 'Counsel in the heart of man is like deep water,' and sometimes it is long there. There are two things that will draw it out; namely, 'A man of understanding' or foes will draw it out; and it was the latter that drew out of good Mr. Philpot truths that will live in the church of God as long as she is on earth, and then she will bask in the glory of them for ever. Then again, the obituaries. What a blessing they have been made to the church of God!

"I can look back many years, for we have had the *Standard* in our family from the very first. It was brought into my father's house by a friend, and taken in regularly from that time, though we were not Baptists, but what is called Huntingtonians; yet the truths in the *G.S.* were what my mother and father cleaved to, and since I have been concerned about the welfare of my soul, through mercy I have cleaved to them also, and I have felt that if all the men on earth forsook such truths as the *G.S.* has maintained, God helping me, I would hang to them whether I get to heaven or not, whether lost or saved; for they are the truths I love."

An old friend of John Gadsby, James Knight of Southport (not a minister) spoke a few words, followed by Edward Porter, minister at Allington. Both spoke of the wonderful effect their first introduction to the *Gospel Standard* had upon them. Mr. Knight said, "I never wish to be happier in heaven than I was at that time"; Mr. Porter, "Through reading the *G.S.*, I was instructed in the Word of righteousness."

The last speaker was Alfred Coughtrey of Nottingham, later Editor of the *Gospel Standard*. He said:

"I find that the truths that the *G.S.* has contended for from the first are the truths of the Bible; and though I knew not the late W. Gadsby, Warburton, M'Kenzie, or Philpot, yet 'the memory of the just is blessed.' Their praise is in all the churches, and the creeping things by which they were assailed have crumbled into dust."

Then he spoke of some of the vital doctrines: especially, man's ruin through sin, and the vital necessity of redemption by the blood of Christ, and the regenerating work of the Holy Ghost. At the end he touched on a practical note (so dear to the founder, William Gadsby):

"One of the greatest privileges you can have, you rich men and women, is to give to the poor: 'Ye know the grace of our Lord Jesus Christ, who, though He was rich, yet for our sakes became poor, that we, through His poverty, might be made rich.' If the grace and spirit of this kind of thing gets into our hearts, doubtless it will open our pockets. We cannot give to a better cause than the cause of Christ."

The doxology was sung and Mr. William Vine of The Dicker closed the meeting with prayer.

The preacher at the evening service was John Warburton (the

younger) of Southill. His text was: "Lift up a standard for the people" (Isaiah 62.10). His divisions were:

    I.  What *Standard* it is we lift up.

   II.  The *Standard-bearers*

 III.  The people for whom it is to be lifted up.

 IV.  The effect.

In a remarkable sermon he spoke essentially of Christ:

"This, then, is the blessed Standard we lift up, and we lift Him up as the eternal Son of the eternal Father, with power to pardon sinners. I say before this immense assembly, for I am not ashamed to own it, that He is the eternal Son of the Father, equal with God in every respect; and woe be to that man who lives and dies denying this grand and glorious doctrine! 'If ye believe not that I am He, ye shall die in your sins.' What! Commit my soul into the hands of anything short of Deity? God forbid! Therefore, I lift Him up this evening to you, poor, needy, helpless and worthless sinners, who feel you are lost and undone and want to feel the power of the Redeemer's blood and have tried all manner of ways to get ease, travelled here and there, up and down; you have wept, vowed and made resolutions, but could get no ease, comfort, or peace to your soul; and Satan has said, 'You will be lost as sure as you are born, and to hell you will go. You have no ground for hope. God has cast you off.' No, no; the Redeemer still lives: 'I am He that liveth, and was dead; and, behold, I am alive for evermore, Amen; and have the keys of hell and of death' (Revelation 1.18). Beloved, our Jesus, our Brother, is God, and

'With heaven and earth at His command
He waits to answer prayer.'

What grand language is that!"

Of the magazine he stated:

"Now there is another standard, and that is the *Gospel Standard* that comes out every month. Says one, 'That is a periodical common with the rest that profess the doctrines of grace.' Of course it is; but I tell you I am not ashamed to own it. There is not a periodical afloat that is to be compared to it in any sense. I have watched it for forty years, and it bears the mark upon it of genuine things, and its Editors have been men taught of God, who have discarded everything dishonouring to

God. Look at that standard-bearer, dear Mr. Philpot. He was something like a man going with strength into the battle-field; everything
gave way before him. Or like a man with a scythe going into a field of
thistles, and when one after another rose up against him he took his
pen, like the man with the scythe, and down they fell.

"Since then God has raised up others. Our present Editor, I believe,
knows the truth, and he has conducted the periodical in an honourable
way and manner. May the Lord uphold him.

"I think it an honour to say I knew the late dear Mr. Gadsby, and
had the pleasure of conversing with him. My father and he lived
together in unbroken friendship. When the G.S. was first started my
father brought a few copies of it to London with him, and it was
approved as maintaining Christian doctrine and experience, and all the
cannons that were fired at it were only like so many pop-guns and a
pop-gun captain could no more batter down the firm Tower of London
than they could overthrow the *Gospel Standard*. Here it is to this day,
and we are met together to commemorate God's goodness in watching
over it for fifty years. I am glad to see such a noble company met
together to uphold it, and I can recognize friends from various parts."

It is stated that "such was the stillness of the congregation that one
might almost have heard a pin drop".

The hymns that were sung were 592 ("Mighty to save is Christ the
Lamb"), 582 ("High beyond imagination") and 631 ("The Lord
Himself be with you all"). After Mr. Warburton had spoken a few
words of prayer, the whole assembly united in singing hymn 730
("All hail the power of Jesus' name") — incidentally, the only hymn
during the day not composed by William Gadsby.

Of the singing John Gadsby commented afterwards:

"I never before heard anything like it, either at home or abroad.
There was no choir, no organ, nor any other instrument; none was
needed. The whole assembly formed the choir. As had been arranged,
Mr. Hinton, the Chairman of the Committee, with his good, strong
voice, led off, and before the second syllable had been sounded, the
whole congregation seemed to have heartily joined in.

"D.S. said, in a letter to me, there was one old woman near to him
'who had a voice like a nightingale, and she sang with all the powers of
her soul, as though she desired heaven and earth to hear'. And the same
may be said of hundreds of others. Referring to the closing hymn (730)

after prayer, Mr. Standeven, of Patricroft, supplying on September 27th at Southport, said he could not express the effect it had upon him; and he, being used to Lancashire singing, knows well what good singing is. And J.K., another Lancashire man, says, 'It was (may I say?) awfully grand; and this was felt by all I have conversed with.' Not grand merely because of voices, but because so many hundred of hearts seemed to be in it."

# 9

## MEMORIES

The time round about the Jubilee was a time of looking back. Memories were aroused, and many came forward with a testimony of what the *Gospel Standard* had meant to them in former days.

John Gadsby, having laid down the *Gospel Standard*, was now (since 1880) editing his *Christian Monthly Record*, and delighted to publish these memories of former days. We give one or two examples:

The following is by E.W., of London:

Regent's Park, Nov. 30th, 1885.

As I have been a reader and a lover of the "G.S." since 1850, I feel bound to add my poor testimony as to its value and usefulness in my own case.

I was brought out of the Established Church, and told by a minister of it that I had committed schism by so doing, which was a great sin. I did not understand exactly what it was: but well remember feeling if I had, God had pardoned it, and to His blessed Majesty was I desiring to look for grace to be led and guided into all truth. I never opened my mouth to confess my sin to any one, but groped my way along.

This was the time a friend began to read to me pieces from the *Gospel Standard*, which I commenced taking, and from that day to this it has been a true friend, to comfort in affliction, to counsel in trial, to cheer when faint; yea, next to the Word of God it has been the *one book* my soul has loved, because the Lord has made it a great blessing to me in numberless instances.

This by S.P. also of London:

> 1, Camden Houses, Peckham Road, S.E., Dec. 2nd, 1885
>
> It was at the close of 1849, when on a visit with my late mother, at Lewes, that a friend gave her the whole of the numbers of the "G.S." for 1848. It was at the close of that year I had been convinced of my state as a sinner, at the grave of an only sister, and was then working hard under a legal ministry for my own salvation. I read these *Standards* over and over, but felt I never could believe that was the way. The terrible war they stirred up in my spirit I can never forget. The pieces that most struck me were John Rusk's; one on the Lord's Prayer in particular. For two years I had a continual battle between the truths they contained and my self-righteous spirit. However, it was the means of opening my eyes to the pure truth of God; for which I can never feel grateful enough.
>
> From that time till the present I have taken in the "G.S.," and hope to do so as long as life lasts with me; for it has many, many times been made a blessing to my soul.

Another by H.M. of Broyle:

> We have taken the "G.S." for more than twenty years, and can set to our seal that the things brought forward are living truths and have often found savoury meat, such as my soul loves. O, what union have I felt to that dear man John Rusk! What reality, what weight, in such writings and other's experiences of the tried and harassed, and those who are helped with a little help! I often get a crumb and sometimes a feast when the Lord Himself draws near. As in water face answereth to face, so do I see that I am walking in the same steps; yet O how far behind.

The following is by Charles Barnes, the minister:

> We read in the Word of God of "treasure hid in the sand." Now I am about to show how I found treasure hid in the mud. It was about thirty years ago that the Lord laid upon my heart eternal matters, so that the cry of my soul was, night and day, "What must I do to be saved?" I was thus a constant and anxious hearer at Providence Chapel, Cranbrook; and on one occasion, as I was walking up that town, I saw a sheet of paper in the mud. This I picked up, and read, and saw at the top,

*Gospel Standard*. This had such an effect upon me that I was most anxious to see more of it; for I knew not whether it was a volume or a periodical, and I went to the minister who preached to us for information. But I soon found he was not at all favourable to it; and the reason was (though I knew not then) because of baptism, he not holding with that ordinance; and as there were so very few of that people who differed from him, I had some difficulty in getting the work.

But the desire to take it was kindled in me, I believe, by the Holy Spirit, and have it I must. So I went to a stationer's, and he sent for it monthly, and I have continued to take it ever since; and I must and will say I have found it a treasure indeed. I have waited for it as much as a merchant does his ship that he hopes to see come into the harbour, laden with treasure from a distant land; and I believe it has been more to me than the merchant's cargo.

## R. Mayell from Chatteris, Cambridgeshire, wrote:

I have intended for some time past to let you know how I became acquainted with the *Gospel Standard*. I think it was in 1847. I was among the Primitive Methodists, at Melksham, Wilts. I was talking with one of the local preachers (Daniel Harding), about the people who met for worship at Ebenezer Chapel, Union Street, and Daniel said they publish a book called the *Gospel Standard*, quite contrary to the Scriptures. I said, "Do they? It is a wonder some one does not tell them of it." Surely I thought they must be an ignorant lot of people to publish a book contrary to the Scriptures. So I said I should like to see it. Daniel answered, "I will show you part of one." So next time he read me a piece by Mr. W. Gadsby, respecting a poor sinner realizing Christ, as his Brother, Friend, Redeemer, Saviour, God, All in All, &c. I said, "That is good; is it not?" He answered, "But they will not allow us all the chance." However, I went to the bookseller and ordered the magazine, and I now say, "God bless the *Standard*! Let the *Standard* live, and not die; and let not its friends be few." And I now testify there is not a man of the nineteenth century who has stood higher in my estimation than the late W. Gadsby, and I have not seen any monthly periodical that I consider so scriptural and truthful as the *Gospel Standard*.

Then from the *Gospel Standard* itself we have the memories of John Gadsby's old, tried friend, James Knight of Southport:

> My father-in-law was a godly man, and he was acquainted with godly people at Preston. One day he went to Preston, and brought back with him a *Gospel Standard*. This was in the year 1843. At this time I was much distressed in mind, not only on account of owing money and no means of paying it, but my sins stared me in the face; for the Lord had not given me sweetly to feel that my sins were put away. I was now removed from the place where my minister lived, and there was no place of truth for a great distance round about; but if there had been, I had not a second coat to put on my back; therefore my little room used to be my place of worship. When I received the "G.S." and one of the Gadsby's Selection of Hymns I will tell you the effect the reading of them had on my soul. As soon as I read the "G.S." and a hymn or two, the feeling of joy that came over me made the workhouse go out of sight directly; for it would have made no difference to me if I had gone there. I never wish to be happier under heaven than I was at that time. One moment I was on my knees, weeping and praying, then up again singing praises to God. I continued week after week in this state through the things I had read in the "G.S." and Gadsby's Hymn Book. The Refiner was at work removing the dross until He could see His own image. I was lost to everything here below, and was swallowed up in God. I am sorry to say never since that time have I been able to get into that blessed state so fully as then. Another divine says, "I passed out of self into God." This was really the case with me; for as Berridge says, I
>
> > "Dropp'd into His sea outright,
> > Lost myself in Jesus quite."

This was the effect the reading of the "G.S." had on my soul the first time it came under my notice.

And, finally, the testimony of Edwin Porter, minister at Allington, Wiltshire (so intimately connected with J.C. Philpot):

> I purpose to tell you a little about the time when I first saw the "Gospel Standard," now forty-four years ago. I was then a youth, working in the fields not far from where Culham Station (Oxfordshire)

now is. When thirteen years of age I had the "G.S." put into my hands by a labouring man with whom I worked. I found something in it that made me tremble; for I saw it contended for a religion very different to what I possessed, or what I heard contended for in the Church of England where I attended. My father was the parish clerk, and had much to do for the bishop and clergy of Oxfordshire; so you may suppose we were not shown by our parents any of these things. I had some convictions of sin at this time, and when I saw children sprinkled I felt assured it could not be right in the sight of God. Through reading some things in the "G.S." that this poor man put into my hand, I went to Abingdon and bought a Bible, for which I paid one shilling.

I began to read the Word of God to see whether things were so or not, and I put a mark to every chapter that I read, and compared it with what I was taught at church. I soon found that the things they taught us could not be found in the Bible, and when I got to the end of the Revelation I read something very solemn indeed referring to the kingdom of Christ and the glory of Christ, "that there shall in no wise enter into it anything that defileth, neither whatsoever worketh abomination, or maketh a lie"; therefore, to be found amongst those who believed a lie I felt would indeed be terrible. I used to go to God and ask Him to teach me, and to overthrow everything in me that was wrong, deliver me from all iniquity, and save my soul. The Lord was pleased to deepen His work in my soul, and though I did not leave off going to the parish church, I went with a heavy heart ofttimes, till at last the time came when the Lord thrust an arrow into my heart, and gave me grace to apply my heart unto wisdom and seek after Christ; and that which I sought He gave me.

I had been at Culham working with this old man who first gave me the *Standard*, and he could not afford twopence to pay for it, so asked me if I would join with him in buying it. I had been engaged in working for the modest sum of 2s. 6d. a week up to the age of fourteen when it reached 5s., and I was glad to give the man a penny towards buying the *Gospel Standard*. I remember once being at work near the turnpike road, away from all men, and was weeping because I felt so miserable, when the late William Tiptaft and John Kay passed, and I thought if any men in the neighbourhood had true religion they had, for it kept them from all the temptations and from all the outward evils religious men went into. I thought "O if I had but the religion that they have," though I knew it was a religion that was hard to flesh and blood. Through reading the "G.S." I became instructed in the word of righteousness, and was brought to renounce the things I had been brought up in, and go to the Abbey Chapel, Abingdon, and hear that man of God, Mr. Tiptaft, and then it was with me as with the woman of Samaria for I could say, "Come, see a man which told me all things that ever I did in my life."

# 10

# THE END OF AN ERA

Often the latest chapters of a book are more interesting, more exciting, than anything that has gone before. Sadly this cannot be the case with the history of the *Gospel Standard*. Why? For three special reasons:

1. John Gadsby's own "History of the Gospel Standard" (published month by month) ends in the year 1871.

2. *The Seceders* by J.H. Philpot deals thoroughly with many matters involved, but terminates with the death of J.C. Philpot in 1869.

3. The wealth of information given at the time of the Jubilee obviously cannot reach beyond 1885.

So far these have been our chief sources, and now it is like scouring the fields when the harvest is gathered in. Later volumes of the *Gospel Standard* never give the stories, the memories, the details as John Gadsby did.

However, following the resignation of Mr. Dennett in 1890 we come to two short editorships, those of Alfred Coughtrey and Enoch Feazey. Sadly, Mr. Coughtrey was only able to write the editorial when he took office in 1891 and then through illness was incapacitated till June (his place again being taken by Mr. Dennett). In it he had said:

"The sanction of the Holy One, and His continued assistance graciously granted, are indispensable, and will be both my guard and strength. I am bound to say I am for peace; but it must be understood that peace at any price is not intended. The pure truth of God, in all its branches, is the only foundation of permanent union and success.

"There appears to me to be a greater need than ever of union in the ranks of all real lovers of truth; for union, well founded, is strength. No doubt we live in a dreadful day. Errors of every form and shade, suited to all tastes, stalk through the land; and as time threatens to close, the day darkens. The old enemy — that arch-enemy of Christ and His church — lifts up his head today as he has never done since before the Reformation. The diabolonians, as Bunyan speaks, no longer conceal themselves in holes, and wait until the shutters are closed, before they come out: they walk the streets in broad daylight. Anti-Christ fills the land. All classes of professing people, let their names be what they may, all appear to unite in one vast body against the pure gospel of God, and against the true church of God. Brethren, the time is short. The solemn state of things, both at home and abroad, fills the brief period with great importance."

He then continued till the end of 1898 when he resigned owing to ill-health and infirmity. He was pastor at Chaucer Street Chapel, Nottingham, but long before his death he had to give up his pastorate, because of ill health and mental infirmity.

His successor seems to have been a little critical of him, for in his first editorial he suggests that Mr. Coughtrey "could have brought more original matter." Nevertheless, it is clear he was a man both of ability and grace, and his successor nonetheless comments:

"With what firm decision, boldness, and plainness of speech did he lay before us the grand truths of the everlasting gospel, solid truths which came warm from his heart, carrying weight and power with them, many of our readers receiving them with warmth of feeling, and with dew, savour and unction into their souls. There was no halting with him between two opinions; no mixing creature doings with the gracious operations of the Holy Spirit in the hearts of poor sinners; no attempt made to blend man's free-will with God's free grace; no toning down, or chiseling off the rough edges of God's unerring word."

The only occasion when the *Gospel Standard* has ever included a photograph was during Mr. Coughtrey's editorship, December 1893. The photograph, on the front cover, was of John Gadsby in his old age. Mr. Gadsby had peacefully passed away on October 12th, 1893,

almost 85 years of age — the end of an era in the magazine's history.
Much of that issue was devoted to his life and work. With passing
time old controversies and personal differences were forgotten and the
zeal of the originator of the magazine nearly sixty years before and his
wonderful generosity since that time were remembered.

Mr. Coughtrey, in announcing his death, said:

"Our dear friend's religion was such as 'endureth to the end.' He was
no changeling. You do not find him in his writings drifting about, first
from one thing and then to another. The old beaten path and the same
truths, held and preached by his dear father, were those which were
dear to him all through his life to its close. . . .

"The church of God has lost one of her oldest pillars, and one of her
best supporters. His gifts to the Societies in connection with the *G.S.*
alone would make such a sum as few people have little idea of, to say
nothing of his kindness to God's poor people in a variety of ways,
which people know nothing whatever about. . . .

"What Judah said to Joseph about his father's life being bound up in
the lad's life will, I am sure, well apply to our departed friend and his
dear *Gospel Standard*; the lives and prosperity of the two were so
wonderfully entwined that the life of the one seemed indeed to be
bound up in the life of the other; and even to the last he showed the
same earnest and affectionate concern in its welfare."

Shortly after his death the *Gospel Standard* announced the commencement of "The Gadsby Memorial Christmas Fund." This was as
a memorial to the name of John Gadsby and his father, and to send
presents of money to those in need at the end of each year. John
Gadsby had always delighted to do this personally, and it was now
felt, following his death, that something should be done in a regular
way. The "Gadsby Fund" is still extremely useful today.

Following Mr. Coughtrey's retirement, the elusive Enoch Feazey,
of Leamington in the Midlands, was appointed Editor, beginning in
January 1899. We refer to him as "the elusive Mr. Feazey" because it
has seemed impossible to glean much about him. Evidently he was a
godly and much loved man, and there are sermons in print that he
preached, letters that he wrote, references to help received under his
ministry — but concerning his life next to nothing is known.

When John Gadsby died he had written:

"We now have no Mr. Gadsby at the helm of our little bark, the *G.S.*, which is still floating on the ocean of time, and sometimes sailing in rough weather, and in deep waters, against wind and tide; but He that hath mercifully stood by it nearly sixty years, and has kept it afloat for the good of His people, we humbly hope will not forsake the *Gospel Standard* now."

And soon it was Mr. Feazey on whom the burden of responsibility fell. On commencing he wrote:

"Thus, after much care and exercise of mind, and a long discussion upon the important matter at the October committee meeting, it was decided by the majority of friends then present that the appointment be placed in our hands, which has surprised us greatly, as we think there are others among us better qualified for the work, and whose judgment in divine things far surpasses ours. But being assured by the friends who carried on the discussion at the meeting that the best feelings of those present were much in our favour, and being voted to the editorship by a large majority, we have accepted the appointment, but with much fear and trembling, knowing, as we do, our ignorance, weakness, and inability for so important an office. After the result of the meeting was made known to us by the Chairman, we sank fathoms deep in our mind, and inwardly said before the Lord, 'Lord, we need wisdom and understanding from above,' and we feel that it will be utterly impossible for us to attempt such a great work if the Lord the Spirit withholds those heavenly favours from us. Our heart, then, is up to the Lord for His benign blessing to rest upon our soul in this, to us, great undertaking.

"We are somewhat encouraged to hope that the Lord's helping hand will be seen on our behalf, and all needed grace given us, by the fact that we feel much meekness of spirit, tenderness of conscience, softness of heart, and much humbleness of mind as we set out upon our new sphere of labour. And we wish to say that our exercise of mind is great, and our strength for the work is small. But we have been, even thus far, greatly helped in our feelings by the many encouraging letters received from our friends, which we feel to value very much, as they have come at a time when such encouragement is greatly needed."

It is interesting to note that the cost of the *Gospel Standard* was still only 2s. 6d. (12½p) a year, including postage.

The new Editor soon had to witness the death of Queen Victoria, the accession of Edward VII, his illness and the postponing of his coronation — matters briefly alluded to in the magazine.

But on May 11th, 1905, Mr. Feazey very suddenly died. His heart was in his work to the very end and indistinctly, when dying, he said that the proofs he had been correcting must be sent back to the printer that morning. He had gone to bed the night before weak and tired after two days' work on the *Gospel Standard*. (None but an Editor knows the relentlessness of his labours.)

Thus, with the death of Enoch Feazey nearly thirty years of short editorships came to an end. It had been a difficult period; Satan had made many attempts to overthrow the magazine, and to assail the truth. Now the next *sixty* years were to see only two Editors.

Yet one wonderful thing can be said of this trying period with all its changes: there was no deviation from the truth as in Jesus throughout the whole of the period, while the high quality of the magazine was, in greater or less measure, consistently maintained.

Many years later J.K. Popham could write concerning the Editors during this difficult period:

> "In their measure (all) the Editors might have said to their readers, 'Those things which ye have both learned, and received, and heard, and seen in us, do; and the God of peace shall be with you.' "

# 11

## A LONG, GRACIOUS EDITORSHIP

In 1905, after the death of Mr. Feazey, it appears that there was some thought of Edwin Picknell of Redhill becoming Editor, but the choice fell on James Kidwell Popham, pastor at Galeed Chapel, Brighton. His gracious editorship was second only to that of J.C. Philpot.

One special feature of his editorship was the appearance of many of his own beautiful, Christ-exalting sermons. (In the last few years, four volumes of his sermons have been published.)

A new feature was the introduction of many more extracts from the godly Puritan and Scottish divines. Mr. Popham had a close affinity with "the sweet savour of Christ" in the old Scottish preachers, and in those still alive. Also, he delighted to publish pieces by James Bourne and one of his own predecessors, Joseph Hatton.

In 1906, a Mr. Thomas Mallett of Geelong, Australia, bequeathed the sum of £25 to the Editor of the *Gospel Standard* for the distribution of the magazine in Australia. This in turn led to the setting up of a Free Distribution Fund so that free copies could be sent, not only to Australia, but to needy persons anywhere. An appeal for further funds for this worthy cause was published under the title "Sow thy Seed."

Mr Beedel, pastor of the Particular Baptist Chapel, Castlereagh Street, Sydney, was able to testify of good done in Australia in this way:

"Only last week, when at Northwood Asylum, where there are over 1,200 men, one came in with a *Gospel Standard* in his hand, telling me *it had found him out.* He had received it from me some time before; he had read it, and a sermon in it of Mr. Philpot's had been greatly blessed to him. His story touched my heart. . . .

"Another remarkable case I may mention. While distributing among the men at George Street Asylum, Parnatta, one day a gust of wind blew a copy of the *Gospel Standard* into the gamekeeper's office; he opened it and read it, and found a sermon preached at the place in England he came from. Attracted by this, he read it, and it was so blessed to him he could scarcely wait until my next visit, so anxious was he to tell me of it. This gave him a desire for more; and now, whenever I go, not less than four or five copies will suffice; and he affirms it is the best reading he has ever met with. He is evidently a living soul, and is now being watered as never before."

Over the years ever since, this work has gone on in obedience to the Lord's command, "Cast thy bread upon the waters," and only in the last twelve months (1985) a letter has been received from a prisoner in the State Penitentiary in Pennsylvania who, remarkably, had been reading a *Gospel Standard* and wished to purchase J.C. Philpot's sermons.

National events did not pass unnoticed and in 1910 special reference was made to the passing of King Edward VII.

Very soon afterwards the death of two former Editors of the *Gospel Standard* were reported. On June 16th, 1911, at the age of 85, Alfred Coughtrey had died. Almost immediately after laying down the burden of the magazine, he had been unable to preach, so that his tongue and pen had been silent for eleven years, or more.

Grey Hazlerigg died on October 4th, 1912, at the advanced age of 94. It was now over thirty years since he had been Editor, but Mr. Popham published a tribute of high esteem, in which he said:

"It would seem that an archangel cannot be employed in a work so honourable, so glorifying to God, so beneficial to elect men as a true minister of the gospel can. And such a minister was the late Mr. Hazlerigg. To how many he was such is known only to God who sent him and made choice of him, that by his mouth many should hear the word of the gospel, and believe. To all such how beautiful were his feet upon the mountains of divine truths, bringing good tidings, publishing peace, bringing good tidings of good, publishing salvation; saying unto them, 'Your God reigneth,' (Isa. 52. 7). Only those who have heard in such a way, with such power receiving the good tidings of good, can understand the sense of respect, love, and reverence which fills the heart for the messenger of peace. To speak personally, it was my mercy and privilege to *so* hear this messenger of the Lord once. Though it is now many years since, the memory of it is fresh, warm, and pleasant as I write this. The occasion was the annual meeting at Edenbridge. His text was Matt. 6. 9: 'Our Father, which art in heaven,' etc. Powerful was the word, penetrating, assuring, comforting. My state of mind on entering the chapel was one full of fear of rebuke; but mercy wrought by God's servant, and effected a marvellous change. How many now in heaven, how many still struggling on their way thither, could have borne, or could bear a similar, perhaps a clearer, more powerful testimony to the glorious work of some deliverance wrought by the ministry of our departed friend! Such hearings are vastly different from the mere 'hearing well,' so common, bearing, alas, no fruit in the hearer, giving no comfort to a true minister.

"In addition to his preaching, Mr. Hazlerigg laboured with his pen. For some years in the 70's, he edited this magazine. Many articles came from his pen; perhaps, if we judge by what has often been said, the most useful of them being those on Solomon's Song. It may be given to every minister to preach one or two very special sermons; or if he is called to employ his pen in Christ's service, to write one or two pieces for some special and abiding usefulness. Many years ago Mr. Hazlerigg preached and published a sermon on drinking the cup which God gives His children to drink. And from his own observations to us a year or two after its publication, we should conclude that at that time he regarded it as *the* sermon for usefulness. . . .

"And he had the high honour to be counted faithful, and put into the ministry; and God enabled him to exercise it profitably. The love and esteem he had from the poor of this world, rich in faith, were a brighter crown than that honour which properly belonged to him as descending from an ancient and honourable ancestry."

During his early years Mr. Popham had written in defence of the Gospel Standard Articles of Faith as connected with the magazine, the societies and the churches. Later in his editorship he felt constrained to do so again, and publish his original article. William Wileman (1848–1944) had been connected both with the magazine and the Committee at the time that a number of new articles had been added to the Articles of Faith in the 1870's. In 1921 not only did Mr. Wileman attack the articles but also hinted strongly that the motives of the formulators were unworthy.

Mr. Popham, in his explanation of the articles, did not fail to admit that the wording could have been improved; but he contended that these were godly men, concerned for the truth. And these "added articles" appeared at a time when the Moody-Sankey campaign had made its inroads in England.

Concerning William Wileman's account of what took place in 1877, it would bear little weight as historical evidence:

1. Why did he wait over forty years before publishing what he did?

2. Why did he wait till all the other nine men present on the occasion were dead, and so his evidence could not be contested?

Moreover:

3. He was writing as an aged man many years after the happenings; and

4. His article appeared in the heat of controversy. The *Christian's Pathway* magazine was constantly attacking the *Gospel Standard* (on innumerable issues) and this attack on the Articles of Faith, and the way they were drawn up, appeared in this context.

Considering these things, what Mr. Wileman wrote cannot carry too much weight. Indeed in the pamphlet *Workman and Warrior*, a short tribute to the life and ministry of William Wileman written by his son in 1944, the author strongly suggests (pages 7–8) that his father did not really believe the doctrine of particular redemption. It is little wonder, then, that he was not too sympathetic to the *Gospel Standard* or the Articles of Faith.

In 1928 the revised Prayer Book was rejected by Parliament. Though a faithful Dissenter, Mr. Popham was not unmindful of the concerns of the national church. In the *Gospel Standard* he wrote against the new measures which would weaken the Church of England as established by law, and likewise rejoiced when the measure was defeated.

In 1932 came J.K. Popham's own Jubilee at Galeed Chapel, Brighton, the services being reported in the pages of the *Gospel Standard*. At this time the love and esteem in which he was held throughout the churches was evident, and Mr. Popham's appreciation of this respect was published.

During his last years as Editor, the "God-honouring movement" was begun, through the pages of the *Gospel Standard* in 1934. There was a clear call for loyalty to the distinctive position of our churches, a position of separation from all other Strict Baptists who in anyway deemed unimportant the doctrine of the eternal Sonship of the Lord Jesus. Pastors, supply ministers, deacons and churches were called upon to re-affirm their adherence (as a weakening had taken place).

A clear statement of the doctrinal position was issued by the Editor in the January 1934 *Gospel Standard*. This was followed by a call issued by Mr. F. Foster, pastor at Patricroft, Lancs., in April of that year. This was prefaced by an introduction by Mr. Popham which read:

> "My earnest endeavour, continued for years, through the *Gospel Standard* to keep open the fundamentally wide difference between 'Gospel Standard' churches and all other Strict Baptists is now being practically and openly supported. For this I humbly thank and praise God. He has enabled me to bear reproach; now others have come to bear it also. Our contention is no mere denominationalism. The honour and glory of our Lord and Saviour Jesus Christ, and the integrity of the ever-adorable Trinity, the Object of true worship, we trust moves us to this action. The disentangling from mixing with other bodies, and again openly declaring that we stand on the historical, God-glorifying separation caused by the declaration of the truth of Christ's Eternal Sonship by J.C. Philpot, I believe will be for the glory of God and the good of the churches. Oh, that the Spirit may descend upon us, animate our feeble faith, and cause us to compass the altar of God, and prevail!"

The whole was headed "A God-honouring Movement."[1]

Month by month the names of supporting pastors, ministers, churches and deacons were published, and on July 13th, 1934, a public meeting was held at the Memorial Hall, Farringdon Street, London. Mr. Popham, through illness was unable to be present, and the chair was taken by Mr. G.D. Clark of Guildford.

A lengthy statement from Mr. J.K. Popham was read, in which he clearly set out the position of the *Gospel Standard*, the stand taken by J.C. Philpot in the 1860s, the cause of the separation of the churches

---

[1] Though this is a history of the *magazine* (not the churches), it is felt advisable to make some mention of "the God-honouring movement" as so much space in the *Gospel Standard* is devoted to it.

connected with the magazine, and the continuing need for that separation. He concluded:

> "Be it given to us to seek by faith and prayer to follow after the things which make for peace in our souls, and with each other; and grace to be diligent that we may be found of the Lord in peace, holding fast the faithful Word; and thus live, as a poor little body, to the praise of the glory of that grace which called us out from a body which openly condemned the Lord Jesus in His highest title, honour and glory, and the ineffable glory of the Trinity in Unity."

Mr. J.C. Fookes, pastor at Bethel Chapel, Luton, followed with an address, and at the end proposed a resolution that our churches continue as a body separate from all other Strict Baptists, by whatever name they be known. The resolution was seconded by Mr. J. Harwood, pastor at Godmanchester, Hunts., who spoke from his own experience of the need of the continued separation.

Mr. F. Foster, of Patricroft (the originator of "the God-honouring movement") then addressed the meeting, followed by Mr. John Kemp, pastor at Ebenezer Chapel, Luton, and Mr. F.H. Wright, pastor at Hope Chapel, Rochdale. Three Committee members spoke in turn: Mr. J.H. Gosden, pastor at Maidstone, Mr. H.E. Carr, pastor at Chippenham, and Mr. Walter Croft, pastor at West Street Chapel, Croydon.

On being put to the meeting the resolution was carried 407 for, 28 against. The resolution read:

> "Now we do solemnly decide and declare that, by the merciful power of God, we assembled as above, while ever desirous of loving all who love our Lord Jesus Christ in sincerity, will continue *as a Body*, known for above seventy years as 'Gospel Standard' churches, entirely separate from all other Strict Baptists, by whatsoever name known."

The following year, 1935, marked the Centenary of the *Gospel Standard* magazine, and as Mr. Popham reached the age of 88 that year, he felt it advisable to lay down the burden of his Editorship. A continual gracious witness to the truth as in Jesus had been maintained for thirty years. And what a barren period in the religious life of England that between the two Wars had proved to be! Truth

denied, a falling away, departures on every hand, diminishing congregations, church and chapel attendance generally becoming
unpopular. But during that period the *Gospel Standard* maintained an
undeviating witness to the doctrines of grace, commonly called
Calvinism, and the necessity of a vital, personal experience of the
truth.

# 12

## THE CENTENARY 1935

The centenary of the *Gospel Standard* was held on Wednesday, August 28th, 1935, again at the Memorial Hall, Farringdon Street, London.

One great difference between the Jubilee and the Centenary Services was that there was no John Gadsby present at the latter! So we have not had the innumerable details preserved.

In the morning at 11 o'clock a meeting was held for prayer and thanksgiving with Mr. J.H. Gosden presiding. The day began with hymn 1 ("Great God! how infinite art Thou!") to the tune *St. Flavian.* Haggai 1 and 2.1–5 was read. Mr. W.S. Cooper, the aged pastor at Lakenheath, prayed, and hymn 882 ("Prayer was appointed to convey") was sung to the tune *Ernan.*

Mr. C.H. Frost, pastor at Chelsea then prayed, the Chairman read Psalm 85, and Mr. S.T. Burton of Coventry prayed.

The meeting was saddened to hear that Mr. J.K. Popham was suffering from throat trouble and most probably would not be present in the evening. A brief address and prayer by Mr. J.H. Gosden followed in which he spoke on the three points: confession, supplication and thanksgiving.

Mr. H.E. Carr, pastor at Chippenham prayed, followed by Mr. H. Patterson, pastor at West Norwood, London, and hymn 720 ("Endless blessings on the Lamb") was sung to the tune *Festus*, Mr. Walter Croft, pastor at West Street, Croydon, concluding in prayer.

Throughout the day the singing was led by Mr. A.W. Light, the well-known preacher, lecturer and author, who had been Chairman of the Companion Tune Book Committee.

By the time 2.30 p.m. had arrived the hall was nearly filled, about 1,000 persons being present. Quite unexpectedly Mr. J.K. Popham appeared on the platform though unable to speak a word. The congregation was touched by the effort he had made, travelling from Brighton though 87 years old, and unwell. Mr. Gosden referred to this as a "gracious token of his unflagging, affectionate interest in our magazine."

Mr. J.K. Popham, in a letter next day, wrote:

"No one doubts that our little denomination (I use that term not legally) is in a low state spiritually; yet by the large gatherings yesterday one or two things may be justly inferred: (a) That there is still a godly remnant among us, for which let us give thanks to Him who alone by His gracious power has preserved it. Seven thousand in a nation professing God, and owing to Him their all (Exodus 20. 23), would appear few and contemptible, *yet He Himself owned them* (1 Kings 19. 10–18; Romans 11. 4,5). So, though we may seem beneath notice, yet if the Lord is among us, keeping us from false and ignorant worship, error of devotion, notional religion, and evil practices, we have much to be thankful for; (b) The atmosphere of the afternoon meeting, the only one I was permitted to attend, was *felt*. It was of a spiritual nature. If I may speak for myself, it was distinctly encouraging. Out of it good may grow, and bear fruit to the praise and glory of God."

The afternoon meeting began with the singing of hymn 362 ("How pleased and blessed was I!") to the tune *Ascalon*. The Chairman, Mr. G.D. Clark of Guildford read Isaiah 62 and Matthew 5. 1–20, and then Mr. J.C. Fookes, pastor at Bethel Chapel, Luton, prayed. Mr. Clark then gave a résumé of the history of the *Gospel Standard*. Among other things, he said:

"But I ask in respect of the *Gospel Standard* periodical: Is it not unique in this, that it has never become susceptible to modern principles? The influence of the press, the teaching in many schools, and the trend of education generally is against those fundamental truths which we hold so dear, and which our magazine is carried on to uphold and set forth.

"The *Gospel Standard*, together with its successive Editors, has remained true and faithful to its first principles. May not these principles be summed up thus: To proclaim in its pages, month by month, the doctrines of free and sovereign grace as revealed in the sacred Scriptures, and to insist that an experimental knowledge of them, by the teaching of the Holy Spirit, is essential to salvation? Today its message is still the same. Now we believe that the blessing of God has most signally rested upon this magazine. Not only in the home country, but in our colonies, as well as in other countries, evidence has time and again come to hand, as the years have sped on, that many of the Lord's people have been convinced of sin, reproved, instructed, edified and confirmed through the instrumentality of its pages. Some who have lived in out-of-the-way places, where they were cut off from the public assembly for worship, have testified to the spiritual help and consolation received through this means of grace.

"It is said of us today that we are old fashioned and out of date; we do not move with the times. Presumably then, we do not move fast enough. How much in our social life is being sacrificed to this god of speed! In the air, on the land, and on the sea, people cannot go fast enough. Many rush on to their own destruction, and human life is little valued by many, in this insatiate pursuit after ever-increasing speed. Yes, the world is moving on, but don't forget it is moving on to destruction. Brethren, in the midst of all the rush and confusion of modern thought and modern pursuits, God's eternal truth, like Himself, remains for ever unchangeably the same: 'Heaven and earth shall pass away, but My Word shall not pass away.' May the future of the *Gospel Standard* magazine ever be marked by a strict and stedfast adherence to the truth as it is in Jesus Christ."

Mr. J.H. Gosden, Editor of the *Gospel Standard*, in a remarkable address based on Psalm 133 emphasized that the basis of real unity is the truth of God. He spoke especially of the Trinity — emphasizing the eternal Being of God; the Holy Ghost's work in regeneration; and the Person of Christ as the eternal Son of God: in this he spoke in similar vein to the speakers at the Jubilee fifty years before: "This is not unity of mere opinion; it is not necessarily entire uniformity of thought; it is unity in and on the basis of the truth of God."

Hymn 372 ("Glorious things of Thee are spoken") was sung to the tune *Austria*, and Mr. John Kemp, pastor at Ebenezer Chapel, Luton, gave an address. He said:

"The great secret of the usefulness of the *Gospel Standard* during these hundred years, I believe to be this — that God Himself was pleased to send it, and He has maintained it up to this day, and thus in the next place, it was not only sent by God, it has been maintained, as we have heard this afternoon, in its Scriptural character. There have been times, as you know, when certain truths have needed to be particularly emphasized, but no truth of the gospel has ever, as far as I know, been left without a faithful witness and maintenance in the magazine."

And again:

"I have often noticed in visiting some of the Lord's poor and afflicted people, that usually their library consisted of the Bible first, Gadsby's hymnbook, and perhaps an old volume or a recent issue of the *Gospel Standard*. Some people point the finger of scorn at such things. I have heard some even remark that people put the *Standard* and hymnbook on a level with the Bible. No gracious person does that, my friends. It is not that: but because they find in the *Gospel Standard* that which is profitable to their souls and helpful, encouraging, and strengthening in regard to their daily life and their afflicted path, therefore it is esteemed. It has been — and is — a useful magazine on account of its scriptural and experimental character."

Mr. F.H. Wright, pastor at Hope Chapel, Rochdale (where John Kershaw formerly preached), next addressed the meeting. (Mr. Wright died little over a year later at the comparatively early age of 51.) He spoke of three things as explanation of "the magazine's success, under the Spirit of God": 1. There has always been an insistence on the majesty of God. 2. There has always been an insistence on the inspiration of Holy Scripture. 3. There has always been an insistence on gracious experience. Hymn 667 ("Immortal honours rest on Jesus' head") was sung to the tune *Toulon*, and the Chairman concluded with the benediction.

At the 6 o'clock service the congregation numbered between 1,200 and 1,500. The hymns at the service were:

1139 ("O God, our Help in ages past") — *Ann's*
318 ("God of eternal love") — *Rhodes*
730 ("All hail the power of Jesus' name") — *Miles Lane*.

The reading was Philippians 3.

Mr. J.H. Gosden preached from Colossians 1. 28: "Whom we

preach, warning every man, and teaching every man in all wisdom; that we may present every man perfect in Christ Jesus." Speaking especially of Christ in His Person, he said: "We preach Him because in our little measure we know Him. And what does the knowledge of Him do? This — it makes you love Him. You cannot know Immanuel without loving Him. Is that a touchstone of true religion? I believe the Scripture makes it so."

Mr. Gosden continued, speaking of Christ in His death, His resurrection, His priesthood, His righteousness, and as Zion's King. He concluded:

"If He gives you a heart to know Him, He will fill your heart with the knowledge of Him in His own time. He will come again. I would warn you, my friends, you cannot escape Him because you do not know Him. If you do not want to know Him, He knows you, and you will have to do with Him. Judgment is committed to that Man whom Jehovah has ordained; and of the judgment 'He hath given assurance unto all men in that He hath raised Him from the dead.' He will come with eyes as a flame of fire, and of those His enemies He will say, 'Bring them forth and slay them.' They will cry to the rocks and mountains to fall upon them and hide them, but they cannot be hid. Some here, though they feel truly unworthy, often full of fear — some here want Him, would rather lose anything than lose their hope in Him; and at times they say with the Apostle, they count all things but dung and loss for the excellency of the knowledge of Christ, and that they may win Him."

Special thanks were later given in the *Gospel Standard* to the Secretary of the Gospel Standard Societies, Mr. W.E. Wallis (who in 1985 is still alive) "upon whom devolved the onerous and hidden work of all the arrangements of the Hall, hymn sheets, accommodation for meals, loud speakers, the recording of the collections, and the multifarious duties connected with the Meetings. We feel it was a labour of love undertaken with his usual pleasant, unostentatious manner."

A facsimile reprint of the first volume of the *Gospel Standard*, August to December, 1835, was on sale, price two shillings (10p) a copy.

Mr. J.H. Gosden's summary of the day was:

"We feel it behoves us to thank the Lord for His condescending help afforded to us and the dear friends who took part in the proceedings of the day. We feel that prayer was answered, and trust that days to come may evidence the Lord's divine approbation more and more. . . . It is our desire to record the Lord's goodness to us on this occasion, that apparently a spirit of unison and concord prevailed."

# 13

# THE LAST YEARS

The editorship that followed that of J.K. Popham was that of a man after his own heart, his own son in the faith, John Hervey Gosden. It is, therefore, no surprise to find that he closely followed the pattern of his godly predecessor.

Mr. Gosden, on assuming the editorship, wrote in July 1935:

"It is with considerable trembling that I address myself to the work which has thus fallen to me through the unanimous vote of the trustees of the magazines, and on account of the resignation through age of Mr. J.K. Popham. No word of mine is necessary to commend our beloved friend's long years of gracious, devoted and conspicuously able editorship, whereby very many of God's dear children have been instructed, edified and blessed. Human applause and human censure alike move a man only when his eye is off God — when he aims not singly at His glory; and their unsteadying effect is proportionate to the absence of divine conviction, power and support. When *these* are enjoyed, gratefully and gladly it is confessed, 'By the grace of God I am what I am.' This is doubtless the heart-felt language of the worthy occupant for 30 years of our editorial chair, who — notwithstanding his 87 years — has kindly consented to yet occasionally contribute to the pages of the magazines, if the Lord will.

"Here it might be fitting to say, kindly and affectionately, once-for-all, that it is my intention to endeavour, by the help of God, to observe the same uncompromising attitude hitherto held in regard to our

71

historic position which came into being through the dividing of
churches on the sacred doctrine of the Person of the Son of God.

"In girding on my harness (for labour) and armour (for defence), my
language is, 'I will lift up mine eyes unto the hills, from whence
cometh my help. My help cometh from the Lord which made heaven
and earth" (Psalm 121. 1,2). And I desire never to have them fixed
anywhere else for help, for defence, for wisdom, grace, mercy, strength
and for reward; but to be enabled to imitate David, 'Mine eyes are *ever*
toward the Lord.' "

From the beginning Mr. Gosden stated that he would not intrude
himself much on the readers but select suitable pieces that are
"unctuous and fitting to edify." Dr. Owen was perhaps his special
favourite, but during his editorship there appeared many beautiful
sermons preached by his brother, Mr. F.L. Gosden, and his friend,
Mr. Jesse Delves. The high calibre of the magazine appealed to a
spiritual mind, especially to one longing and thirsting for Christ.

The practice, which had begun under Mr. Popham, of reporting
the Annual Meetings of the Societies, held at Gower Street Memorial
Chapel, London, continued, as did the practice, established under his
predecessor, that the Editor should preach the evening sermon on that
day. Later, in 1951, Annual Northern Meetings at Manchester were
commenced, and likewise reported.

Soon the nation was mourning the loss of King George V. Mr.
Gosden wrote suitably on the occasion and later, as representative of
the Gospel Standard churches, officially attended the coronation of
George VI. A letter of loyalty was addressed to the King at this time
and later to his successor, Queen Elizabeth II.

It was in 1944 that the Bethesda Fund was commenced, and in
1948 the first Bethesda Home for aged people in connection with the
*Gospel Standard* was opened at Redhill, Surrey. There are now six such
Homes, with a seventh expected to open in the near future. Reports
concerning the work, which has been wonderfully supported, have
often appeared in the pages and on the wrapper of the *Gospel Standard*.
This is not recorded merely as a point of denominational interest but
as the working out practically of the precious truths advocated in the
magazine.

In 1946 a Library was established at Brighton, which includes one
of the finest collections of free grace books in the country. (A lovely
new building to house the Library was opened in 1981.)

Mr. Gosden's editorship covered the difficult period of the Second World War. He continued right until his death on June 21st, 1964. Thus two editorships had spanned almost sixty years — a wonderful favour to the magazine.

In his last sermon at the Annual Meetings only two months previously, he had said:

"All we have if we have not Christ is but destitution, barrenness, emptiness; but with Him, whatever your state is, you are rich, and sometimes you may say, I am content, I am happy, all is well. When can that be? Not when you discover you are not such a great sinner as you thought, but when the Lord comes and claims you for His portion, as it says here: 'And pardon our iniquity and our sin, and take us for Thine inheritance.' If the Lord pardons our sins, He will own us and take us to Himself, because His forgiveness is the result of His redeeming Sacrifice."

These were the very truths so dearly loved by the founder of the *Gospel Standard*, William Gadsby.

The magazine being left without an Editor, there was deep concern as to who should follow, and in July 1964 Mr. Sydney Frank Paul was elected. Mr Paul had been a deacon at Galeed Chapel, Brighton, since the days of Mr. J.K. Popham and had been a fellow member there with Mr. J.H. Gosden, so he followed very much in their tradition.

Mr. Paul wrote in the September issue:

"We feel much our insufficiency for the solemn and important work, and lack of grace and gracious experience in the things of God, and would earnestly solicit the prayers of our readers that more grace may be given, and strength and ability according to our need, so that the spiritual character as well as the literary standard of the magazine may be maintained, and the Lord's blessing still rest upon our denominational periodical."

In one sense this could be described as a "caretaker" editorship. Mr. Paul was over 80 years of age and it was obvious that he could not continue for long. Nevertheless, he was most highly esteemed as a gracious man, and a man of ability, though he was not a public figure. (Apart from John Gadsby he is the only Editor who was not also a minister.) He was able to continue quietly and graciously for the next six years.

Mr. Paul continued till the end of 1970 when he felt it prudent that another should be elected. The following year, on September 30th, he died, aged 88. His pastor, Mr. F.L. Gosden, said of him:

> "He was an example to many. I do not know of another quite his equal for his self-control. He was self-possessed and he exemplified that word in Philippians 4. 5: 'Let your moderation be known unto all men.' So that we have not just lost a person; we have lost an influence, and therefore the loss is in proportion to the gift. For he *was* a gift, a gift to the denomination, but the Lord has taken him."

By this time a younger man was serving on the Committee, Benjamin Ashworth Ramsbottom, pastor since 1967 at Bethel Chapel, Luton, and a native of Haslingden in Lancashire. It was Mr. Paul's wish that he should succeed him, and this was also the unanimous decision of the Committee. He thus became the youngest Editor of the *Gospel Standard* (apart from the joint editorship in 1840). Strangely, when Mr. Gosden had been asked before his death if there was anyone who could be Editor in years to come, he immediately mentioned the name of Mr. Ramsbottom.

Mr Ramsbottom, in his first editorial, January 1971, stated his desire to follow in the same steps as his illustrious predecessors:

> "Our editorship begins in solemn times. We feel it must be as when we first began to preach: 'leaning on all-sufficient grace.' It is now over 135 years since William Gadsby and his son John 'ventured to launch their little vessel into so wide an ocean' (to use their own words in the first *Gospel Standard*). Since then, the Lord has blessed us with a succession of godly, able editors whose desire has been to exalt Christ, abase the sinner, set forth the precious doctrines of grace, insist on vital, gracious experience, and contend earnestly for the faith once delivered to the saints.
>
> "The substance of the first Editor's favourite expressions has ever been found in its pages — speaking of Jesus: 'Honours crown His head for ever'; and of the gospel: 'O the riches of matchless grace!' May this be the spirit still of the *Gospel Standard*.
>
> "Thinking of the precious heritage of the past and ourselves, our thoughts have gone to the second chapter of Haggai: 'Is it not in

comparison of it as nothing?' Yet that meaner building, the second temple, was to be honoured by the immediate presence of the Lord Jesus Himself and there in that much less glorious building, His own glory was to be displayed. May the Lord Jesus honour these pages and may they be perfumed with the sweet savour of His name. Our one desire is 'that in all things He might have the preeminence.' We long that the *Gospel Standard* may contain a sweet savour of Christ — His name as ointment poured forth; and may it be to many 'the savour of life unto life.' It is the Holy Spirit's work to cause this: 'Awake, O north wind; and come, thou south; blow upon my garden, that the spices thereof may flow out.' J.C. Philpot, in almost his last New Year Address, said, 'We would come, month by month, simply, quietly, unobtrusively, without loud knock or noisy ring, and lie by the side of the Bible and the hymn-book, speaking the same language, breathing the same spirit.' "

\* \* \*

What of the *Gospel Standard* today? In the last century there were numerous Baptist magazines; for the most part even their names are no longer remembered. But through mercy the *Gospel Standard* still continues, but not merely continues: it still maintains the same precious truths on which it was founded.

This is a day in which there has been a revival of interest in Calvinism. Our godly forefathers would be amazed at the books now flooding the market — some of them real Christian classics. But there is a spirit of worldliness abroad and very little of the power of vital godliness.

We believe the *Gospel Standard* still has a living witness to bear — to the doctrines of God's free and sovereign grace; to the importance of clear views concerning the Person of the Lord Jesus Christ; to the necessity of separation both from worldliness and the religious world; to the need for godly lives answering to a profession of the Redeemer's name; and, not least, to the vital necessity of the Holy Ghost's work in the sinner's heart:

"True religion's more than notion,
Something *must* be known and felt."

The *Gospel Standard* still seeks to contend for a religion which is

God's work, not man's; which honours Christ, not the sinner; which will stand the test; and which will take us to heaven at last.

In setting up our waymarks, and raising our high heaps (Jeremiah 31. 21), it is, we trust in the spirit of the psalmist: "Not unto us, O Lord, not unto us, but unto *Thy* name give glory, for Thy mercy and for Thy truth's sake."

NONE BUT JESUS!

# PART II

# *The Lives of the Editors*

# WILLIAM GADSBY
## 1773–1844

*It is much to be regretted that Mr. Gadsby did not leave anything at all in writing concerning his life or spiritual experience. The following is by the Editor.*

When God has a work to do, that work must be accomplished; yet how mysteriously and by what unlikely means does He work! Who would have thought that a small, ragged, barefooted boy, receiving hardly the bare essentials of education, and growing up "as far from God as sheep can run," would one day be one of the most honoured ministers in the churches of truth—indeed the founder, instrumentally, of forty churches—and that his name and work would still be honoured over two centuries later? Yet so it was with William Gadsby.[1]

On January 3rd, 1773 (or thereabouts—the exact date is uncertain), a ninth child was born into the family of a poor Warwickshire roadman, John Gadsby. The child was named William. The cottage in Attleborough, near Nuneaton, where he was born, has long since been demolished, but an interesting pen sketch may be seen in the chapel at Attleborough.

We know little of William's early days—just sufficient to catch a glimpse of a lively little boy, full of mischief and frolic, running almost wild about the village, or nursing a younger child almost as soon as he is able to hold it in his arms; a little boy being punished for throwing away a piece of bread, or, feeling he is badly treated, fleeing from home disguised as a hunchback. Yet already a fallen nature was manifesting itself, especially in dreadful swearing.

At the age of thirteen, he was apprenticed to a ribbon weaver, and ran to great lengths in sin. Already he was a leader among his companions, entertaining them for hours together to their great amusement and delight. As he put it, "I was the life of their society, and they seemed as if they could not live without me."

But "the appointed time rolled on," and about the age of seventeen, the Lord began to work in his heart. He strikingly describes this:

> "When the set time came, He arrested me, broke my heart and brought me to stand before His throne as a guilty criminal, brought me to sign my own death warrant. I gave God leave to damn me if He would. I had nothing to offer, and I could do nothing to save myself."

---

[1] It is remarkable how the memory of his name has survived in some parts of the country. Some years ago, a worldly man, on hearing of our religious connections, exclaimed, "Why, you're a Gadsbyite!"

Some of his workmates tried to force him to go with them as formerly, but he so solemnly spoke to them of hell and damnation that they were glad to be rid of him.

The Independent Chapel at nearby Bedworth ("black Bed'orth" as it was known on account of its wickedness) was where he now began to attend. His mother soon had to warn him that he would have to go without shoes as he was wearing out his only pair by the constant journeying there and back! There was a godly zeal in William Gadsby's religion from the beginning.

It would appear that his soul was brought into gospel liberty after a few months of deep and sore spiritual distress. Speaking of this in after years, he said:

> "But O! God's peculiar love that was shed abroad in my heart by His blessed Spirit, and which brought me to feel the love and blood of Christ, led me to trace something of the wondrous work of His wonder-working grace! Then how my hard heart was melted! I was brought to His footstool with all humility, simplicity and godly sincerity; filled with gratitude and thanks for God's unspeakable mercies in opening these great mysteries to my poor soul. I was then solemnly and blessedly led to believe in God's free mercy and pardon, and could look up and say, 'He loved *me*, and gave Himself for *me*.' I recollect the time when God was graciously pleased to reveal pardon in my poor soul at first. O! what sweetness and solemnity and blessedness there were in my poor heart! I sang night and day the wonders of His love."

Soon a period of trial followed in which he was allowed to backslide, and was well taught his ignorance and helplessness, Satan roaring, "Where is your peace with God *now*? Where are your meekness and humility and your tenderness of heart *now*? Where is your power in prayer *now*? Where is your trust in the God of Israel *now*? And where are YOU?" No peace could be felt till he found that Ezekiel 16 exactly described his case—the blessing, the backsliding, the desperate wickedness—till, as he read on, at length he cried, "This is my case. Whatever is this people's lot must be my lot. Damned or saved, I must go with them!" But when he reached the last verse, the word most powerfully entered his heart: "That thou mayest remember, and be confounded, and never open thy mouth any more because of thy shame, when I am pacified toward thee for all that

thou hast done, saith the Lord." "They're safe! They're safe!" he cried
out, and his deliverance was complete.


Eight miles away at Coventry there was an old Baptist cause where
in former days the renowned John Brine had been pastor. At this
time, a new chapel had just been built in Cow Lane. Through
meeting the assistant minister, who often preached at Attleborough,
William Gadsby was constrained to meet with the Coventry Baptists.
He often spoke in later years of how he was never late for the seven
o'clock Sabbath morning prayer meeting, though having to walk
every step of the way. Here he was baptized on December 29th, 1793,
shortly before his twenty-first birthday. The aged pastor, John But-
terworth, a member of a remarkable family from Goodshaw in the
Forest of Rossendale, Lancashire, was too old and feeble to baptize; so
Gadsby was baptized, along with twenty-one others, by the assistant
pastor, James Aston. Mr Aston (almost prophetically) remarked that
he could "see something in the young man, although so illiterate and
uncouth, that seemed blessedly to prove that he would sometime or
other be made useful to God's dear family."

Shortly afterwards, Gadsby became closely attached to a young
woman about two years his senior. She was Elizabeth Marvin, the
daughter of a stocking weaver at Hinckley, about five miles away
from his home. Elizabeth was one of eighteen people who had just
been baptized and formed into a Particular Baptist church at
Hinckley by Mr. Aston. Partly through this friendship, but mainly
because his health was suffering through the arduous nature of his
work, Gadsby left Attleborough and began to learn stocking weaving
in Hinckley.

The Hinckley years form a most attractive part of William
Gadsby's life. It was here he was married to Elizabeth, where they first
set up their home, and where their three eldest children were born.
Here he joined the newly-formed church, now meeting in Hogg
Lane. And it was whilst living at Hinckley that he first preached.


Preach? Gadsby was determined he never would. He prayed to die
rather than preach. He continually cried, "Do not let me preach,

Lord. Send by whom Thou wilt send, but not by me." He even sat in his night shirt on the cellar steps trying to catch a cold and die rather than preach. Then the Lord settled the matter. With divine authority and power the word was spoken: "But God hath chosen the foolish things of the world to confound the wise; and God hath chosen the weak things of the world to confound the things that are mighty; and base things of the world, and things which are despised, hath God chosen, yea, and things which are not, to bring to nought things that are: that no flesh should glory in His presence." This was enough. "Well, Lord," was the prompt reply, "if this is the way Thou workest, Thou never hadst a better opportunity, for Thou never hadst a bigger fool to deal with."

It was on Whit Sunday, 1798, at the age of twenty-five, that William Gadsby preached his first sermon, in an upper room in Bedworth, from the words: "Unto you therefore which believe He is precious." How appropriate this text at the very beginning of that long, Christ-exalting ministry, during which he would so often exclaim, "Honours crown His head for ever!" Though many were astonished that this rough-looking young man, so clownish in his appearance, should attempt to preach, the godly marked the power of the Word, and also the exemplary life of the preacher.

At this time, he used to travel about during the week, taking the stockings he had made to Leicester, Coventry, Nuneaton and other places. It was on one of these journeys, having only half a crown ($12\frac{1}{2}$p) with which to provide for his family, that he gave it all away to a poor man in distress—only to receive a gift shortly afterwards of half a guinea ($52\frac{1}{2}$p) from a man he had not seen for years. But his mind was on his preaching continually—so much so that, after he had ruined a pair of stockings, his wife said, "Look here, William, it's time you gave up either preaching or weaving."

The barn at Hogg Lane now became the scene of many of his labours. What trying days these were! Years later he said of his Hinckley days:

"I preached to a number of poor people in an old barn and truly we had many precious visits from the Lord, which made the old barn a consecrated place to our souls, notwithstanding the thatch was off in so many places of the roof that we could see the sky through the numerous holes, so that when it rained the people had to remove from one part to another during preaching to prevent getting wet through; and what was worse, we were too poor to get it repaired. An additional torment was that our enemies (who consisted chiefly of professors of religion) often broke our locks off, and did us much mischief."

One hole in the roof was just over the pulpit, through which at times stones were thrown at the minister while he preached. On one occasion, the barn was broken into, the pulpit taken, and an attempt made to sink it in a pond—but the pulpit (which may still be seen at the Editor's home) still floated. At last they said the devil was in it for they "could neither sink the parson nor his pulpit." Yet amidst all this, the Word had free course and was glorified, sinners were blessed, so that it was resolved to attempt the building of a chapel.

Eventually a chapel was built (and by this time Gadsby was prospering in business). Remarkably, this chapel still stands, though closed many years and now part of a large hosiery factory. Also, a chapel was built for him at Desford in 1800, Gadsby's practice at this time being to preach twice at Hinckley, once at Desford; then the following Sabbath, twice at Desford and once at Hinckley. The chapel at Desford has long been demolished; but the burial ground can still be seen, not far from the village church.

But it was not at Hinckley nor Desford but Manchester where the Lord had ordained that most of his life should be spent and his preaching signally blessed.

"There was as much prospect of the mountain of Gibraltar coming to Manchester as I!" exclaimed William Gadsby not long before his death. Yet how remarkable the unfoldings of providence in bringing him there! Really, he invited himself. Hearing that the people at Back Lane Chapel (as it was then known) were without a minister, and being anxious to raise funds for the building of the new chapel at Hinckley, he wrote saying that he had business in Manchester, and would willingly preach three or four Sabbaths. His business was to beg for money.

How much could be written concerning his first remarkable visit to Manchester! The people were divided between those who agreed with Andrew Fuller's duty-faith writings and those who opposed them. Gadsby made a great stir among the Fullerites, and the longer he stayed, the more people came to hear him. The Word entered many hearts. One godly member was so impressed by the power attending Gadsby's announcing the opening hymn ("Awake, my soul, in joyful lays") that he was persuaded this was to be their pastor. At his first appearance many were astonished; he was at that time very thin, and dressed in a coarse brown coat, drab trousers, and wearing a coloured neckerchief—in fact, "Not a bit of black except inside me," as he said. But the doctrines he preached had a gracious effect, and the hearts of many of the people were united to him. It was on this occasion that the well-known John Warburton, then a poor weaver, came with his heart full of prejudice but, feeling so blessed in his soul, went home with his "very soul knit to him as closely as Jonathan's was to David." Soon the good old veterans were saying, "This is the man for us; let us arise and anoint him," and they began to cry mightily to God to make a way.

It was during this first visit to Lancashire that one who heard him, said: "Before he had spoken ten minutes, I saw more beauty and glory in Christ than I had ever seen before. My cup of joy overflowed. I saw that this glorious Christ and His finished salvation were mine."

The outcome of all these events was that, after much opposition had been overthrown, William Gadsby, at the age of thirty-two, left Hinckley to become the pastor at Back Lane Chapel, Manchester (now Rochdale Road). His farewell sermon was preached at Hinckley on September 29th, 1805, from the text; "The grace of our Lord Jesus Christ be with you all. Amen."

The time would fail to tell of all the happenings during the thirty-eight years that William Gadsby laboured in Manchester. It was during this period that so many of his precious hymns were written, as well as the publication of his Selection, designed as a hymnbook "free from Arminianism and sound in the faith, that the church might be edified, and God glorified." And how abundantly his prayer has been answered—that "the dear Redeemer will be gracious to make this selection of hymns a blessing to His people"!

An interesting event took place about the year 1831. A quantity of spoiled sheets of Gadsby's hymns were being used as wrapping paper in a cheesemonger's shop in London. A stranger, who bought some cheese (or bacon), on unwrapping it read:

"Pause, my soul, and ask the question
Art thou ready to meet God?"

and the Holy Spirit so fastened the words upon his conscience that he
was convinced of his state as a sinner, and ultimately brought to a
saving knowledge of Christ. But what effect Gadsby's hymns have
had at other times over the years, only eternity will reveal.

Various books and pamphlets were written during the Manchester
years; these varied in subject matter, but especially he wrote on the
gospel as the believer's rule of life—this being one of the chief
differences between himself and other Calvinistic ministers. It was
also during these years that the *Gospel Standard* was first "launched
into the wide ocean" by Gadsby and his energetic son, John, a
successful Manchester printer, William Gadsby at first writing the
Annual Address, and also contributing articles under the nom-
de-plumes, "A Lover of Zion" and "A Soldier".

But it was upon his *preaching* that the Lord's blessing most evidently rested, and as a *preacher* that he made such a marked impression
during his lifetime.

What was it in William Gadsby's preaching that made such an
impression on his contemporaries (for that he made a tremendous
impression there can be no doubt)? Most certainly it was the divine
power, unction and gracious authority that attended the Word he
preached. J.C. Philpot felt that he was the greatest minister of his
day.

Wherever he preached, there were crowded congregations,
whether in his own chapel at Manchester, or during his annual visits
to London—where sometimes as the people were coming out at the
end of one service, they found others queuing to make sure of a place
at the next. There seemed to be a special suitability in his ministry for
the cases of burdened, broken-hearted sinners, many of whom could
find no relief in much of the dry, formal preaching that prevailed
among so many of the Baptists at that time. The Holy Ghost clothed
the Word with divine power, and warmth, life, love and liberty
attended it. How difficult it is for us to gain any real impression of the
atmosphere that must have prevailed among these crowded congregations in those days of spiritual prosperity!

He would open the service by giving out a hymn, usually verse by verse; and often his slow, drawling manner would prejudice a new hearer against him. Then after reading from the Word, he would pray. His pulpit prayers were unusually short (seldom above five minutes), but they were singularly his own, and from his heart. After the second hymn his sermon commenced—often, after taking off his glasses and slowly surveying the congregation, with some striking, weighty statement. "His voice was wonderful." wrote Dr. Halley, Principal of New College, London. "I heard him once in the old Free Trade Hall of Manchester. When other speakers had made strange efforts to be heard, sometimes in vain, he seemed to me, sitting near him, to be speaking in a pleasant, conversational tone; but the voice of the old man rolled like an equable wave of sound across the great hall and filled the ear of every auditor."

He would solemnly open up the depths of the fall and the aboundings of sin, often touching on things another dare not even mention. Often under the leading of the Holy Spirit his remarks were so pointed that they brought the hearer under deep conviction. On one occasion when speaking of infidelity, two men who had just attended an infidel meeting almost fainted away, and on more than one occasion, people who had acted dishonestly had to confess it when the service ended and seek to put things right.

Then he would set forth what he delighted to call "the riches of matchless grace," dwelling on the glories of Christ, His fulness, His eternal union with His church, His finished work, His suitability in His offices, and then sweetly emphasizing the blessed invitations of the gospel. It was said, "His heart went, as it were, direct into the hearts of the Lord's people." There were, undoubtedly at times, coarse expressions and many eccentricities, but the solemnity with which he spoke, especially of the sufferings of the dear Redeemer, soon outweighed this. How beautiful is the following example of the sacred, solemn manner in which he spoke on the sufferings of Christ!

"Bless His holy name, honours crown His brow for ever and ever! O my soul, adore Him! He stood in His people's law place, called their sins His own, took their debt as His own, cancelled it by His blood, groaned, and sweat, and bled, and died. 'He died the just for the unjust, to bring us to God.' Can you think lightly of sin? Can you call it a trifle, while it tore the heart of our dear Christ, and horrified Him? His soul was in an agony so that He lay on the earth, and cried out, 'My soul is exceeding sorrowful, even unto death.' He drank into His holy soul the hell that His children must have endured. Yea, He put out the flames of hell with His heart's blood that my soul might obtain eternal blessedness. Then adore Him my soul, and bless His precious name!"

One hearer said of him, "There was a power attended his ministry that I hardly ever felt under the ministry of any other man"; and another stated that those who had never heard him could have "little idea of the living energy, life and power in the preacher during his delivery." Indeed, one aged saint wrote: "Ah! if you had but heard that voice of his, rolling like peals of thunder, and seen those eyes of his, like balls of fire piercing through the congregation, you would never have forgotten it while you lived." This last was the testimony of one who, as a young man, went to mock, but was cut down in deep conviction as Mr. Gadsby solemnly announced his opening hymn, "Alas! and did my Saviour bleed?"

And there was a *lasting* effect of his preaching; it was not just momentary impression. During his early years at Manchester, between five and ten on an average were added to the church each month, many of whom were eminent in godliness. One was a very poor woman who lived in a cellar. When Mr. Gadsby visited her before her death, she was lying on a straw bed in a most filthy state. (Her daughter was lazy and dirty, and failed to look after her dying mother.) The cellar was littered with old bones, old rags, and all sorts of rubbish and dirt. When the dear, dying saint, lying amidst all this squalor was asked how she felt, "O!" she exclaimed, "I don't think the Lord deals as mercifully with anybody as He does with me? He is most precious to me, and His visits are most sweet."

Perhaps the most touching account of the power of the Word under William Gadsby's ministry is that of the little dying cripple boy he was asked to visit. Never having seen the lad before, he concluded there was some mistake, till the little boy informed him of how he had crept into the gallery steps after the service had begun. He gave a most blessed account of the Lord's work in his heart. Coming from a place where he had heard nothing but the law, and bitterly feeling its condemnation, he happened to enter Mr. Gadsby's chapel when the text was, "Christ is the end of the law for righteousness to everyone that believeth," and under the sweet influence of the Spirit, was brought into complete gospel liberty. This was at a time when Gadsby was longing that the Lord would work in the hearts of a few well-to-do young men in his congregation. "But," he says, "the Lord at the same time was at work upon the heart of a poor cripple upon the gallery stairs that none of the people seem ever to have noticed or known."

Perhaps the most lasting effect of his ministry is to be found in the *forty* causes of truth he was instrumental in forming, some of which still continue. In his labours he was untiring, preaching at home four times each week, and usually three times elsewhere, going many miles by foot, often over wild moors; and then, besides his annual London visit, preaching in various distant parts of the country.

May it never be forgotten that as a background to his ministry, he patiently endured one of the sorest of trials—the dreadful mental affliction of his beloved wife. For well over twenty years, until his death, she was a continual trial, often plagued with a jealous spirit, and constantly misunderstanding him. He had to prove in deep waters the precious truths that he preached.


If William Gadsby made an impression, blessedly so, on the church of God, he equally made an impression, though of a different sort, on the world, and the religious world. Stigmatized as an Antinomian (because of his belief that the law is not the believer's rule of conduct), despised, opposed, treated with contempt by Church and Dissenting ministers alike, he lived to see his enemies, in great measure, at peace with him. And the secret was the God-glorifying life that through grace he lived. He came to be respected and honoured as a man by those who hated the truths he preached. After his death in "A Tribute of High Esteem and Love," J. C. Philpot (not given to flattery!) issued the challenge: "Who ever found a visible blemish in him?" whilst the brief memoir published the same year stated: "For years his enemies watched for his falling, but, by the grace of God, he maintained an unblemished character to the last. No minister of the Lord of life was ever upheld by the hand of God in a more consistent and blameless life for so long a period. His walk and conversation were an ornament to the pure and sound doctrine he preached; and yet, at times, O the distress and trembling fears he had lest he should be left to fall into some sin, and disgrace the blessed truth of God, such was the working of corrupt nature within, and the feeling sense of his own weakness! But the Lord most graciously held him up, and brought him honourably through all."

His tender spirit, his love of children, his kindness and sympathy, and his humility were ever apparent. Especially was he renowned for his kindness and liberality to the poor—of whatever creed. It was a poor Irish woman who said, on hearing of his death, "He once kept me from starving when my own priest would not give me a farthing." It is estimated that nearly half of his regular income he gave away.

When in his old age he broke his leg, the Manchester papers said: "Any cessation of the activity of such a man is a public calamity." A religious leader in London, who opposed Gadsby's doctrinal beliefs, wrote of him: "No minister in Manchester lived a more moral life, or presented to his hearers a more beautiful example of Christian discipline and self-control." And on the day of his funeral, thousands lined the streets of Manchester to show their respect.

But what was he in his own eyes? "Less than the least of saints, and the chief of sinners"; or, as he would say, "Less than nothing, and vanity." It is very typical of Gadsby's religion, and that of his friends, that when John Kershaw preached his funeral sermon before a crowded congregation, the text was: "Less than the least" (Eph. 3. 8)!

In one aspect of his life, Gadsby differed from almost all other well-known ministers—the active part he took in public affairs. For this he has been severely criticised by some. But, right or wrong, it is certain he exerted a wonderful influence in the city of Manchester. His sympathy for all who were oppressed was so deep that many a good cause gained his interest and active support.

When a severe famine prevailed in Ireland (many having to live on sea weed), Gadsby advertised a special service at which £40 (a large sum in those days!) was collected. When he heard of a poor soldier unjustly sentenced to a severe flogging, he again had a collection, and bought the man off. Whilst in London he made what efforts he could to arouse sympathy for the Lancashire poor—the papers suggesting that other ministers should do likewise. Frequently he would appear on a public platform on such issues as the repeal of the cruel Corn Laws, which kept bread so dear; temperance (believing that strong drink had ruined thousands); the grievances of Dissenters; the distress of the hand-loom weavers; whilst his pointed criticism of the ill behaviour of King George IV toward Queen Caroline caused the Government to send the deputy constable of Manchester to hear him and observe his views. (What minister of truth would so arouse the Government's interest today?) Invariably when there was to be a collection for any good cause, Mr. Gadsby was appointed to make the appeal—his special ability in this direction causing people not only to put in all they had with them, but sometimes a note also, promising more! And be it remembered that there were sometimes as many as 8,000 to hear him at such public meetings.

If William Gadsby honoured the Lord in his life, the Lord honoured him in his triumphant death. He was able to preach on his last Sabbath on earth, thus fulfilling a desire not to be laid aside for long. One present made a note in his Bible opposite the text (Isa. 43. 2: "When thou passest through the waters, I will be with thee"): "Mr. Gadsby preached this sermon with very great fervour, but with very great difficulty of breathing, especially in the evening, when it took him four minutes to ascend the pulpit, having to stop upon every step. But the Lord was very gracious to him in supporting his mind, although suffering in body. He was got home with much difficulty." The complaint was inflammation of the lungs.

On the Tuesday he had to remain in bed. He was at times harassed by Satan, his poor wife was especially trying, and he suffered much. But now he proved the blessed support of the things he had long preached.

Just before the end, when it was felt his voice was gone, he most solemnly and affectionately prayed for the church and his family. Shortly afterwards he said, "There is nothing too hard for Christ; He is the mighty God—from everlasting to everlasting. He *was* precious; He *is* precious." Then raising his left hand, for his right was cold and motionless, he exclaimed, "Victory! victory! victory!" Then after a short sleep, he testified that he was on the Rock.

"Is He precious to you?" asked his friend and fellow-member, John Ashworth, who was constantly with him.

"Yes," he firmly replied. "King, Immanuel, Redeemer, all glorious!"

"You will soon have done here."

"I shall soon be with Him, shouting Victory! victory! victory!" raising his hand, "for ever."

Shortly afterwards he said, "Free grace! free grace! free grace!" and fell asleep in Jesus. It was Saturday, 27th January, 1844.

So lived and died William Gadsby. The Lord had a great work for him to do and enabled him honourably to do it. In his desk, when he died, was found a slip of paper on which he had written his own epitaph. "Let this be put on my stone," it read. And surely nothing could be more fitting:

> "Here rests the body of a sinner base,
>     Who had no hope but in electing grace;
> The love, blood, life, and righteousness of God
>     Was his sweet theme, and this he spread abroad."

See also:
*Memoir of William Gadsby, 1844*

# JOHN M'KENZIE

## ?[1] – 1849

*T*here *is no really connected account of the life of Mr. M'Kenzie, minister*
*at Preston, Lancs. We are, therefore, reproducing an extract from* The
Seceders *where J.H. Philpot (J.C. Philpot's son) has tied together numerous*

---

[1]  No date can be traced in the old *Gospel Standards* for Mr. M'Kenzie's birth. J.H. Philpot gives
it as "about the turn of the century" i.e. 1800. *Brief Memorials of Gospel Ministers* gives his age at
death as 56. A manuscript note by Fred Windridge, who helped J.H. Philpot with *The Seceders*,
states that the Preston church book gives his age at death as 40.

*unconnected threads. We have added extracts of two of his letters.* The
Seceders *describes him as "a very genuine and lovable man, simple, earnest,
sensitive, humble, upright and deeply taught, with an intelligence as sound as
it was clear, and a most fervid devotion to the cause of truth."*

*After his death Mr. M'Kenzie was the subject of a vicious attack by
Frederick Tryon of Deeping St. James, Lincs. (1813–1903)—the man who
also attacked J.C. Philpot and John Warburton. Mr Tryon contended that
Mr. M'Kenzie was a deceived character. This called forth a pamphlet in his
defence by William Brown of Godmanchester* A Stone from the Brook, *and
an article by J. C. Philpot in the* Gospel Standard.

John M'Kenzie has not informed us when he was born, but he must
have been about as old as his century. Like most young Scots he had
received a sound education and been carefully brought up. Until he
finally settled at Preston in Lancashire, he had been what we should
now call a commercial traveller, walking from place to place with his
samples and his order-book on his back.

Convinced in his soul of sin and guilt in 1832–3, he laboured and
struggled hard for heaven by works. Having on September 1st, 1833,
joined the Independent community at Cannon Street, Preston, of
which a Mr. Carnson was the pastor, he was soon after appointed
superintendent of their Sunday school on Snow Hill, and began to
deliver addresses after school hours on Lord's day afternoons to the
older girls of his class, until two ministers and two deacons stopped
him.

"About July 1834," he tells us, "my eyes were opened to see the
doctrines of grace and God's method of salvation—that eternal life
was the gift of God through the righteousness of Jesus Christ. This
gave great relief to my mind, as I was grossly ignorant of the doctrines
of grace, and even of the meaning of the word 'grace,' thinking the
only way to heaven was making my soul fit for heaven by holy
devotions, holy works and holy frames and feelings. At this time also
I saw that the characters spoken of in Matt. 5. 8–11 presented the
feelings of souls changed by the grace of God. These characters I
found to be a true and exact description of my feelings, which greatly
comforted and encouraged me."

"I have wondered," we find him writing later on, "to see language
penned thousands of years ago describe so exactly the feelings of my
own soul; but this is the mystery of God's blessed Book." And he
might have added, its beauty.

But a far more graphic account of M'Kenzie's conversion is to be found incidentally in a description of his own call to the ministry contributed at John Gadsby's request to the *Christian's Monthly Record*, by James Fairclough, of Garstang in Lancashire, a farmer by occupation, and a preacher well known and loved in the North, who was of about M'Kenzie's age. It must have been in the summer of 1834 that they first met, and the record is well worth preserving.

"An old man, a shoe-maker, who lived near me," writes Mr. Fairclough, "told me, one day, there was a Scotchman who came that way every three weeks and called at his house about five o'clock, and was very punctual as to time. He considered him a very nice sort of man and would like me to have some conversation with him. I met him (M'Kenzie) the next time he came, but he was very shy and durst scarcely speak to me. After we became acquainted, he told me what his feelings and views of me were—that the doctrines I preached led to licentiousness. People say that we say, 'Let us do evil that good may come.' But what says the apostle? 'Whose damnation is just.' He told me afterwards that he looked upon the old man I had sat under, the late John Shaw of Nateby, as something like a viper, and he would bite and leave the poison behind him; and that I was of the same kind, though not quite so old and bad as he as yet.

"The second time we met he left the impression upon my mind that I preached that we may continue in sin that grace may abound. But the next time we met what a change had taken place! The man was completely broken down. He had been seen by some of the neighbours, while crossing the fields, under the hedge and in the ditches, praying; and they called him 'the mad Scotchman.' He had been expecting to get perfect in the flesh; but, instead of that, like the woman with the issue of blood, he got worse and worse. He began to open to me the exercises of his mind in an indirect way by asking what I should think of a man who felt so and so; describing his state and the dreadful bondage he was labouring under, varying his manner of relating his feelings several times. I felt the man was opening the burden of a broken and contrite heart, and that he was really speaking of himself, however much he might strive to disguise it at times; and to every inquiry he made, I believe I was happy to answer him by some sweet promise or portion of Scripture, which was suitable to comfort his broken and contrite heart.

"The last I brought to bear upon his hungry soul was Christ's sermon on the mount: 'Blessed are they that hunger and thirst after righteousness,' etc. I made a little comment on the passage. I said, 'It does not say they will be blessed merely when they are filled; but it says they *are* blessed *now* who do hunger; for that hunger proves that they are possessed of a principle of divine life having begun in the soul.'

"From that moment, as he expressed himself, the scales of ignorance and his bondage under the law fell from his eyes; the Bible became a new book; the way he looked at it, and had been instructed to look, was completely reversed; his old (legal) things passed away, and a clearer view of the plan of salvation was opened to his spiritual view."

Inspired by this revelation, for it can be called no less, M'Kenzie, as already mentioned, began to speak a little, though as yet only in the school-room, to a class of big girls about the doctrines of grace as unfolded in John 3. 3–8 and Isaiah 62. 12. But he soon found himself arbitrarily silenced, and on his refusal to recant he was formally excommunicated by the Independents of Preston on May 12th, 1835 (barely six weeks, be it noted, after J.C. Philpot for the very same reason had formally excommunicated himself from the Church of England). M'Kenzie, too, felt drawn to the Particular Baptists, a few of whom met in a hired room in Cannon Street, Preston, and several of his former hearers joined them with him. Eventually he was baptized at Blackburn by Mr. Worrall, September 6th, 1835, exactly a week before Mr. Philpot was baptized at Allington.

In the May following the friends at Preston prevailed on him to become their pastor, and they moved to the Vauxhall Road chapel on December 4th, 1837.

Shortly after this he wrote: "For a considerable time back I have had exceeding fears of the reality of my Christianity, because I could not feel my own interest in the work of Christ satisfactorily; nor could I feel the Spirit bearing testimony to my spirit that I was one of the sons and heirs of God, in that decided manner which I knew the Word of God set forth. I knew exceeding little of the bright and pleasant side of the Christian's experience; the black and painful side I have felt much and long. A sense of sin, guilt, vileness, darkness, doubts and fears; the workings of rebellion and tribulation, were my general feelings. But I well knew this was only one side of the question, and that there was a more decided and satisfactory revelation of Jesus to the soul, and a more feeling and distinct testifying of the Spirit to the conscience of our sonship, and a plainer handling of the 'earnest penny' than I had ever felt. Consequently, I found myself as one 'weighed in the balance and found wanting'; and such passages as the following would hunt me and pierce me to the heart: 'The Spirit Itself beareth witness with our spirit, that we are the children of God'; 'He who hath sealed us is God'; 'Ye were sealed with that Holy Spirit of promise'; 'God hath sent forth the Spirit of His Son into your heart, crying, Abba, Father.'

"I thought the Spirit never had thus borne witness to mine, and that I had never been stamped with the living seal of God, nor could I say, 'Abba, Father.' And Paul confidently saying, 'Christ *loved me*, and *gave Himself* for *me*,' cut me to pieces. My tongue stammered, and I could not say plainly, 'He died for me.' When such passages overtook me, I would take refuge in knowing I was the subject of doubts and fears, despondency, darkness of mind, weakness, blindness, and ignorance; hungering and thirsting after righteousness; tossed with tempests, and not comforted; seeking water, and finding none, and plagued with sin and Satan's temptations; for the Word of God has spoken of such feelings as being the feelings of the living family of God. Consequently, I concluded I must be a child of God, and would then rest and comfort myself from this indifference as much as I could; but, time after time I was roused from this *refuge of lies*, by such scriptures as the above, and by the thought that a real experimental Christian, taught of God, like a ladder, had two sides, the dark and the bright side; sorrow and joy, weakness and power, captivity and deliverance, tribulation and peace, mourning and gladness, fears and confidences, despair and hope, the warring of sin and the reigning of grace. . . .

"On the 15th of June, as I was reading John 8. 31–36, the Comforter was pleased to shine on the words and in my heart with such glorious light and power that the very words sounded in my ears as if spoken directly from Christ's own mouth. In them I saw and felt Jesus as the *law-fulfiller, sin-bearer*, and *absolute* Saviour of poor law and sin-bondaged souls in such a clear and glorious light, that I stood amazed and astonished with wonder at the goodness, mercy and rich grace of God to poor souls. The glorious and blessed freedom I beheld in Christ for His people ravished my heart, broke it to pieces and filled it to the brim with a glowing gladness and rejoicing, so that I could not refrain from blessing and praising His precious name.

"The following passages were also made very sweet to my taste: 1 Cor. 15. 55—57; Rom. 3. 21—24; 7. 24, 25; Gal. 3. 13; 4. 1—7. I

now felt as visible a change in my soul as there is betwixt light and
darkness. I looked for my trouble, sorrow, and distress, but I could
not find it; it was gone; the Lord had done it, and it could not be
reversed; 'When He giveth quietness, who can make trouble?' 'The
Lord killeth, and maketh alive; He woundeth, and His hands make
whole.' I could no more see any trouble now than I could rejoice and
feel peace before.

"There was a complete change—'the oil of joy for mourning, and
the garment of praise for the spirit of heaviness'; 'Instead of the thorn
came up the fir tree, and instead of the brier came up the myrtle tree';
'The desert rejoiced, and blossomed as the rose'; 'In the wilderness
waters broke forth, and streams in the desert'; 'The thirsty land
became springs of water'; in the dragon's den grew reeds and rushes.
Jesus was exceedingly precious to my soul; 'His fruit was sweet to my
taste'; Himself 'altogether lovely and chief among ten thousand'; 'His
left hand was under my head, and His right hand did embrace me.'
And what made it altogether so satisfying and dear to my soul was
that I felt as persuaded as I did of my own existence that it was the
blessed Comforter that was shining into my heart, and revealing Jesus
so gloriously, and making the truth of God so sweet; the change in my
feelings was so clear and sovereign, and the delight, pleasure and
gladness I felt so precious and supernatural-like. Like Abraham, I saw
Christ's day and was glad, and like Moses, Deborah, Hannah and
Mary, 'my soul magnified the Lord, and my spirit *rejoiced in God* my
Saviour'; for His 'anger was turned away, and He comforted me, and
did excellent things for me'."

At what date he married his first wife, to whom he was deeply
attached no less by spiritual than by natural affection, I have been
unable to discover, but he lost her a fortnight before Christmas 1839.
I have a suspicion that she died of consumption and may have
conveyed the disease to him, for in those days even the doctors scouted
the idea of consumption being catching and no precautions were
taken. "Many and many a time," he wrote to a friend immediately
after her funeral, "we have conversed together on spiritual things, as
if there had only been the Lord and ourselves in the whole universe;
but, alas! all is gone." And he adds a postscript, which shows what
blessed comfort a godly faith can bring to the afflicted:

"P.S. I have just opened into the fifth chapter of Job, and O! how
God has blessed it to my poor soul, but particularly the 19th verse.
My eyes now run tears of joy, and my heart is melted in love. I feel as if

God's own mouth were speaking to me, and I can believe, though with trembling, what He says. I feel Him in my heart and I love Him. Do read it, and may God bless it to your soul."

On March 19th, 1842, M'Kenzie had a special manifestation of the divine love and mercy:

"I then turned to the 4th chapter of Romans again (my heart being soft) when suddenly my heart was filled with glory and love to God, so that I could scarcely refrain from kissing the leaves of the book. The very name of God in the print of the leaves fired my soul with love. I felt heaven let down into my soul. The mercy and love of God and Christ overwhelmed my soul, and such ardent love did I feel to God that my poor heart felt as if it would have broken. I knew not whether God loved me or I loved Him the most. I felt as if the Holy Ghost had come down and filled my heart, and taken possession of it, as I know He did. I felt my heart was not my own, the Holy Ghost, entirely independent of me, had taken hold of it, and filled and blessed it.

"And O the sweet, heavenly, and powerful heart-breaking feeling I had at this moment cannot be conveyed to you in language. The love of God was abundantly shed abroad in my heart, and joy unspeakable and full of glory rose out of it. I felt no sin, no guilt, no wrath; it was all put away out of my sight. Nothing was laid to my charge; my vile sins appeared without guilt or sting; peace with God was in my heart. And O how sweet did His goodness and mercy appear! I felt and knew that the blessed Spirit was in my soul; I had the witness in myself.

"While in this blessed state I could do nothing but sob, and weep, and praise, and adore with a heart broken with love and mercy, while such expressions as the following burst from my heart and lips, as it were involuntary, 'O what is this? What is this? What is this? O bless Thy name for evermore, for evermore, for evermore; Thou hast saved me, saved me, saved me for ever! Blessed God, my God, my Father, my dear Father, bless Thee, bless Thee, bless Thee, bless Thee, for evermore! Loved for ever!' These and many more such expressions burst from my heart and lips, as it were whether I would or no. And all this time I was weeping as if my heart would break with love and blessedness. The blessed feeling was so heavenly that I was fully assured it was the Holy Ghost in my heart. It was the earnest of eternal glory.

"The height of this sweet and ever to be remembered manifestation of favour and love continued, as near as I can think, from five to ten minutes, and more or less from half to three quarters of an hour. O the blessed feeling never can I forget. Happy man! Favoured creature! O, why should the adorable Lord love and manifest His love to so vile a wretch as I? O, why should He let down heaven into my soul, and fill me with the Holy Ghost, and then seal me with the Spirit of promise?"

In September 1843, he came to London in fear and trembling to preach and collect money for the debt on his chapel. He proved, however, so acceptable to the people at Zoar, Great Alie Street, that he was pressed to come again, and two of his sermons have been preserved, one delivered on August 25th, 1844, and the other on October 20th in the same year. It was a year later, I conjecture, that J.C. Philpot heard him preach at Eden Street Chapel, London, "with that melting savour and power that I have scarcely felt under preaching, either before or since."

M'Kenzie had married again at some unspecified date a lady some twenty years younger than himself, who had left the Church of England, thrown in her lot with the Preston Baptists and been baptized. She, too, while staying in London with her husband, very nearly died of cholera, in September 1845. (She departed this life eventually in her 50th year in 1871, after twenty-two years of widowhood.)

By this time, 1845, M'Kenzie had become in considerable request as a preacher. Isaac Harrison engaged him to "supply" at Leicester, and in October 1847, the Eden Street friends, soon (1854) to remove to Gower Street, gave him a call to preach to them for six months with a view to his election as their pastor, but he could not make up his mind to accept it. He had previously been invited to become minister to the friends at Liverpool, and he was much inclined to consent, as the thin congregation at Preston disheartened him. Yet on March 6th, 1848, though it was a snowy morning, he baptized ten new members in the river Ribble there. Forty years later one of the "ten," Margaret Thompson, was often heard to speak of the peace of mind and the comforting of the Holy Spirit which she had felt in her heart on that occasion. She wouldn't mind the snow, she said, nor being baptized again, could she enjoy what she did that morning.

On January 28th, 1849, he preached his farewell sermon at Preston, and the following week his first sermon at Liverpool. In the mysterious but unerring providence of God, a month later, on March 3rd, 1849, the newly appointed pastor had a sudden haemorrhage from the lungs, bringing up about a pint of blood. It was the beginning of the end. In hope of recovery, he spent three months at a hydropathic establishment at Darley Dale, Derbyshire, returned to Preston July 25th, and never again left his room, dying of intractable haemoptysis on August 12th.

See also
*Fragments of the Experience of John M'Kenzie, 1850.*

# JOSEPH CHARLES PHILPOT

## 1802–1869

*A*mong *the Editors of the* Gospel Standard, *William Gadsby alone excepted, none has been more widely known than J. C. Philpot. During his long editorship the magazine was read and loved as far away as the Australian bush, or the Crimean battlefield, or the vast spaces of the United States.*

*In his editorials, reviews and meditations he was able to make the profoundest truths understandable to the simplest of people, and brought before them things of which they would never otherwise have heard. But it was the unction and dew that rested upon his writings that made them so dearly loved by the people of God.*

*Ten volumes of his sermons have been reprinted in recent years ( of how many other nineteenth-century preachers can this be said? ). These are esteemed not only in our country but in Scotland and the United States and, translated into Dutch, are widely read in Holland. His preaching was marked by clear views of gospel truth; an ability to set forth the deepest truths in a simple manner; a wealth of similes from nature to open up and explain the things of God; and a clear discernment of the vital distinction between a mere profession of Christ and a true saving knowledge of Him.*

*"In Philpot we have an example of natural learning sanctified and put to a good advantage by the influence of grace and the teaching of the Holy Spirit. And the immense good which resulted from the culmination of these two blessings, both natural and spiritual, we may observe in his sermons and writings which have been handed down to us."* (Gospel Standard 1965).

*The following account is taken from* Further History of the Gospel Standard Baptists.

Joseph Charles Philpot was the son of a clergyman, the Rector of Ripple, near Deal in Kent, being born there on September 13th, 1802. Both his parents were of Huguenot extraction, and it will be seen were intimately connected with the Church of England. When only nine years of age, he was sent to the Merchant Taylors' School in London, but had only been there a few months, when he was taken ill with chest trouble, which had already made some gaps in the family. He was sent back home, but became so much worse that it was thought he would not recover. These were not however the Lord's thoughts, who had a work for him to do in years to come. But the illness left him with a weak constitution, which was to be a daily cross throughout his life.

When sufficiently recovered, he was sent back to London, but this time to St. Paul's School, where he remained for six years and had the reputation of being one of their best scholars. He must then proceed to a University, as his father wished him to become a clergyman, and in October of 1821 he entered Worcester College at Oxford with an open scholarship. At the end of three years' study, he passed his final examination with great success, being one of the four who were placed in the first class, with a degree in Arts. While at Oxford he was again very ill with inflammation of the lungs, but was once more spared to recover, and continued there to obtain a Fellowship, while earning an income by training pupils.

So matters advanced according to his own and his parents' wishes, and although of high principle and living a moral life, he was notwithstanding "dead in trespasses and sins, and without God and without hope in the world." But in the Autumn of 1825 there came a providential change in his life, which proved to be in the purposes of God a prelude to a saving change in his soul. A wealthy Irish gentleman had called at Oxford to obtain a tutor for his sons, and this led to Mr. Philpot being engaged in this capacity, and his consequent removal. It seems that the engagement hinged upon what may have seemed a trivial event, and yet proved to be a turning point in his life. In one of his sermons in later life, Mr. Philpot recalls the remarkable providence thus: "A gentleman sleeping in Oxford, instead of going off early the next morning, remained two or three hours later. That circumstance gave me an interview with him, which resulted in my going to Ireland. Upon that simple incident then, of a gentleman staying a few hours in the town, hinged the whole work of grace in my heart."

Another apparently trivial, but remarkable, providence preceded his journey to Ireland to take up his new post. He had been to Leicester on some business, but when returning, his coach was delayed at Oakham for about two hours; and to pass away the time, he walked about the town and eventually entered a bookshop—always an attraction to his studious mind. There he found a copy of *Hart's Hymns*, which he had never met before, but purchasing it, he walked on into Burley Wood reading the contents. He was much struck with the truths so beautifully expressed in the hymns, upon which he ever afterwards set such a high value. He little thought at the time what they would be in his future life, nor that he would in years to come be the pastor of a Strict Baptist chapel in that very town.

It was in the Spring of 1826 that he went over to Ireland to commence the tuition of the gentleman's two sons, in a secluded spot not far from Dublin. The first year was happily spent, as he had all that the natural mind could wish; and his attachment to the family in which he was now called to live was no doubt much sweetened by the affection which he began to feel towards the sister of his two pupils. But it was here, in this very tender spot, that it pleased the Lord to bring "one of the greatest sorrows" of Mr. Philpot's life, and by means of the deep affliction that it was, to wean his heart from the world and bring eternal things with much weight and concern on his soul. The ardent affection between the tutor and the young lady did not meet with the approval of the father, and had to be broken off, and Mr. Philpot returned to Oxford. But the work of grace had begun, and here we may again quote from one of his sermons:

"In the beginning of 1827, in the early Spring, the Lord was pleased to bring upon me a very great trial and affliction, which I cannot name, but it was one of the greatest sorrows I ever passed through in my life; and it was in and under that affliction that the Lord was pleased, I have every reason to believe, to begin His work of grace upon my soul, and to do for me the things I have spoken of, in giving me the light of life, planting His fear in my heart, pouring out upon me the Spirit of prayer, and communicating those other sealed evidences which I have laid before you; for though not without a hope in God's mercy, I was not favoured until some years after with any special manifestation of Christ."

On his return to Oxford, although a Fellow of his College, Mr. Philpot found himself unable to settle down again among his old associates. The work of grace in his soul had made a barrier to old friendships, and he was regarded with distrust and coldness by his former colleagues, and eventually the Provost informed him that his new religious tenets would exclude him from further advance in the College. This led him to seek retirement as a parish clergyman, and in 1828 he was appointed to the joint curacy of two neighbouring villages, Chislehampton and Stadhampton:

"I soon found there was no mixing together the things of God and man. Persecution from the heads of the College fell upon me, which much severed the tie, and broke to pieces the pleasing prospect I was indulging of worldly advancement. A great gulf seemed placed also in my feelings between my former friends and myself; and one day in particular, in the year 1829, as I was sitting on my horse near the College gates, it was so impressed on my mind that Oxford was no place for me, that I gladly turned my back upon it, and went to reside permanently at Stadhampton."

As there was no vicarage at the village, he took rooms in a farmhouse, and being made himself to feel the solemn importance of eternal matters, he entered into the duties of his curacy with much earnestness and zeal. Although weakly in body, he did not spare himself, but laboured often beyond his strength. On the Lord's day, it was his practice to spend some time in the Sabbath School before the morning service, during which he usually preached for an hour. After the service he was expected to have lunch with the Squire; but he soon found this was unprofitable and had to be relinquished, which brought a good deal of reproach. After the afternoon service, he would again visit the School and question the children about the sermon, explaining to them what they could not understand. In the evening, he usually gave an exposition on some portion of Scripture in his own house, where a goodly number would attend. Besides these duties, there was a prayer meeting on Tuesday evenings at Chislehampton, and a lecture in the Schoolroom at Stadham on Thursday evenings; and he was unwearied in visiting from house to house to read and pray with the people.

During the Spring of 1829, a further providence occurred which had a marked connection with his after-life, leading him to leave the Church of England, and eventually to cast in his lot with the Gospel Standard Strict Baptists. It was the practice of some of the clergy in those parts to meet together once a month at one another's houses, and at one of these clerical meetings Mr. Philpot came in contact with William Tiptaft, who was then the Vicar of Sutton Courtney. From the first these two became specially drawn together, finding a knitting of heart to heart as they discussed together the truths of the gospel and compared the exercises of their souls. This led to Mr. Philpot being asked to preach in the church at Sutton Courtney on a week evening, and writing of this he says:

"The middle aisle, which is unusually large in Sutton Courtney church, and was then in front of the reading-desk, was completely thronged, one might say jammed, with hearers—strange contrast to most of the parish churches, which even on a Lord's day present a miserable attendance. And of whom was the congregation made up? Almost wholly of poor men and women. Labourers were there in their smock frocks and weekday clothes, almost as if they had just come out of the fields; poor women in their cotton shawls, with a sprinkling of better-dressed people in the pews; but a thorough plain and rustic assembly had gathered together to hear a sermon on a weekday evening—an event which had not probably occurred in that church or neighbourhood since the days of the Puritans."

In the Winter of 1830–31, these two clergymen were brought into more continued and intimate contact owing to the fact that Mr. Philpot was again brought low by an attack of his chest trouble, and in this afflicted condition was kindly nursed and attended by his friend Tiptaft, who took him into his own house for several weeks until he was well enough to get out-of-doors again in suitable weather. Mr. Philpot then had a period of further rest with his mother at Walmer, and in the meantime had arranged for another clergyman, Charles Brenton, to take charge of his parishes. This seemed to prevent Philpot's return to his duties, as he was unwilling to displace his substitute. During the year 1831 however, a circumstance occurred which brought Brenton to the decision of leaving the Church of England. He was expected to read the Church Burial Service over a wicked man who had died without any sign of repentance; and to avoid offending his own conscience by so doing, he abruptly left the Established Church. This made the way for Mr. Philpot to return to Stadham, which he did at Christmas in 1831, feeling that the Lord still had a work for him to do there.

William Tiptaft, who had seceded from the Church of England before Brenton, now had a chapel built at Abingdon, and as he had by this time become intimate with some of the Particular Baptists, he invited John Warburton of Trowbridge to preach at the opening of the new chapel. This soon led to Mr. Philpot being introduced to Mr. Warburton at the house of Mr. Tiptaft, of which circumstance he writes as follows:

"It was some time in the year 1833 or 1834 that Mr. Warburton came to Abingdon to preach at the chapel of my dear friend Mr. Tiptaft. I went over therefore to Abingdon, about eight miles distant, to see and hear Mr. Warburton. I was then, and had been for some time, a good deal exercised in my mind about eternal things, and went with many fears and under much bondage, both on account of my position in the Church of England, which I was then beginning to feel, and the state of my own soul, which was then passing through varied trials. . . . Under these circumstances I went to Abingdon, feeling my own want of grace, and therefore with more fears than hopes, as about to see and hear a servant of God so eminently possessed of it, and anticipating rather a frown than a smile, both in the pulpit and in the parlour. I afterwards learned that the poor dear man, having heard I was a man of great learning, was almost as much afraid of meeting the Oxford scholar as the Oxford scholar was of meeting him. But how much better grounded were my fears than his, and how much his grace outshone my learning! He received me however with much kindness, and talked pleasantly and profitably on the weighty matters of the kingdom of God. I heard him very comfortably in the evening; and the next morning after breakfast, he would have me engage in prayer, which I did with a trembling heart, but seemed helped to express simply what I knew and felt. . . . I afterwards learned that my feeble lispings had given me an abiding place in the dear man's heart, and laid a foundation for that friendship and union which has subsisted unbroken ever since between us."

Mr. Philpot's trouble about continuing in the Established Church still increased, and in 1833 he felt he must refuse to send any children from his parish to be confirmed by the Bishop, while his outspoken complaints about the practices of neighbouring clergy brought much reproach upon him. His weakly constitution also added to his difficulty of thinking of relinquishing his living and also his College Fellowship, and thereby giving up his whole income. But in March 1835 matters came to a head, and after preaching to his congregation at Stadham, he made the startling statement in the pulpit: "You have heard my voice for the last time within these walls. It is my intention to resign my curacy, and to withdraw from the Church of England; for I cannot longer continue in evil that good may come." His people were struck dumb with astonishment, and we are told "that the sounds of weeping were heard on every side; there was not one that did not feel it acutely, for he was beloved by all." So "like Abraham, he went forth, not knowing whither he went, but counting with Moses the reproach of Christ greater riches than the treasures of Egypt, and little foreseeing either what the Lord in His providence would do for him, or in His grace would do by him." Besides resigning his living, he wrote also a letter to the Provost of his College, relinquishing his Fellowship.

In the meantime, Mr. Joseph Parry, a farmer at Allington in Wiltshire, had heard of Mr. Philpot through his friend Mr. Tiptaft, and had been over to Stadham church to hear the young curate. This had commenced what proved to be a life-long friendship, and after Mr. Philpot had left the Established Church, he went to reside with his friend at Allington. After selling up most of his treasured books, he came to Allington on June 5th, 1835, and remained there until July, preaching at the chapel. He was baptized there on September 13th by Mr. Warburton, and often preached for that minister at Trowbridge until in June 1836 he left Allington for Oakham. In July 1838 he was married to a daughter of Dr. Keal and made his home at Stamford, from whence he visited Oakham each fortnight from Saturday to Wednesday, to preach for the friends there on alternate Lord's days and Tuesday evenings. It was in this way that he became established as the joint pastor of the Oakham and Stamford churches.

This settlement of Mr. Philpot as pastor over the joint causes could not but be a great disappointment to his friend Joseph Parry, who doubtless hoped that he would be led to settle at Allington; but the way in which the former was led and influenced to take the step is reflected in some of his letters to Mr. Parry during that period. Writing to his friend on July 25th, 1836, he says: "The opening for truth at Oakham and Stamford is very great, and persons come from distances which put your lazy Wiltshire professors to the blush. Twenty miles is not thought much of as a distance in this country. Yesterday morning was very wet, and this thinned down the congregation to what the Dissenters call comfortably full; but the weather clearing up, the afternoon congregation was overflowing."

Again on October 24th he writes: "The friends at Oakham have much pressed me to stay the winter, to which I should not have any great objection, as the climate is mild, the friends kind, and the door for preaching wide. The last Lord's day afternoon on which I preached being very fine, the congregation was overflowing. A person at the door counted fifty who could not get in; and on last Wednesday evening, which was moonlight and a beautiful evening, we had considerably more than at Allington on the Lord's day afternoon. I do not mention this as though it were anything, for novelty will bring a congregation; and I dislike a crowd, as it usually shuts me up, and seems to draw back anything like a flow of unction and feeling."

It was not mere numbers that attracted Mr. Philpot to Oakham and Stamford, as he here intimates, but it was no doubt the liberty which he realized in the pulpit, and the leading of the Spirit in his own heart. In another letter dated November 14th, it is evident that his mind was being drawn from Allington, as he feels he must disclose to his friend:

"I hinted in my last letter at the probability of my staying the winter in these parts; and as the friends here and at Stamford are very urgent that I should do so, I seem inclined to listen to their wishes. I do not however think it right to decide upon a point which affects you as well as them, without first writing to you on the subject. I am encouraged to continue here a while longer, as the people profess to derive profit from my ministry. At Allington you know, the Winter congregation is often very scanty. I find the climate here and at Stamford much more suitable to my weak chest than the cold blasts

which blow so chill and strong over your unsheltered Downs. . . .
You recollect that when I first came among you, I never promised to
tie myself to Allington, and have always considered myself as a
temporary supply, who was at liberty to go away for a shorter or
longer time, or even altogether, without its being considered that I
violated any engagement or broke any promise."

It is obvious that Mr. Philpot was preparing his friend for the break
which was to come.

It was in the following year, 1838, shortly before his marriage,
that he began to think of making his home in Stamford, especially as
the friends there invited him to become their permanent minister. To
this he refers in a further letter to Mr. Parry: "I was sorry to learn that
you were so much troubled at the mention which I made in my last
letter of my intention to settle here. Believe me, my dear friend, that
had it not been for my being under the necessity of fixing on some
settled place of abode, I should have paused very long before I
relinquished my post at Allington." The settlement as pastor of
Stamford and Oakham did not mean that Allington was altogether
forsaken, as Mr. Philpot used to visit them every year so long as his
health would allow.

It was not until 1843 that a Strict Baptist church was formed at
Oakham, when Dr. and Mrs. Keal and others were baptized, and the
Doctor chosen as deacon. A church was also constituted at Stamford,
when Mr. de Merveilleux and John Morris were baptized and made
deacons. Mr. Philpot was enabled to continue amongst the two
Congregations for twenty-six years, when his health failed so much
that, under medical advice, he relinquished the joint pastorate and
retired to Croydon. Previous to this, in the year 1856, he received an
invitation to become the pastor of Gower St. Chapel, London; but he
felt too much attached to his flock to think of leaving them.

Mr. Philpot's health suffered a serious breakdown in the Summer
of 1847 through an attack of inflammation of the lungs. He tried
hydropathic treatment at Malvern, but it was so rigorous as to seem
only to aggravate his condition, and he returned rather worse than
better. He then went to his mother at Plymouth for a month's rest,
and received more suitable treatment for his health, which was
recovered sufficiently for him to resume his labours in the following
Spring. Other comparatively short breaks there were owing to ill-
nesses, but it was not until 1864 that he felt he must give up the
pastorate. In April of that year he wrote a letter to the joint churches,

in which he says: "I have not really known what it is to enjoy sound health for more than thirty-three years, and for the last seventeen have been liable to continual attacks of illness, such as I am now suffering under. . . . My own ill-health for the last few years has left you for weeks sometimes without the preached word. And as we know that a congregation is first brought together chiefly by the ministry of the word, this circumstance has a great tendency to thin and weaken our assembly."

A more serious attack in the following Summer, and his medical adviser, Dr. Corfe, warned him that he was unfit for continuous labours and that the Stamford climate was too cold. So he writes again to Dr. Keal, who of course appreciated the medical side of the case, and says: "These continued attacks warn me that I cannot go on labouring as I have done. I cannot sacrifice my health and life, as I certainly shall do if I continue my ministry at Oakham and Stamford. . . . I shall much feel leaving my people and the friends with whom I have been connected so many years, and no other cause would have induced me to do so. But again and again, and especially of late years, I have been laid aside for weeks together; and it is but a gloomy prospect to look forward to a succession of attacks of a similar nature. . . . I wish to make it a matter of prayer that the Lord would direct my path, nor do I wish to come to a hasty decision; but as my year is up at the end of October next, and I cannot stay another winter at Stamford, it is in my mind not to go on beyond that time."

A similar warning was given to Mr. Lightfoot, then deacon at Stamford, and there seemed no course for the two churches but to accept the resignation, which they did with much sorrow and reluctance. The parting sermons were preached at Oakham on Lord's day, October 2nd, 1864, and the following week-evening. Speaking on the Lord's day he said: "It is now more than twenty-eight years since I first opened my mouth in this pulpit to preach the word of life, and very nearly twenty-six since I was permanently settled as the minister over this congregation; for at that time the church here of which I am the pastor was not formed. In that space of time, more than a quarter of a century, I have lived to witness great changes. . . . I myself have grown grey in your service. I have given you the best part of my life. I have spent upon you whatever strength I have had, both of body and soul, and freely given you of both whatever the Lord has freely given me. . . . But my failing health, and the attacks which I have had for several successive springs of illness warn me that I cannot go on as I have done."

At the close of the evening service, he thus addressed his affectionate farewell: "And now brethren, I bid you farewell. The God of all grace be with you and bless you most abundantly, that every prayer and petition which has been offered up in this place for you as a church and people, and for you in the congregation also who love and fear God, by myself and others, may be fulfilled richly in your heart's experience. I shall not be able, as I could wish, personally and individually to take my leave of you all; but thanking you for all the kindness, forbearance, affection, and liberality which you have shown me for many, many years, I now in the name of the Lord bid you farewell."

Public expression to the esteem and affection in which he was held by friends at Oakham was given in the form of a testimonial consisting of a handsome sum of money collected from the church and congregation. The Stamford friends presented him with a silver goblet and purse of gold. But there were some who were ready to take up false reports against the good man, attributing the resignation to divisions in the churches, or dissatisfaction with their pastor; or even a sordid motive in the latter, desiring to better himself or to seek a more exalted sphere of usefulness. This was an added trial to that of his failing health, and necessitated an explanation which appeared in the *Gospel Standard* of 1864, in which he speaks of the "grief and lamentation" among his congregations, that he was compelled to leave them, and points out his declining health which unfitted him for his pastoral office, to which was added his editorial labours.

So having had to retire from his pastorate at Stamford and Oakham, Mr. Philpot came to live in Croydon, where he felt it a privilege to sit when able under the ministry of Mr. Covell, as well as to supply in his pulpit when necessitated by the pastor's absence. The two ministers became very friendly, and their mutual esteem can be gathered from some of Mr. Philpot's correspondence, in which he calls his fellow-labourer, "Brother Frank." Writing to Mrs. Peake of Oakham he says: "We much like Mr. Covell. He generally comes to see me once a week and sits some time. We agree very well on most points. I find his conversation spiritual and profitable, without any affectation and cant." Again in a letter to his friend Joseph Parry of Allington he writes of the West Street Pastor: "He is a good man and has a good experience with a very fair gift, having a great knowledge of Scripture and much readiness in quoting it suitably and appositely. He is very friendly and generally spends an hour with me once a week."

Thus Mr. Philpot occasionally occupied the Croydon pulpit or was able to be present to hear their stated pastor; but although he benefited by the drier climate his weakness continued, and towards the close of 1869 an attack of bronchitis, which it was at first hoped would pass away as previous ones had done, proved to be the means appointed to bring his valuable life, with his ministerial and editorial work, to an end. Just before he departed he looked earnestly upwards and then closing his eyes said: "Beautiful!" He was asked what was beautiful, but was unable to give a direct answer, and presently said with a failing voice, "Praise the Lord, O my soul!" and so breathed his last on December 9th.

This was indeed a great loss to our little denomination, and especially to his family and his close friend, Mr. Covell, upon whom now fell the sad duty of committing the poor body to the tomb. In the midst of a storm of wind and rain this took place in the Croydon Cemetery amidst a large gathering of friends from all parts of the country. "Know you not," said Mr. Covell, "that a great man and a prince is buried this day, proving that all flesh is grass and the glory of man as the flower of grass. The gold of acquired literature that our dear departed friend possessed, and the silver of human eloquence to speak it forth, now lie silent in the dust; but John said he 'heard a voice saying, Write, Blessed are the dead which die in the Lord. Yea saith the Spirit, for they rest from their labours and their works do follow them.' It is done; the conflict is over; the spirit has fled. Let Zion's children weeping kiss the rod and gird on their robes of deepest sackcloth."

See also:
*Letters and Memoir of Joseph Charles Philpot, 1871;* reprint *1981. The Seceders* (3 Vols), 1930, 1960. A small, paperback edition of *The Seceders* is currently in print.

# JOHN GADSBY

## 1808–1893

*J*ohn Gadsby was the sixth (and youngest) child of William Gadsby. No life of him ever appeared. Printer, publisher, editor, author, traveller, lecturer—he was never a minister.

We have gathered together what information we can, and supplemented it with his own account of his spiritual experience. This he gave in a lecture in the Shetland Islands in 1864, which he later republished. His own experience is given in bits and pieces, in a disorderly way, with a description of Eastern customs. We have extracted this, and tried to fit it together.

114

John Gadsby was born in Manchester on November 19th, 1808, three years after his father had commenced his long pastorate there. He was apprenticed at an early age to a Manchester printer but became so efficient that, moving to London, he was earning four guineas (£4.20) a week as a compositor. In London he regularly heard Henry Fowler preach at Gower Street Chapel and James Wells at the Surrey Tabernacle. He was so fond of James Wells that he persuaded his father to invite him to Manchester—but, sadly, much controversy resulted. Returning to Manchester, his own business prospered till eventually it was felt prudent to transfer it to London.

John Gadsby was a most energetic, go-ahead-man—ardent, enthusiastic. At his funeral his old friend, Robert Moxon of Bury, said: "He was all activity, all energy, all push, all tact. He had not a quiet bone in his body, and was only quiet when asleep."

Most of his life he was unwell, suffering from a severe chest complaint, at times vomiting blood. Because of this he travelled extensively abroad. It is difficult to follow all his journeys but he was away for long periods in 1846–7, 1850–1, 1852–3, 1856, 1859–60 and in 1872 he visited the U.S.A. In 1888 he stated that he had visited Egypt nine times.

Much of his travelling was in Palestine (Israel), following which he published two volumes of *My Wanderings*, relating what he saw to Scripture. These books at one time had immense popularity, and are still a wealth of information. The *Illustrated News of the World* remarked: "We are not surprised at the popularity of Mr. Gadsby's work; it is exactly the kind of work to please the majority of his countrymen." Many other books written by other authors were published by him.

He also lectured (on occasions at the Metropolitan Tabernacle). The following is a typical advertisement for 1858:

"EASTERN LIFE. Mr. J. Gadsby's Illustrations of Biblical and Oriental Life will (D.v.) be given as follows: BRENTFORD (Town Hall), Jan. 4, 6 and 8. HACKNEY (Manor Rooms), Jan. 9, 11 and 12. LONDON (Music Hall, 16 Store Street, W.C.), Jan. 13, 14 and 15. BRISTOL (Broadmead Rooms), Jan. 20, 21 and 22. WORCESTER (Guildhall), Jan. 25, 26 and 27. BIRMINGHAM (Oddfellow's Hall), Feb. 3, 4 and 5. LEAMINGTON, Feb. 8, 9 and 10. ST.IVES Feb. 17, 18 and 19. MARCH, Feb. 24, 25 and 26. SLEAFORD, March 1, 2 and 3. At Half-past Seven each evening."

Also on the the wrapper of the *Gospel Standard* were advertised various mementoes that could be bought—water from the Red Sea; sand from the Arabian desert; leaves from the Garden of Gethsemane, etc.

Warm-hearted, generous to a degree, it is only fair to mention that John Gadsby spoiled himself by his egotism.

For many years the *Gospel Standard* was owned personally by him, as was the *Friendly Companion*, which he started in 1857, and re-started in 1875. By a generous Deed of Gift he handed over the magazines to the Trustees of the Gospel Standard Societies in 1878. In his later years he commenced another magazine, which he owned privately, and which he edited till his death, the *Christian's Monthly Record*. This was a most interesting magazine. It has been described as "religious titbits" but its fourteen volumes are a mine of information, and contain some most valuable sermons and letters.

John Gadsby was married three times, losing his first wife when young, and his second in 1871.

J. H. Philpot in *The Seceders* gives his recollections of a visit of Mr. Gadsby to his father in Stamford:

"I remember him as a spare and very hirsute little man with unkempt, grizzled beard and moustache, bright eyes and an engaging smile." (The only picture that has appeared in the *Gospel Standard* is the one of John Gadsby which was printed in 1893.)

Despite persistent ill-health John Gadsby lived to the age of 84, dying on October 12th, 1893. In his life he engaged in many controversies and certainly was not without his faults, but the Editor of the *Gospel Standard* wrote:

"Our dear friend's religion was such as 'endureth to the end.' He was no changeling. You do not find him in his writings drifting about, first from one thing and then to another. For a number of years together, you will find that his religion and his people were the same, without the slightest change. The old beaten path, and the same truths, held and preached by his dear father, were those which were dear to him all through life to its close.

"His exceeding kindness to the poor of God's people for a number of years, in such a variety of ways, and that, we believe, for Christ's sake, is by no means trifling as evidence that he was prompted by no mere love of applause, but as flowing from principles far higher and purer in their nature. We know that he has been accused of being influenced by unworthy motives in the bestowment of his goods; but we believe that nothing could be more unfounded, nor could the accusers know anything really of the person they thus accused. Not many men, perhaps, have received more ingratitude for their kindness than Mr. Gadsby; but nothing of this kind could stay his hand, for it was kept open to the very last.

"We venture to think that no unprejudiced person could have been present on the occasion of the funeral, and witnessed the scene which presented itself on that day, when the spacious building, Rochdale Road Chapel, Manchester, was filled by an assembly consisting of many hundreds of God's dear people, with their ministers, for several miles round, as well as from a greater distance—expressing by their presence and appearance the greatest interest during a service which lasted about two hours—without coming to the conclusion that our deceased friend was held in the highest esteem and affection."

*But it is time to let him speak for himself:*

It was the sun which shone on the 19th of November, in the year 1808, which first shone upon me; if, indeed, the sun were visible at all in Manchester on that day; a question exceedingly problematical, as my native town is not proverbial for sun-shinings, especially on a November day.

Like the rest of the human race, I was "shapen in iniquity and conceived in sin"; or, as the margin reads, *warmed* in sin. I was the *slave* of sin, just as those born in Abraham's house were Abraham's slaves. Sin was my master. I ate and drank at his table and obeyed his commands. I was "under" him (Rom. 3. 9); and not under him merely as a hired servant, at liberty to leave his service upon giving due notice to quit, but I was "concluded" under him (Gal. 3. 22), under him for ever, unless a Redeemer could be found. I had, by my own "act and deed," "sealed and delivered" the conveyance, or compact; and, so far as any power of my own could aid me, had no means of escape from its covenants or their consequences. As with Paul, so with me. I was "sold under sin"; and gave proof that in my flesh dwelt no good thing. I had sold myself by my iniquities. I was not only born in sin, and compelled to remain in sin's service until I became of age, as it were; but I sold myself to him when I arrived at maturity, and did his work more readily after that than I had done while in my minority. I was Satan's slave, and loved his service well; so well that it was my delight to remain with him and obey him in most things; and I should have lived and died in his service had not an almighty arm rescued me.

All this time I was tolerably regular in my attendance at a place of worship and almost everybody thought I was a very steady young man; but my master did not trouble about this. Satan has no objection whatever to his slaves attending church or chapel. He is quite willing, too, that they should be, as I sometimes was, liberal and charitable; and, indeed, sometimes even urges them to be so, as it serves to quiet conscience; but they are slaves, merely whited sepulchres, all the time.

I once, when a compositor in London, cheated my employer out of work to the value of some pounds; but when the Holy Spirit showed me something of the evil nature of sin, I never rested until I had made up every farthing, with interest. And well do I remember, on one occasion, when on the very verge of falling into one of the greatest sins I was ever tempted to commit in my life, being cut short by Joseph's words: "How can I do this great wickedness, and sin against God?"

There were some things, however, which my master never succeeded in compelling me to do; such as to throw myself into what are called the grosser sins of human nature. And this in later years often filled me with wonder, even after my eyes were opened to see the state I was in as a sinner before God; for never, perhaps, was youth more exposed to temptations or who had more opportunities to fall in with the temptations than I had. But when light shone into my soul, then I understood it all, and was enabled to say, in this as in other respects, "By the grace of God I am what I am!"

The most fascinating scenes were often placed before my eyes, the delights of the sins to which I am referring were, not only by Satan, but also by my sinful companions, vividly portrayed; but fearful as were the forces employed against me—persuasions, allurings, jeerings, so far from being drawn or impelled onwards, I more and more recoiled from them. Not because I felt that the sins were sins against a holy God; such a thought rarely entered into my head; but because I dreaded the consequences; not only having read of such consequences, but having seen them in some of my companions. O what a black page I could write here! What a mercy that either reading, or seeing, or anything was made the means by God, in His providence, of restraining me!

The singing-club, the card-table, the theatre, betting on horse-races, dancing-booths and the like at fairs were my delight.

I once spent £10 at Greenwich fair, dancing, or rather jigging, for I never learnt to dance, in the Crown and Anchor booth, until nearly 2 o'clock in the morning, paying for all my companions, and brandy flowing as freely as water into a horse-trough from a spring, though I was myself a teetotaller. I was never, indeed, intoxicated in my life, except, perhaps, once when a boy, through a friend (?) having given me a glass of wine.

In my younger days, I never knew what it was to want money, except as a result of my own extravagance. When a compositor on the "Sun" newspaper, I often earned my four guineas a week, and when appointed reader of that paper, i.e. "corrector of the press," as non-professionals always put it, my standing salary was £3. 2s. 7d. per week. I was allowed to be the quickest and cleanest compositor in London, the "whips" or "crack men" from other offices, being brought frequently to work against me, and bets being laid on the event.

For the amusement of my companions, I gloried, not only in singing foolish comic songs, but in forging ridiculous lies, and confirming them with the most awful oaths. Well do I remember, on one occasion, in the singing gallery of my late dear father's chapel, using a most awful oath. One of the congregation who stood by corrected me; when I exclaimed, "I'll be — if ever I swore in my life!" My face burns while I record the fact. O if the Lord had taken me at my word! Some friend, I never knew who it was, reported the matter to my father, and he was the means of making me feel so ashamed of myself that from that day to this I believe a profane oath has never polluted my lips. Many times afterwards did one quiver on my tongue, but it never escaped. And, I repeat, into the grosser sins, as they are called, of human nature I was never left to fall. O the restraining and preventing mercy of God!

At one time I had free admission to the Surrey Theatre, London, and went two or three times a week; now I am kept from having the slightest desire to visit one at all.

Notwithstanding all that I have said, I must add that I never remember the time when I was able to sin without some qualms of conscience; not exactly, as I have said, because I felt I was sinning against God, but because my education had taught me that it was wrong, but I always brushed those qualms aside as an elephant brushes aside the canes which are in his way in a jungle. And even here I see the restraining power of God.

In 1833 I lived at Chelsea. I had before this been impressed with the thought that if I died as I then was, I should die in an awful state. I had left my ungodly companions altogether, had married, and had a child; but I rarely attended a place of worship, often staying at home to attend to the child, as for some time we had no servant, and my poor wife was laid up sick. Still, as I had begun to reform, I was determined, as I thought, to have everything right as soon as possible. But one Sunday morning I found that my wife had forgotten to order any meat for dinner, and I went out to procure some. I thought nothing of it until I was paying the money; and then such a horror seized me that I was literally almost blinded. I felt as if I had been entombed in ice, and could hardly tell how I ever reached home.

This was the climax. This sin lay with tremendous weight upon my poor soul. I now began in earnest to pray that some way might be opened that I could regularly attend chapel, read my Bible, and be everything which a man ought to be. Sometimes I argued thus with myself: "If the doctrine of Arminianism be true, I will do all I can to be saved; and if not true, and I am lost, *the fault will not be mine!*" How awful! However, my prayers became more and more earnest, and I more and more anxious. And how were my prayers answered? By the solemn hand of death.

I went to the office as usual one morning, returning home about five o'clock in the afternoon and found that my wife had been seized with cholera. In a few hours she was a corpse. I rushed out of the room in a state of madness, and these words sounded in my ears as though some one really shouted them out: "I will answer thee by terrible things in righteousness." Instead of asking the Lord to have mercy on me and prepare *me* for death, I exclaimed, "Righteousness! What righteousness can there be in that, to snatch my wife from me in such a way?" Alas, Alas! Such was my rebellion.

But it was in righteousness after all; for by this means the Holy Ghost gave me my first lesson as to how I stood before God. All before this had only been outside; but now I felt I must know something I never yet had known, or I must be lost for ever. I strove hard to make myself believe that as I had not fallen into such and such sins, there might be hope for me; but a host of sins which I had committed, and others I had projected, appeared to rush into my mind at once, and stopped my mouth; and I was constrained to confess before God, for the first time, that I was a sinner, a *great* sinner. Such was my first lesson.

I then was compelled to acknowledge that I had no claim upon God to save me, and that if He did so, it must be of His own free and sovereign will; and I felt that if I were lost for ever it would be no more than I deserved; and I was led, consequently, anxiously to inquire how matters stood. Then it was that the parable of the Pharisee and the publican came to my mind; and from my very soul I cried out, "God be merciful to me, a sinner." Satan told me it was a "stereo-typed" prayer. But stereotyped or not, I felt that it suited me. If I never before knew what prayer was, I did then; and I felt that I could part with all I had if I could only be assured that that prayer would be mercifully answered.

About this time I visited Manchester, and heard a Mr. R. in my father's pulpit. He said that some hated or avoided sin, not because it *was* sin, but for fear of the consequences. I felt that that was my case. In the evening I heard my father in continuation, as it were, on the subject. He described the way in which we could distinguish whether our desires to keep from and our hatred of sin were of God, or were only mere nature; observing that if we hoped by so doing to merit God's favour, and were never delivered from that, it was not from God. Here again I was condemned; and in that state returned to London. I was not satisfied that my strivings and anxieties were anything but natural.

In this respect I was favoured above many. I believe one of the happiest days of my father's life was that in which he first learnt that my mind was exercised about eternal things. Neither was it a trial to me to leave my companions; for I had long before become disgusted with them, and given them up, without the slightest idea of the matter beyond its immorality and expensiveness. But I had afterwards to endure a temptation of another kind—that all I knew I had learnt from my father and the ministry of other good men. It is true they described my feelings most minutely; but had I not heard the same things from my youth up, and might they not now be only just coming fresh to my mind? Yet, I would say to myself, "I was never concerned about them before. How is it I am concerned now?" And over and over again did I wish I had never sat under the sound of the gospel; for then, I thought, I could have no doubt about the genuineness of my feelings.

For months was I tried with this, and could meet with no one similarly exercised; until, on one occasion, I went to hear a good man (the late David Denham[1]), who was led to speak upon the subject. The Word was blessed to me; and from that day to the present I cannot call to mind that I have ever been very much exercised on that point.

[1] (1791–1848), the hymnwriter

I for some time had a hope in my breast before I realized the blessing of adoption. I read and heard the Word, and over and over again I had a hope that I should be found right at last; but never had I had so good a hope as on one occasion when hearing a minister (Mr. H. Fowler) preach, on November 8th, 1833, from Lam. 3. 25: "The Lord is good unto them that wait for Him, to the soul that seeketh Him." While expatiating, as Mr. F. did, on the blessedness of being able to wait, I said to myself, "But I have waited so long." "How long have you waited?" exclaimed Mr. F., as though he had read my very thoughts. "Fourteen years? For Abraham had to wait that time; but he got the promise at last." "No," I said, "I have not waited as many months." "And the longer you have to wait," continued Mr. F., "the sweeter will the fulfilment of the promise be when it comes."

This was enough for the time. A great weight was taken off my mind, and my heart rejoiced. This was "rejoicing in hope." (Rom. 12. 12). I felt willing to wait, though I dare not say I waited very patiently. I wanted more than this. There was the promise, and I in some measure rejoiced in it. But it was not until the following Tuesday that it was fulfilled in my experience; and that was by the application of Psalm 130. 4.

I could scarce refrain from standing up and addressing all the compositors in the office; and at one time it was impossible for me to read the proofs. Not only could I not fix my mind upon them, but my eyes were so filled with tears that I could not distinguish the lines, much less the letters, and I had more than once to give up, and go to my lodgings. One of my companions, who with another had always taken my part when, just fresh from the country, I hardly, in business matters, knew my right hand from my left, listened attentively, and then begged of me to quiet myself, or I should assuredly become like my poor mother, I having told him that, poor dear woman, she had not had her reason for many years. I confess I felt for a moment shaken; but it was *only* for a moment. *Quiet* myself, indeed! He might as well have desired me to fly.

O how I longed for the Lord's day to come, that I might make known my joys to my friends! My new Master had my whole heart, not half of it only; and with that whole heart I praised Him, and spoke loudly in His praise to others. This was in November, 1833.

I had been in an exceedingly desponding state, but had had some encouragement from a letter from my dear father, in which he dwelt much upon the passage: "Blessed are they which hunger,"; and still more encouragement from the fact that a minister I went to hear in the evening, and of whom I then thought well, took the same passage for his text; but my encouragement was, indeed, only temporary; for it was suggested to me: "How would you be, were you now to be laid on a death-bed?" And I dared not attempt to answer the question. A trembling literally came all over me. I retired to rest lower in mind than ever, without having received the assurance that I was hungering and thirsting in a right way, though the remarks in my father's letter and those from the minister were very similar, and I felt persuaded that *they* could not have learnt them from each other.

In the morning, however, as I awoke, that passage came with great force and sweetness to my heart: "There is forgiveness with Thee." It came with such power, indeed, that I felt in a moment that I was forgiven. My sins seemed gone for ever, and, like the psalmist, I sang aloud on my bed. The question I have just referred to was again suggested to me; but, with tears in my eyes, I really laughed at it. I felt quite ready to die, and thanked God for giving me the victory through Christ, and exclaimed, "O Grave, where is thy victory? O Death, where is thy sting?" I saw forgiveness in a light I had never seen it in before, and I felt that it was mine. Both my body and soul rejoiced. I felt as though I had not a sin about me. I was as light as the air I breathed, and my soul was in a transport of joy.

Well do I remember getting up to dress, and sitting on the side of the bed, unconscious of the time, until at last I had really to scramble, as it were, to get off to my duties. I seemed as if I were in a new world. I was tolerably well acquainted with the Bible, but that also appeared new to me, and the promises in it, which came to me fast one after another, seemed to be mine; as, indeed, I believe they were and are.

I well remember, one Lord's day morning, about this time, when going to hear a minister in the south of London, accompanied by a son of the late dear Warburton, being a little late, the people were singing that hymn:

"My God, the spring of all my joys."

And the words were so sweet to me that it seemed almost as if they were angels who were singing; and I could join them heartily.

That I experienced these things, I *never* for a moment question, though I often doubt whether it was anything more than natural. The remembrance of it is sweet to me at this moment. I see the room, and myself sitting upon the bed, hastening to dress myself, yet hardly able to do so. I see all as though it had occurred only yesterday. *Was* it only the elating of my natural feelings? I can only say, though I have experienced providential deliverances almost miraculous, though I have more than once been snatched from an apparent death-bed, though I have been blessed with temporal mercies above many, and have seen and acknowledged the good hand of God upon me in marvellous ways, I never, on any other occasion, experienced anything like this. What I experienced in the Wilderness of the Temptation, as described in "My Wanderings," was of a softer kind, though equally blessed; nor do I believe that my natural feelings could by possibility, under any circumstances, be worked to the pitch of joy that I felt on both occasions. At any rate, if they could be, they never have been.

I went in the power of this for some time, and devoured greedily psalm after psalm and chapter after chapter in the Sacred Volume. I sang and rejoiced with the psalmists, and gloried with the apostles.

I trust, if I am not most awfully deceived, I know what it is to be as certain that my sins are forgiven as that Christ died on the cross, and yet at the same time to feel ready to tear myself to pieces on account of those very sins. And could I willingly renew them or augment their number? Alas! Alas! The longer I live the more do I feel a will within me desperately striving to make me do the very same things again, and worse. But, bless the Lord, I have another and a better will not less desperately determined I shall not. I use the word *desperately* unqualifiedly; for the struggle within is sometimes *most* desperate; so desperate that it sometimes seems that the better part would be conquered. And O how I have to cry, "O Lord, hold Thou me up, or I shall fall!"

When my soul was set at liberty under the gospel, I had no more doubt that God intended me to be a minister than I had of my own existence. The whole Bible seemed to be opened up to me. I purchased a little book, "Clarke's Scripture Promises," and every promise appeared to be mine. Yes, and I could expatiate on them too. If I read, "The Lord is good to them that wait for Him, to the soul that seeketh Him," I saw that there was a *waiting*, and a *seeking*. I saw that there was a God, omnipotent, able to perform what He had promised, and that He not only promised to *do* good to the waiters and seekers, but that He *is* good to them—good now, and will be good for ever. If I read, "Blessed are they which do hunger and thirst after righteousness," I saw that the promise was not only made for the future, but that the assurance was given for the present—they *are* blessed. If I read, "The Lord heareth the poor, and despiseth not His prisoners," I could see that these poor were *the Lord's* prisoners, not Satan's; and I believe one of the sweetest days I ever had in my life was the one in which that passage first struck my mind, and when I was led to meditate upon it; and I thought that *that* must be the first text that I should preach from. I pictured to myself crowded and admiring congregations and fancied, in the pride of my heart, that I should as far outstrip my dear father as he outstripped all the ministers in his day or since. But I soon learnt the truth of what my father says in his *Nazarene's Songs*:

"Young Christians oft please their vain mind
   With wonders they hope to perform;
But soon they come limping behind,
   Their courage all failed in a storm."

I have often thought of and wondered at one circumstance in my life. When I commenced business in Manchester, my best patron was the late Sir (then Mr.) Thomas Potter. The morning (Lord's day) on which I was baptized by my dear father, on leaving the vestry after the service I found a messenger waiting for me from that gentleman. "Mr. Potter," said he, "wishes to see you immediately. He wants some posting bills printed at once, to be on the walls before daylight in the morning." I replied, "I will wait upon Mr. Potter as early as he pleases in the morning, but I feel that it would be a sin to go now." "That answer will not do for Mr. Potter," said the messenger. "Depend upon it you will lose his support if you do not go." "I shall be very sorry for that," I responded; "but I must risk it. Tell Mr. Potter that I will be at his house by one o'clock in the morning, if nothing prevent; and if that will not do, I must bear the consequence."

The circumstance of Christ being baptized, and of the Spirit taking Him into the wilderness immediately afterwards to be tempted of the devil, came into my mind and I felt as bold as a lion in resisting the temptation.

I was up soon after midnight, and at the house. Mr. P. was exceedingly angry, and sent me the copy of the bill to the door by a servant. However, the bills were on the walls by daylight. After

breakfast, I went to Mr. P.'s warehouse, and had to endure a scolding
which was far from agreeable. He finished up, however, by saying,
"Well, I suppose I must look over it this time, as you are a good sort of
fellow on the whole."

Looking back over my life, I am a monument of God's care and
goodness. I once, when a boy, fell from a load of hay, at Bubnell,
Derbyshire, and was just snatched away from the wheels of the wagon
in time to be saved from being under them. A woolpack once fell
upon me in Piccadilly, Manchester, and stunned me; but, to the
surprise of everyone about at the time, did me no serious injury. A
straw-bonnet maker's block once fell upon my head, and made a gash
in it, the mark of which remains. How was it I was not killed? Once
when on Snowdon, in North Wales, I was so charmed with the
enchanting echoes that are to be thereon heard, the echo sweetly
singing, as it were, all the parts of music, echoed and re-echoed until
they died away in the distance, that I went to the edge of a precipice
that I might hear the more distinctly. A stone gave way from under
my foot. I slipped and fell. My brother-in-law seized hold of me by
the collar, and saved me from being dashed to pieces down the
precipice. Was it by mere "accident" that he was there? One Christmas, when a youth, I was going to a village a little way from
Stockport, when a "gentleman" in the coach (there were no railways
then) "happened" to be going to the same place. I readily joined
company with him, as the night was very dark and the way lonely.
But, when we arrived at Stockport, an old companion "happened" to
be at the coach office, preparing to return to Manchester by the coach
in which I had arrived. Seeing me with the aforesaid "gentleman," he
called me on one side, and said, "Do you know who that man is?"
"No," I replied. "Why, he was only let out of the New Bailey prison
last week"; and, at the risk of losing the coach, he started off with me
as hard as we could run until I was out of danger. Was all that mere
"accident?" I was once with a companion in the Olympic Theatre,
London, to see Madame Vestris. Two police officers came to the seat
behind us, and called out, "You two come out; you are two known
thieves!" My companion and I both thought he was addressing us,
and I trembled like a leaf; not that I *was* a thief, but fearing I had been
mistaken for one; but they were two men behind us who were
addressed. I was, however, so frightened that I never went to a theatre
afterwards. Was *that* an "accident"? When a boy, I was afflicted with
scrofula. My left arm was greatly affected. Our family doctor set an

issue right in the elbow-joint of my left arm; so that to this day I cannot properly bend my arm; and then said nothing could save it but amputation. My dear father was then in London and heard of a medicine (Dr. Webster's English Diet Drink) which had been made exceedingly useful in innumerable cases. He sent some down for me. Not only was my arm saved through it and with the blessing of God, but all scrofulous affection removed from my system. Was it by "accident" that my father heard of that medicine just in time to be the means of saving my arm, and probably my life? In 1843 I was given up for consumption. Some did not believe it possible I could live for twelve months. I was ordered to winter in Malta, etc.; and as pulmonary symptoms, such as the expectorating of blood, etc., appeared again and again, again and again I had to winter abroad, my last journey being in the beginning of 1874. At Jerusalem, in April, 1864, I was attacked with fever, dysentery, etc., and subsequently reduced to about 90 lbs. in weight. In the following June, being then at my own house, I expectorated not less than a quart of pure pus, from a large abscess in one of my lungs, so the doctor said; and from that time for ten years I had no serious chest ailment. Was it by "accident" that I had dysentery, which was the forerunner of this manifest improvement? And so I might go on. I sometimes think no man living has been more watched over and favoured by my Father in providence than I have, though I had not, at one time, eyes to see it.

For several years prior to 1846 I had been living in a way that I should not like to be transcribed on my forehead. Yet I was rarely absent from the Monday night prayer-meeting or the Tuesday night preaching; so that none but God and myself knew the state I was in. But my severe chest attacks in 1845 and 1846 caused me to think a little as to my state; but it was only a little. Did I seek for manifestive forgiveness? I was so hardened that I often seemed not to care whether I was forgiven or not.

The death of my dear father in 1844 had made some impression upon me; but it was not enduring. Then came my dangerous illness while in Malta at the end of 1846, and my subsequent journey to Egypt and the Holy Land. I began to be filled with bitter remorse. I did not wonder that God had afflicted my body, but I did wonder how it was He had so prospered me in providence, and that He had not blasted everything I had undertaken. I saw no deliverance; while death from consumption, according to the opinion of my doctors, was drawing nigh.

O! how well I remember, while on the French steamer going to Constantinople, how my past life was opened up to me! I had been baptized by my father, received into church fellowship, and attended to the precious ordinances of God's house. But O! what was I then! How I had departed from the good old paths, and been taken captive. True enough, while at Malta, I had, under the ministry of a Scotchman, been somewhat relieved; but I was still left a captive. Then came my journey from Egypt through the desert to Jerusalem. I was far from being insensible of the goodness of God to me in that "great and terrible wilderness," having been enabled to set up therein my "Ebenezer—Hitherto hath the Lord helped me"; but I was still not as I wished to be. When in the church of the Holy Sepulchre, as it is called, at Jerusalem, I felt a softening of heart which caused my tears to flow, and I had a sweet hope that I had an interest in Christ's sufferings and death; which was as an anchor to my soul, notwithstanding that it was suggested to my mind that I was every whit as superstitious as the poor pilgrims who were crossing themselves and kissing the priest-made relics. But I was still not able to say, "I know that my Redeemer liveth." Then came my journey to Jericho, through the Wilderness of the Temptation, and there it was that I proved the truth of the Lord's promise: "I will heal their backslidings, and love them freely."

In about three hours from the time of our leaving Jerusalem, our guide announced to us that we were entering into "the Wilderness of the Temptation." "The Wilderness of the Temptation!" I exclaimed; every circumstance at the same time rushing into my mind connected with that awful period when Christ was "driven into the wilderness to be tempted of the devil." And was it really *here* that the Saviour fasted for 40 days, while Satan hurled at His holy soul every temptation which ever was or ever will be endured by all His redeemed family? Well might the challenge be given, "Behold, and see if ever were sorrow like unto my sorrow!" And well might I, as in sincerity and truth I did, boldly answer, "Never, never! Impossible!" And I had such a sight of His sufferings, and so powerful an application to my soul of His redeeming love and pardoning mercy that I was overwhelmed with grief and joy; while my own sinfulness, unworthiness and backsliding so covered me with shame that I would fain have hidden my head; and yet I could hardly believe it possible it was a reality, though my heart was broken and my eyes ran down with tears.

I well remember, and in some degree feel the power of it now, that, after the challenge had been, as it were, given, "Behold, and see if ever were sorrow like unto my sorrow," and I had answered, "Never! *Never*! Impossible!" I had the assurance that those sufferings were for *me* so powerfully impressed upon my heart, that if an audible voice had declared it from heaven I could not have been more certain of it. And well also do I remember that after my guide had missed me, and stopped for me, and looked at me with astonishment, for I was saturated with tears and perspiration, that my mind was carried back to Jerusalem, and I was led to reflect upon what I had there witnessed, and what the Redeemer had there endured for *me*.

It is not possible, while my reason is continued, to forget the blessing I experienced the latter end of 1871 and early part of 1872, after the sudden death of my only daughter, leaving two young children, and the death, eleven days afterwards, of her beloved mother [Mr. Gadsby's second wife]. It was the sorest temporal trial I ever experienced in my life, except, perhaps, the loss of my dear father in 1844. Both wife and daughter were taken to glory, and the trial was so blessed to me, that for more than three weeks I had almost uninterrupted peace; and felt that I could shout out, in holy triumph, "Glory, honour, praise, and power be unto the Lamb for ever. Jesus Christ is my Redeemer. Hallelujah!" Never can I forget how those precious Psalms, 46, and 86, filled my whole soul! O! what an unspeakable mercy to have our trials thus sanctified to our soul's good, and to be enabled to say, "Even so, Father, for so it seemed good in Thy sight." I desire that the following verse by my father be put upon my tomb:

> "For me Christ shed His precious blood;
>   For me He in the winepress trod;
> He magnified the law for me,
>   And I for ever am set free."

See also:
*Slavery, Captivity, Adoption, Redemption,* 1876
*My Wanderings* (2 Vols.), 1872

# GREY HAZLERIGG

## 1818–1912

M r. Hazlerigg came of a noble family, his father being the 11th baronet. Educated at Eton, he had kissed the hand of William IV and carried the colours of his regiment in Manchester when Queen Victoria was crowned. However, through grace, he was brought to cast in his lot with the despised people of God.

There are still those alive who remember him and at least one aged member at Zion, Leicester, was received during his pastorate there. The vast Zion *chapel was filled to capacity during his ministry, and we understand that twenty-four persons were baptized during the last year of his life (he was ninety-four when he died). He, personally, was unable to baptize them, but preached the sermons at the baptismal services.*

*J. H. Philpot, in* The Seceders, *describes his boyhood memories of Mr. Hazlerigg in 1862.*

*"I remember him as a slim, dapper, little man with a pale, thin face and an aristocratic nose."*

*He was made a blessing to his own mother, Lady Hazlerigg, who was brought to know the truth when almost sixty-five years old.*

*Dearly loved by his own congregation, one wrote:*

*"How can we speak of him without our whole soul pouring out its thanks to God for such a pastor? A perfect gentleman, both by birth and by grace, a prince among preachers, of rich and rare gifts, full of sympathy with the poor, the tried and the afflicted, a clear exponent of experimental truth, but unflinchingly severe against all inventions of error."*

*The following is taken from his own account, at the beginning of his* Letters to a Mother.

In my childhood I used to be at times greatly affected with religion. How this came about I cannot say. I do not remember that any of my friends had anything more than the ordinary Christ-and-Mammon-combining religion. One governess I had when a very little boy used to make me kneel beside her, and say, "Let the words of my mouth, and the meditation of my heart, be acceptable in Thy sight, O Lord my strength and my Redeemer." I remember, however, periods when for days together I enjoyed much peace of mind, and even desired to die, that I might not sin again. Such a season I had when confirmed at Eton by the then Bishop of Hereford. I broke off for a season from my childish and youthful follies and vain ways and enjoyed a kind of peace in so doing. Some experience of the power of sin, and great ignorance as to the right way of overcoming it, made me fear at such times that I should again be overthrown and fall before the power of the enemy.

At times I used to be greatly troubled with terrifying dreams. In one night I woke up three times in great consternation, having dreamed that the end of all things was come, and the world was on fire. I merely relate these things as they certainly produced some effects, and had a considerable influence upon my mind. My conscience was in some degree awakened, and though exceedingly ignorant, I had enough light to make me uneasy. My conscience accused me because I did not come up to the scriptural standard of forsaking all for Christ's sake, and following Him wholly, which I saw was the will of God and essential to salvation. Such words as these: "Ye cannot serve God and mammon"; "Ye are dead, and your life is hid with Christ in God"; and others of a similar nature, but of which I had only a dark, legal, and carnal conception, made me feel that I lacked what was essential to true Christianity, and fell short of the standard of the gospel.

A degree of respect to religion was produced in my mind, and certain slumbering desires to be found right in the Lord. But in spite of all this, I was a poor, ignorant, sinful and sinning creature; sometimes repenting and sorrowing, and then again sinning against the light of a partially-instructed conscience. I could sin, and be sorry; until at length I could sin but I could not be sorry as before; though I think at this very time the real wound in the conscience began to be deeper.

In my eighteenth year I went into the Army; and though greatly preserved from some forms of sin, my life was one of vanity and evil, according to the course of this world, and far off from God.

In my nineteenth year came a change. The Lord, I believe, drew nearer unto me, and to this period I trace back the real work of grace upon my soul. If not then begun, it was at that time carried on with a prevailing power. One day I was sitting by a brother officer at dinner, or mess as we called it, and I reproved him for some scoffing remarks he made about Christianity. I was a sort of professor; he was a kind of infidel. He turned around sharply upon me, and said, "As for you, you profess what you know nothing about." This went home like an arrow, and drove me to my Bible and my knees in reading it. For about a week I read my Bible on my knees before the Lord. Truly I soon began to find that my brother officer was right. The Word of God began to take hold upon me and influence me in a way it had never done before. Amongst other portions the fifth of Matthew greatly affected me.

With some intervals, my mind became more and more absorbed with the subject of religion. I left off my former ways, became separate, as far as was possible in my position, from my former companions, and gave myself entirely, so far as was consistent with my duties as an officer, to one thing, seeking the salvation of my soul. The truth concerning my natural state as a sinner, the true character of God as holy, just, wise and good, the way of salvation by faith in Christ, the terrors of hell and the blessings of heaven, were more and more opened up to my sight. These discoveries, accompanied with many temptations, the workings of lusts and corruptions, and especially infidel objections which Satan began to inject into my mind, together with the fear lest I should fall away and go back to the world, and sin as too often I had done before, sank me very low, and made me extremely sorrowful. I could not enjoy the world as before; I did not enjoy the things of the heavenly kingdom, though at times I had such visitations from the Lord as encouraged me and sustained my spirit.

In this state, one morning these words were very sweet to me: "When I shall awake up after Thy likeness, I shall be satisfied with it." I saw that in this life I must have tribulation; the satisfaction was reserved for the world to come. One day, I was in prayer before the Lord, particularly fearing lest I should fall away and not attain to salvation, when suddenly there broke in upon my soul a heavenly light, accompanied by a full persuasion that I should be saved and obtain eternal life. This filled my heart with faith, love, humility and godly fear; and I broke forth immediately into singing, crying out, "I shall be saved! I shall be saved!" This was like a new and divine life breaking forth suddenly in my soul, filling it with glory, immortality, and joy.

The comfort and assurance derived from this visit lasted, as far as I can remember, for some time; but at length I was greatly robbed of it, and one thing that tended to do this was reading in some book that persons might experience such things as these and yet fall away and come to nothing. I was at this time as one feeling my way in divine things, without any one to guide me. Indeed, I knew of no one who could in the least degree enter into my case. I was very ignorant as to many things pertaining to salvation, and both men and books rather misled me than guided me aright. I began then to sink again, and to sink lower and lower into trouble. I went into deeper convictions and deeper exercises of mind.

As I thus saw more and more of my native blindness, and got deeper into the wilderness, the words in Isaiah were sweet and helpful to me: "I will bring the blind by a way that they knew not," etc. They gave me hope that the Lord would thus lead me.

I saw now clearly that all depended upon faith; that he that believed should be saved. At times, in reading or meditating, faith would spring up and come into lively exercise. In the Lord's light, as shining in the Word, I saw light. Then I felt happy and assured. Then I was persuaded I was a believer. At other times I was swallowed up in all sorts of questionings — Had I faith? Was God with me, or not? Was I sincere? and so on. When the Lord shone in upon me in reading or prayer, then I knew that I was sincere, believing, etc.; but when He withdrew, then I was restless again, tossing to and fro. Part of this time I was at home on leave of absence. Then I returned to my regiment again, and this produced new trials. Still the Lord gave me resolution, and enabled me to profess, and be separate from those living in sin. "My heart is fixed" etc. (Psalm 57. 7) was with me. But I was fearfully harassed. Infidel doubts bewildered and shattered my mind. Legality mightily prevailed over me, and swallowed me up. Floods of evil, vile, filthy and abominable thoughts were about this time poured upon my mind, so that I was in great trouble.

At times, however, as I told a brother officer who professed, I had periods of joy and peace which I would not part with one moment of for all the pleasures of this world. Once these words were very sweet: "I am the Way, the Truth, and the Life." At another time the Lord seemed exceedingly present with me as I read about Him as seen by John in the first chapter of the Book of Revelation. These were bright if transient breakings in of divine enjoyment into my soul. The language of my heart was, "Give me Christ, or else I die"; or, as I expressed it in my simple prayer, that I might be viewed as one abolished and received in Christ only as from the dead.

One day I was engaged in reading and prayer. I had just taken up a book to read, when suddenly the Lord descended by His Holy Spirit into my soul, filling it with the joys of heaven. I broke forth into praise and adoration with these words: "My Father, my Father." My thought was, "Well, what can heaven itself be more than this?" My soul was at once filled with love, joy, peace, faith and a godly awe. I remember that three-quarters of an hour passed away while I was upon my knees in this state of mind, and it seemed hardly a minute.

After this I again sank into deep waters, my many temptations overwhelming my soul. Beneath the exercises of my mind my health seemed to quite give way. On this account, and because the army seemed undesirable for a Christian, I sold my commission, and returned home. I was exceedingly out of health, and passing through the most violent temptations. My days seemed gone like a shadow, and amid the incessant distractions of my mind day after day passed by, as Job says, like the swift ships. . . .

One day, when I was reading the Bible I lit upon the sixth chapter of Hebrews, and it was as though its terrible judgments had struck me, for it was at once suggested to my mind that this was exactly my case, that I had fallen away after experiencing the things Paul writes about. I remember how my soul was instantly overwhelmed with the deepest anguish; how the greatest horror fell upon me. I thought that I had sinned beyond hope and the possibility of being saved; that it was impossible to renew me again unto repentance. A poor person at this time came to the door and begged. I relieved her; but it was with this feeling—that she was welcome to all I possessed; for what was the good of possessing anything, seeing I must be eternally lost. If I lived, thought I, for a hundred years, it would still come to this—I must be lost, for I well knew in my heart that God's Word could not possibly be broken.

This fear and horror would come upon me from time to time for the space of about six or seven years. At times I used to be comforted again and walk for a while somewhat comfortably and at peace with God. But again and again I kept falling before the power of inbred corruption. A legal spirit and the strength of nature were still powerful in me. All my surroundings, too, were of a carnalizing, delusive nature. Thus my way was full of infirmity and evil, and again and again this would come with overwhelming power upon my soul—that the terrors I had felt were certainly well-grounded, and harbingers of eternal misery.

Being at this time a professed member of the Established Church, I was taught that it was right, having been confirmed, to attend the Lord's Supper. I attempted to do this, but well remember the dread that fell upon me when the awful words about a man's eating and drinking his own damnation were read. I could endure no more. In horror I have risen up and left the place of worship, leaving the worthy communicants to partake. I dare not remain, being, I feared, reprobate and unworthy. . . .

I was like a person in a consumption; sometimes rallying for a season, but again falling beneath the power of organic disease. At length the Lord seemed to speak this word concerning me, "Ephraim is joined to idols; let him alone." The Lord will not have His people halved between Himself and the world. No; the judgment of

Solomon is, "Give her the living child, and in no wise slay it." There is a giving over of a child of God to Satan for the destruction of the flesh, that the spirit may be saved in the day of the Lord Jesus.

I went at length to Cambridge University, with some idea of going into the Established Church. But I found all my religion bit by bit taken from me. It was as if the Lord, as in Ezekiel (10 and 11. 23), took His departure from me. Mathematical studies and wrong associates quickly robbed me of my religion. I had, indeed, periods of strong compunction and bitter tears, particularly in hearing sermons; but I felt myself too strongly entangled to disengage myself, though I earnestly desired that it might be effected for me. All this time, under a tolerably cheerful outward appearance, I was secretly wretched. I was not really one with those I to some extent associated with. I was not happy in the midst of gaiety. There was, I believe, an aching void, an inward restlessness and dissatisfaction. At times, too, I was stung with remorse, thinking that now surely nothing remained for me except a fearful looking for of judgment and fiery indignation. . . .

Once, when in Ilstone Church, I was sweetly visited with a spirit of prayer which vented itself in a crying unto God in the name of Jesus. And now the name of Jesus began to be exceeding sweet to me so that I besought the Lord I might never have any gods but Him. Other lords beside Him had had dominion over me. In His strength I desired now only to make mention of His name.

One day, as I was walking, the words of Jacob were very sweet to me, being turned into prayer: "If Thou, Lord, wilt bring me again to my father's house in peace, then shall the Lord alone be my God." The words, too, of David were with power in my heart: "Then will I teach the wicked Thy ways, and sinners shall be converted unto Thee." Thus I seemed to vow vows. I seemed to have at times a vehement desire that the Lord Jesus Christ should be made glorious in the parts where I was dwelling: my own native parts. . . .

I was led about this time to set up family worship in our house again and to pray to the Lord that it might become as an altar in the land of Egypt. I soon saw the good effects of this in a greater seriousness in the family, and I had one or two remarkable seasons of prayer about some of its members. Thus I was struggling forward into rest. I was sweetly drawn by the mercies of God, and the High Priesthood of the Lord Jesus, as revealed in the Hebrews. I was awed and aroused by Paul's words: "How shall we escape if we neglect so great salvation?" "Today, if ye will hear His voice, harden not your hearts." These words, as applied by the Lord, at once aroused and alarmed me and yet encouraged. . . .

At length the Lord gave me rest and peace. He kept me still waiting upon Him. At one time I was tempted to try and assure my heart and give myself peace by a process of mere reasoning. I tried to argue thus: "Those who believe shall be saved, says the Scripture. I have believed; I shall be saved." But it would not do. Such a process brought no rest to my soul. The Lord showed me that I must wait upon Him for peace. This, in His own time, He gave me. He must speak peace to the heathen, and create the fruit of His own lips. Blessed are they, therefore, who wait for Him.

When I was thus waiting upon the Lord for a sweet sense of His favour to my soul, I was sorely tried by the temptation to believe that the Lord now did no miracles. He had done His part in dying for sinners. Now the sinner had to do his in a way of repentance and faith. All was done by the Lord that would be done; salvation depended, therefore, on the sinner's performance of his part. The conditions of the gospel were—Repent, and believe. Here I was at a stand. These conditions I could not fulfil. Thus the very gospel, if this were it, condemned me. I was feelingly, as Erskine writes, "quite powerless to repent, believe, or pray."

One day, when in Carlton Church, if my memory serves me rightly, a sweet relief from this temptation came to me. These words were applied with power to my heart: "I, if I be lifted up from the earth, will draw all men unto Me." I felt the drawing virtue of the cross of Christ. A crucified Christ brought, I believe, not only pardon, but faith, repentance and a receiving heart at the same time with Him. He makes the believer and gives him His crown.

But it was not by one or two visits, however sweet and powerful, that I was made to rest. The principal way the Lord took to establish my soul in the fulness of the blessing of peace, after all my wanderings and toil, was to pour the Epistles of Paul into my soul with the sweetest flood of light and life and liberty. I used to take them up to read. Scarcely would my eye have run through a verse before the mountains dropped with sweet wine, and the heavens rained down righteousness and blessedness in Christ, so that I had little more to do than to mount up into the sweetness of full communion with God in Christ. My soul seemed filled with the old wine of the everlasting love of God, like the bowls of the altar. All seemed perfect indescribable immortality and peace. Or perhaps I should begin to read, and all would appear death and condemnation, and then anon the Lord Jesus Christ would open my eyes, and the Holy Spirit would pour light and life and glory and peace into me. I had not to labour in those days for my spiritual food, but to eat that which grew of itself. It was a jubilee time to my soul in which it returned to its rest in Christ after a long legal toil, travail, and trouble.

Two great things which brought me into this state were—(1) I was enlightened to perceive, and enabled to believe in, the free access for sinners into the very holiest of all through the blood of Jesus; and (2) I was shown the completeness of the believing, coming sinner in the perfections of the Lord Jesus. These two things freed my soul from the burning wrath of God felt in it, and from legal trammels. I felt the blood of Jesus, sweetly again and again applied to my soul, speak peace therein, and I saw my access to the Father by the Spirit, through faith, as complete in Him. I saw the law buried, and sin crucified, the old man condemned and executed, and I felt the power of these truths in my own soul, freeing my conscience, crucifying my flesh, and bringing me experimentally into the fellowship and enjoyment of the risen life of the Lord Jesus Christ, where was no law, no sin, but God in Christ by the Spirit All in all. This filled my heart with love to God as made known to me in the Lord Jesus, with love to His people, and with an earnest desire to save men's souls and impart my blessings to others. I remember one day, when I was reading in Paul's Epistle to the Romans, through fatigue I fell asleep, as I was thinking upon verses 25 and 26 of chapter 3. I soon woke up, and immediately these very words came with sweet light into my soul, discovering to me the Lord's blessed way of justifying a sinner by faith in the blood and righteousness of Christ. I used to be exercised as to the possibility of a just God pardoning and blessing me; but He showed me that He could be just, yet justify the ungodly who believed in Jesus.

One day, when feeling in a spiritual sense a filthy leper, a man, as I often felt, full of leprosy, the Lord sweetly by faith plunged me into His blood and gave me fellowship in His resurrection. This visit was from the account of the cleansing of the leper in Israel, and answered in experience to the poet's words:

"Dipped in his fellow's blood,
    The living bird went free:
The type, well understood,
    Expressed the sinner's plea;

Described a guilty soul enlarged,
And by a Saviour's death discharged.''

I experienced in my own soul this plunging in Christ's blood, and this
sweet liberty of heart and conscience before God. One day, in hearing
a preacher, I was most sweetly blessed as he expounded Leviticus 16. I
saw my sins laid upon the head of Christ, and carried away by Him
into a land of forgetfulness, no more to bring me into condemnation.
At another time the same preacher sweetly pointed out that the
believer in the Lord Jesus had already passed through sin and death
and judgment and hell into life and glory and blessedness. This he
had already done in the Person of Another. Therefore his standing in
Christ was better than that of Adam in innocency. Adam could fall.
The believer in Christ must live for ever.

The Word of God was indeed sweet to me in those days. Not only
Paul's Epistles, but the Bible generally, from Genesis to Revelation,
was full of Christ. He was the Rose of that Sharon. His fragrance filled
its pages. A sweet savour of Christ was everywhere. Before, the Bible
had been a great book; now, it was everywhere a sweet book to me.
Christ was the sum and substance of it, and nothing in those days had
any charm to me except that which had Christ Himself in it. His
words were found, and I did eat them and He Himself as in them was
the food and the joy and rejoicing of my heart. Christ was all. Oh,
how sweet were the words of Paul: "Of Him are ye in Christ Jesus,
who of God is made unto us wisdom, and righteousness, and sanctification, and redemption." Though I saw Him to be the Holy One of
Israel, I could rejoice in Him. I had conceived of Him as a hard Man;
but now I beheld Him as John writes: "We beheld His glory, the
glory as of the only-begotten of the Father, full of grace and truth."
He seemed all grace to me. Full of grace were His lips. As a holy,
harmless High Priest, I saw He just became such an one as myself. He
was separated from sinners in order to receive sinners to His glory. He
could touch a leper and turn leprosy into purity; but contract no
defilement in so doing. An infinitely eternally holy High Priest I saw
was God's provision for, and not against, a sinner. I had known Christ
after the flesh, thought of Him in a carnal way, now I knew Him so no
more; but I trust, under the teachings of the Spirit, all had become
new, and my soul was blessed and happy in the enjoyment of a
crucified, risen Saviour. His Name was sweet to me in those days. His

very Name, Jesus, was as ointment poured forth. He was grace itself
to my wounded, sin-sick, ruined soul, and I loved Him. . . .

From the earliest days of the divine work upon my soul I had had
strong impressions in reference to the ministry, and my own ordina-
tion to it. Strong desires to be useful unto others in this way visited
my heart when the Lord was graciously with me. These desires and
impressions kept returning again and again. Portions of Scripture,
too, were from time to time applied to my mind, stirring up these
desires, and producing a persuasion that the Lord had designed me for
this work. Thus the blessing of Moses (Deuteronomy 33. 8–11) to
Levi was at times very powerful to me. I used to be led to pray, like
Solomon, for wisdom. Satan would sometimes come in and tell me it
was all the pride and naughtiness of my heart. My friends, seeing me
thus seriously affected, often wanted me to go into the Established
Church. But they knew not the agonizing conflict of mind I was at
times going through. For days together I used to be smitten with a
horrible dread, so that my very teeth chattered with fear and trembling. Another great barrier, too, was the terrible infidel infestments
and filthy blasphemies poured into my mind. So dreadful were these,
and so did they intermingle with my attempts even to think upon
divine things, that at one time I tried not even to think upon such
things, but to get away from them. How could I minister to others
when I seemed to myself more like an infidel reprobate than anything
else? I never thought that children of God passed through such scenes
as my soul had to journey through. If at times I was intending to
comply with these desires of my friends, something would occur to
prevent. This was more particularly the case about the time of my full
deliverance. I was just on the point of going into the Church; but
circumstances occurred to hinder, and then my great trouble of soul
put an end to such intentions and at length, instead of taking orders
in the Church of England, I felt constrained to become a
Nonconformist.

But as I was returning from what I look upon as a sort of Babylonish
captivity in my soul, the old impression concerning the Lord having
some design to use me in the ministry also returned to me. The Lord
seemed to revive in me the desires and heart of a minister. He stirred
my spirit up, and I used to think of the way in which He stirred up the
spirit of Samson in the camp of Dan. He gave me, too, sweet and
precious promises concerning these things. Zechariah 3. 7 and Psalm
2. 8 were very powerful and sweet to me in a way of application. But

principally Jeremiah 1. 7. I was feeling my own utter insufficiency for the Lord's work when these words came sweetly in. The Lord also showed me how He could, and I trusted would, use me in His work as a man like myself used his own hand. I hoped I belonged to the Lord, and was a member of His mystical body, and I trusted He would use me as such to His glory. . . .

I had been accustomed to use in our family worship a book of prayers; but after a time the Lord led me to cast aside such props, and then He enabled me to pour out my soul before the Lord as before a Father. By the power of the Holy Spirit I could do this in public. I had previously in private been enabled freely to do so in the name of Jesus. My mother at length allowed us to meet in the hall at Carlton where we resided; and there I spoke not only to our own family, but to some strangers who came in from time to time. Then I was invited to speak at Leicester and in other places. All I can say is that the Lord helped me from time to time in the work, and overflowed my soul with His blessing. I was somewhat ignorant of systematic divinity. I only knew that I was myself a lost sinner, and Christ by the Father's gift and the Holy Spirit's operation a sweet and all-sufficient Saviour for me. It was my delight to tell to sinners round what a dear Saviour I had found; to point to His redeeming blood, and say, Behold the way to God. I used to have hours of sweet communion before ministering, and the glory of the Lord was present in ministering. . . .

For a long time I was now deeply exercised about the ministry. Often thought I should give up; but this I could not do. Fresh invitations to preach would come in. It was hard work, but I went forward. I have gone into the pulpit with the temptation upon me that the Lord would strike me dead. Yet my conscience would not allow me to give up, and I have gone forward with this feeling,— "Well, I will venture on His grace. I will try and speak His truth as He enables me. I dare not in conscience do otherwise; I will try to do His work, and leave events with Him."

The following is from *Further History of the Gospel Standard Baptists*.

Mr. Hazlerigg was constrained about this time to leave the Established Church by a powerful application of the Words: "Come out of her, My people, that ye be not partakers of her sins, and that ye receive not of her plagues." This raised a considerable storm, and his mother was urged to exert her influence on her dissenting son, instead of which, however, she abode with him, and allowed him to hold meetings in the hall of their house at Carlton, where they often realized the favour of the Lord. The time came when the house at Carlton had to be broken up, and Lady Hazlerigg had to decide whether to live with her other son at Nosely, or still keep up a house of her own. The question was settled for her in this way. One day, as her son Grey went forth to preach the gospel, she was watching him riding down the road, when these words fell upon her heart: "Where thou goest, I will go; thy people shall be my people, and thy God my God." She determined to go to Leicester and provide a home for him there.

When Mr. Isbell left Leicester in 1861, Mr Grey Hazlerigg was appointed as his successor at Trinity Chapel, preaching for three months at a time, with three months' intervals between these times, during which intervals he went away. He felt this arrangement very burdensome to his mind, so that after eleven years he said he could not continue any longer. The church then chose him as their pastor, but even then he was not allowed to have control of the pulpit. One stipulation made by the Harrison family when the chapel was built was, "that the sole right of control of the pulpit be vested in the hands of the family, who maintained the ministry." Under these circumstances, Mr. Hazlerigg rightly felt he could not continue, and told the church that "he was compelled to resign his pastorate and the ministry of the chapel. He believed nothing but the fear of God made him take that step. The church then took the matter up, and sent a deputation to the Harrison family, to ask that Mr. Hazlerigg might be allowed to invite the supplies on behalf of the church. That request was peremptorily refused. A month's consideration of the matter was requested, but at the expiration of that time a similar answer was given, being to the effect that if Mr. Hazlerigg wanted to go, he could go when he liked."

The church had no alternative, but must either give up their pastor or their place of worship. The latter course was chosen without hesitation, and in 1872 practically the whole of the church came out with their pastor, and decided to build a chapel where they could worship in their own way, and invite those ministers approved by the pastor. Mr Hazlerigg's last sermon was preached from the words, "Thou has brought me into the dust of death", so expressive of his feelings at the time. The friends met for prayer in the Masonic Hall on March 11th, and for a preaching service on Wednesday, March 13th, and afterwards the prayer-meetings were held in a room given up by Mr. Brown on his premises in the High Street, while the Lord's day services were held at first in the Temperance Hall, and afterwards in the Masonic Hall and the Corn Exchange. The Lord's blessing so attended the preached word that during the year 1872, nine members were added to the church, these being baptized by Mr. Hazlerigg at St. Peter's Lane Chapel, which was kindly lent for the occasion. Eventually a site for the new chapel was chosen bordering on one side on Humberstone Road, and Erskine Street on the other. The chapel was called Zion. Opening Services were held on April 15th, 1873.

Soon after the opening of Zion, Mr. Hazlerigg was married to Miss Clarke of Loughborough, the ceremony taking place on June 24th, 1873, in the Independent Chapel, and the service being conducted by Francis Covell, who preached also at Zion on the previous Monday evening from the words: "The times that went over him" (1 Chr. 29. 30). Mr. Hazlerigg was then fifty-five. Four years later, when passing through a great family trial, he preached a remarkable sermon at the Eastbourne Anniversary from the words, "O My Father! if this cup may not pass from Me except I drink it, Thy will be done." On his 70th Birthday, March 13th, 1888, he was presented by Mr. J. Hack, the senior deacon, with a purse containing 280 new Jubilee sovereigns from the Church and Congregation, the meeting being presided over by Mr. Wakeley.

In March of 1896, Mr. Hazlerigg slipped when walking in the town and fractured his thigh, but he was granted a recovery and was able to walk again with the aid of a stick. A further domestic sorrow was experienced in the death of his wife in 1901. Mr. Hazlerigg outlived her eleven years, and passed away to his eternal rest on October 4th, 1912, at the age of ninety-four.


See also:
*Letters to a Mother, 1886*

# CHARLES HEMINGTON

## 1830–1904

*M*r. *Hemington was dearly loved and highly esteemed as a minister of truth. From 1856 to 1871 he preached regularly, without ever formally becoming pastor, at (the strangely named) Corpus Christi Chapel, Plymouth. From 1871 to 1904 he was pastor at the Old Baptist Chapel, Devizes, Wilts.*

*It is a pity he left no record of his life for the brief memoir published in*

*1904, from which the following is taken, is very fragmentary. J. K.
Popham, who compiled it, had little to work on.*

*In a review of that work one who heard him wrote:*

*"Soon after the time when as a lad we were attending an academy near
Tottenham Court Road, Mr. Hemington was serving Gower Street pulpit
with a view to the pastorate. The chapel was in its old-fashioned state, with
its old-fashioned pulpit, and if we remember correctly it was generally crowded
on Sabbath evenings. In those days sinners were sinners, grace was grace, and
duty-faith was held in abhorrence. Among those firm old Strict Baptist
ministers, who at that time were wont to preach in that chapel, Mr.
Hemington took a foremost place."*

Charles Hemington was born at Over, Cambridgeshire, the 30th of
July, 1830. He was educated at a private school conducted by Mr.
Triggs at Ely. In his youth, though delicate, he was addicted to sport
by gun and rod, and "walked according to the course of this world,
according to the prince of the power of the air, the spirit that now
worketh in the children of disobedience," and was by nature a child
"of wrath, even as others."

Of this period of his life he spoke in a sermon he preached in Gower
Street Chapel in the year 1872. He said, "I was a poor, blind,
ignorant, dead sinner. Well, I had a will, and I followed that will;
and whither did it lead me? Downwards, downwards, to the theatre,
to profligacy, to sin, to vice, to cursing, to swearing." While thus
living, "Sutton Feast" was approaching, and he, with his companion,
was warmly anticipating it. But the Lord had other thoughts concerning both these young men, and instead of their being companions
in sin they were made one, by invincible grace, in seeking mercy,
mourning over their sins, their state as sinners before God.

The subject of this account was brought into the liberty of the
glorious gospel of the blessed God before his friend, but not long, for
they were baptized together, and joined the church at Sutton.

Of one of the early manifestations of God to him, Mr. Hemington
speaks in the sermon above quoted from. Continuing his reminiscence he says: "But at a subsequent period of my life, I spent another
season in London; and that was some years after the Lord in mercy had
opened my eyes, had set my sins before me, and my secret sins in the
light of His countenance. At this time I was truly low and sorrowful.
The friend with whom I was staying not being able to accommodate
me with a bed, I had to procure one where I could. I slept in Oxford

Street; it was a Saturday night. I got up on the Sunday morning, fell upon my knees in much distress, dejected and downcast, and I begged of God that He would give me a blessing that day. I wrestled and pleaded with Him that He would give me a little comfort, a little hope, a little faith to believe in Him as being my God. I came here to this place; the first time in my life that I ever crossed the threshold of your chapel doors. I heard the Word; and I heard it with blessed power. I will not mention his name, but the good brother that preached here that morning knows about it. He preached from the words, 'I am your brother and companion in tribulation.' I sat just a few pews before him, with my eyes in tears, with a softened heart all the time of the service; and I was able to bless God for His manifested mercy."

Of the beginning of his ministry we have two notices; the first written at the end of the first year of his preaching, the second contained in an address by himself at the celebration of the twenty-fifth year of his pastorate at Devizes—the fortieth of his ministry. The first is an extract from a letter (*c.* 1857):

"Plymouth,
"*March 8th.*

"We are very hungry and very lean, and must have one of God's anointed servants who has full authority to go in before the Lord for provisions, and bring them out with his face shining with oil, and his words coming from the Lord right into our souls. . . . We have a second Rudman[1] here, a Mr. Hemington, a man of great talent; and the Holy Ghost is bringing in his ministry with Divine and with extraordinary power. These are golden days, as when brother Rudman was in Trinity Chapel. Mr. Hemington is in Stonehouse, the chapel Mr. Isbell[2] left; and all the afflicted ones get food. He is about twenty-two years of age; has been preaching, at times, one year. He is here for three months.

"James Greenslade."

The second is as follows:

"The celebration of a silver wedding between a pastor and his congregation is not a frequent event, and certain proceedings which took place on Wednesday night at the Old Baptist Chapel were very interesting. Mr. C. Hemington was invited to the pastorate of the

[1] Joseph Rudman (1826–1854), pastor at Trinity Chapel, Plymouth
[2] George Isbell (c. 1814–1860), J. C. Philpot's brother-in-law

church in June, 1871, and the completion of the twenty-fifth year of
his ministry there was a fitting occasion for the members of the church
and the congregation to testify their esteem for him.

"It was mentioned *inter alia* that the church had now been in
existence about 250 years. The greater part of the church as it existed
when Mr. C. Hemington came had been removed by death, but the
membership was larger now than it was then, not reckoning the
increase of strength which came by the amalgamation with the
community from Salem Chapel. Though often labouring with much
weakness of body, and sometimes under much discouragement, their
pastor had been divinely strengthened.

"Mr. C. Hemington, who delivered an address of considerable
length, accepted the presentation as a sincere, warm, and hearty
expression of their good feeling to their minister, of their mutual love
and affection. Twenty-five years, he remarked, made a considerable
gap in a man's life, and those twenty-five years added to fifteen years
of constant labour at Corpus Christi Chapel, Plymouth, told him very
plainly that his labours might soon cease.

"His ministry was a somewhat remarkable fulfilment of his beloved
mother's impressions about him even before he was born. She had
strong impressions (she believed, of God) that the child would be a
minister of the Gospel, and when he was lying in his cradle an old
friend of hers, a venerable servant of God, said to her, 'That child will
be called to preach the gospel.' In ignorance of this he formed
impressions of his own in reference to preaching even during his
childhood, and they followed him all through his youthful days until
such time as God called him by His grace. It was about two years after
he had been baptized, and became a member of the church, that his
mouth was opened. The deacons had some predilections in their
minds about him, but they said nothing about it until one Sunday,
when there was no minister, the senior deacon asked him to read a
chapter in the Bible and, if he felt ready, to make a few remarks. He
read and spoke for half-an-hour upon the parable of the Prodigal Son,
and that was the first time he had ever spoken in the chapel, though
before he had spoken at the Sunday school treats, which in
Cambridgeshire were differently conducted to those here.

"After that he went about speaking in the counties of Cambridge,
Lincoln, Bedford and Huntingdon, until such time as Dr. Marston,
their late greatly esteemed pastor (though he was not pastor of any
church then), came down to Cambridgeshire to preach where his

parents lived. He heard him with such comfort and delight that a strong bond of union was established between them. At that time Dr. Marston was greatly exercised about two places, Plymouth and Devizes, and he told him that while there was a better opening for him at Plymouth in reference to his profession as a doctor,[1] he felt he preferred to be united as a minister with the friends at Devizes. One night the doctor came to his house, and referring to the affection he had professed for him, asked him to give practical proof of it by preaching for him for six weeks at Corpus Christi Chapel, at Plymouth, expressing the hope that in the meantime his own course would be made clear to him. He (Mr. Hemington) at first refused, and his mother cried at the idea of his going 300 miles away, but ultimately the doctor prevailed upon him.

"He went for six weeks, without the slightest desire to be pastor, and intending to return to his parents' home; but the people would not hear of his leaving and he still had their signed requisition asking him not to leave them. He consented to go back for three months, then another three months, then six months, but refusing formally to accept the pastorate; and so he went on for fifteen years, virtually the pastor but never formally recognised as such. In that fifteen years he never once had an unpleasantness with the people of the church, and he believed the bond of attachment was stronger when he left than it had ever been.

"Sometimes in those days on his way to Gower Street Chapel, in London, he would come round Devizes way to visit the Old Baptist Chapel and stop the night with his old friend, Dr. Marston; and he remembered going with him once to see one of his patients. She was lodging in a house in the Castle Grounds, and he little thought then that the room where he saw her would be his own bedroom for fifteen years, for it was the house which he now occupied.

"After being fifteen years at Plymouth, circumstances transpired which caused him to think it was the will of God he should step into another field of labour. Gower Street sent him a unanimous invitation, but at the same time there was a unanimous wish he should fill the pulpit at Devizes, and he felt more drawn to it than to the church in town, for various reasons he need not go into, and ultimately he came here. They knew how frail his constitution had been, and what weakness he had had to grapple with, and nothing astonished him

[1]  C. H. Marston (1827–1870). He was also a homeopathic doctor of ability

more than that he should be still with them at the end of twenty-five years."

He goes on to say how it was sanctified:

"But O! that one night in particular, when our soul was so much blessed, and when the joy of the Lord came down hour after hour, dripping like dew from Jehovah's throne into our poor aching heart; when every verse in that precious hymn of Hart's, 'Faith in the bleeding Lamb,' etc. seemed to drop with the very unction of the Spirit, like so many bits of solid heavenly comfort, into the very centre of our soul. Never, we think, shall we forget that night of prayer, and praise, and comfort, and joy; so blessedly did the dear Saviour of sinners reveal Himself to our faith. We had shed floods of tears for our dear suffering child; but that night we could sit and think of Christ, and shed tears for Him. It was in truth a precious season in our experience, and time of unequalled domestic sorrow. C. H."

The Lord gave His servant many proofs that He had set before him an open door at Devizes, and that a divine blessing rested on his labour in Word and doctrine among an affectionate people. These proofs prevented his acceptance of a warm and affectionate invitation to become the pastor of the church at West Street, Croydon. Where the Lord sent him, there he remained, much valued by his own church and congregation, highly esteemed in the town on account of his manner of life, and because he identified himself with all good works, and especially with every effort to preserve our Protestantism.

In March 1900, the sharpest, heaviest, and most bitter of all his natural sorrow and losses befell our beloved friend in the death of Mrs. Hemington, after a long and painful illness. The bereavement, though expected, prostrated him. But the Lord sustained His servant, and made him a monument of supporting, comforting love.

We next come to September 1900 from which date to July 1903 very occasional notes of varying experiences were made in a small book. The following are taken from these notes.

"*September 25th,* 1900.—I do hope that I felt yesterday a little reviving in my bondage. The Lord dropped, I hope, once again a whisper of His goodwill in Christ towards me, which caused a sensible rising of hope in my soul, and a feeling that God will save me. I have told the Lord on my knees that such was the feeling I had. In reading one or two of Mr. Pierce's[1] letters, I felt them good to read.

[1] Samuel Eyles Pierce (1746–1829)

He sets forth Christ, and faith in Him, and the Word of God, which are what I most need the Holy Spirit to bring me more into."

"*March,* 1901.—My sinkings, my fearings, my despairings of late have been distressing in the extreme. Still, again and again I have been blessed in soul. I have risen up from my heaviness and depression and been helped to believe in God, and to take comfort in His truth. Sometimes in reading Owen on *The Glory of Christ* I have felt my heart drawn out to the Person of Christ in a blessed way; and have, I hope, time after time seen and felt things pertaining to Christ which I never could have seen and felt had I not been led and wrought upon by the Holy Spirit. What help and instruction, and comfort, too, I have found in reading again Mr. Gilpin's[1] *Life and Ministry.* What good it has done me! I can also say the same of Richard Dore's[2] experience. Most blessed has it been again made to me. True, soul-saving religion is set forth in it, and I have felt this morning (March 21st, 1901) a comfortable hope that I have got that religion. Different hymns have also been made most helpful and comforting. O that the Lord would bring me to know Him, and love and serve Him more!"

"*December 3rd,* 1901.—I have experienced a great change in my state of mind, between what my low and desponding state has been for some time past, and what it has been since speaking to the Lord in prayer on Sunday afternoon. Since Sunday, and all yesterday, I have been much impressed with the changed condition I have been under. I have felt my gloomy and miserable thoughts, feelings, and reasonings to be wonderfully removed. I have felt more resting upon the truth of God, and more comforting hope of salvation through Jesus Christ. I have felt that I could more leave myself with the Lord, and in His hands to save me, and pardon me, and bring me out of all my troubles, and be my support and comfort in death, and my Portion for ever. Therefore I hope the change I have experienced has been the Lord's work, and the effect of His gracious visitation upon my spirit.—C.H."

"*Weymouth, July,* 1903.—I have been reading Luther whilst at Weymouth, and the Lord has made the reading a blessed time with my soul. O what a greatness have I seen in God's precious truth! How blessed have I felt it to be, sweet and precious indeed! Surely my poor soul has been wonderfully helped and comforted time after time.

---

[1]  Bernard Gilpin of Hertford (1803–1871)
[2]  One of Huntington's hearers

Yesterday was Sunday (July 26th); as I was walking to chapel, my thoughts ran out to the dear Lord Jesus, and tears came into my eyes."

These are the last words he wrote in the small diary. And very suitable and beautiful words they are with which to close an occasional record of an ever-varying experience.

On Friday evening, April 8th, 1904, Mr. Hemington attended the prayer-meeting at his own chapel. He read Psalm 29, making special comment on verses 5 and 11, and said "very impressively," "When walking to chapel this evening, I said, 'Lord, I want rest, and I want Thy eternal rest.'" He added, "These words have been much upon my mind, 'Blessed are the dead which die in the Lord.'" His concluding prayer was much noticed and felt by some who were present. One of his old and much-attached members remarked to some on leaving the chapel, "I wish he had not prayed that prayer."

On Sunday, April 10th, he preached at Gower Street, London. His text in the morning was 1 Cor. 2. 9: "But as it is written, Eye hath not seen, nor ear heard, neither have entered into the heart of man, the things which God hath prepared for them that love Him." In the afternoon of the following day, as he was on his way to visit his old friend and brother in the ministry, Mr. Adams, he was knocked down by a railway-van, and died from shock, the result of the accident, on April 30th. Thus three weeks after this dear man and servant of God had felt Rev. 14. 13, and preached from 1 Cor. 2. 9, he realised both those blessed portions of God's Word.

During the three weeks of his illness he suffered much at times, but his mind was kept stayed on the Lord, and he uttered many gracious words. Almost his first words on recovering consciousness after he was knocked down were, "If I had been killed on the spot, I should have gone straight into heaven." Often he said, "I have never had one murmuring thought." To Mr. Hazelton he said, "I think it is God knocking at the door, telling me my work is nearly done." To one who had gone some distance to see him he said, "How kind to come to see me! I am much knocked about, and suffer great pain in my head, but my mind is kept quiet, and, though I have no ecstasy, I have no murmuring. I feel much for my people, but I think my work is nearly done." This quietness was remarkable, for Mr. Hemington had always a strong natural dread of death. To Mr. J. Chivers, one of his deacons, he was enabled to write in pencil a letter to read to the congregation, "the dear people of his flock, both of the church and congregation. . . . It has been a comfort to me in this time of calamity to my poor body to know that I have a people who esteem me, and who will sincerely sympathise with me in my present shaken and bruised condition, and I know that the dear young people will do so. . . . I am dreadfully shaken, and according to my present condition and feelings I fear it will be some time before I shall be recovered to my normal condition. The mercy is that I am alive, and have no broken bones. I am in God's hands, come life or death. I have been kept very quiet, and have seen too much mercy in the way the Lord has dealt with me to complain. Kindest love to all; brethren, pray for us."

For several days before the end of Mr. Hemington was scarcely conscious, but amongst his last utterances were his parting words to his friend, Mr. Moss, of Croydon: "O, Mr. Moss, what a mercy it will be to get to heaven!"

Thus was taken to God's rest—God's eternal rest—one whose work was done. God makes no mistakes, but it is not always easy to bow to a truth that has no exception. The loss the only surviving child has sustained is truly irreparable—humanly. The gap made in the church at Devizes is very great, while many in various parts of the country have a sense of loss as they think of the kind, faithful, affectionate friend who has been taken from them.

On the day of the funeral the great respect in which the deceased minister was held was abundantly manifested. His long and blameless life in the little town drew forth marks of respectful recognition and mourning on every side, as the long procession of mourners, resident in Devizes and many other parts of England, moved from the Old Baptist Chapel, where a service conducted by two personal friends of the deceased, Mr. J. K. Popham, of Brighton, and Mr. J. E. Hazelton, of London, had been held. At the grave Mr. Popham gave a short address, and then committed the mortal remains of an elect, ransomed, quickened sinner to the earth till the resurrection morning. There the sacred dust remains. "It is sown in corruption; it is raised in in- corruption. It is sown in dishonour, it is raised in glory; it is sown in weakness, it is raised in power. It is sown a natural body, it is raised a spiritual body. There is a natural body, and there is a spiritual body."


See also:
*Memorial of Charles Hemington, 1905*

# JOSEPH HATTON

## 1821–1884

*M*r. Hatton, pastor at Smallfield, Surrey, for 35 years and at the same *time, in later years, at Shaw's Corner, Redhill, Surrey, was a well-esteemed minister. The following account is from his memoir, compiled by "M.B." We are favoured to have so much of it in his own words so little introduction is needed.*

*Eli Ashdown said of him: "His writings want no commendation from me. Nay; I should but show my vanity by attempting to bestow any. He wrote and spoke knowing much of the depths of the fall and the helplessness of a sinner under the convincing power of the Holy Ghost; feeling the plague of his own heart, and the need and sweetness of the Person, merits and work of the Lord Jesus Christ brought home to the conscience. . . . He was raised up and graciously qualified to preach the preaching which the Lord had bidden him."*

"I was born January 8th, 1821, at Warrington, Lancashire. My parents being God-fearing people, I was brought up under the sound of the truth, and in my younger days had a good example set before me, and was restrained from mixing in bad company and visiting places of amusement. For all this I heartily thank my parents; for I think it is a great mercy to be kept from the vanities of this world in any measure. My father,[1] indeed, was a minister of the everlasting gospel, from whom afterwards I received much help. I was always fond of reading the historical parts of the Word of God, so that I became acquainted with the Bible when very young. From this it will be perceived I was moral, and had a knowledge of the truth in the letter, so far as my mind could understand it. Therefore I have nothing particular to relate, until it pleased God of His abundant mercy to beget me again unto a lively hope by the resurrection of Jesus Christ from the dead.

"This took place about the year 1835, whilst I was reading the account of the children of Israel under the command of Joshua, recorded in Joshua 10. When I came to these words: 'And he said in the sight of Israel, Sun, stand thou still upon Gibeon, and thou, Moon, in the valley of Ajalon,' they entered into my soul like an electric shock. I had been literally electrified many times before this, but I had never felt anything like what I felt now; for my whole body shook, and I was filled with fear. I can well remember bathing my eyes, and wondering what was the matter. Then suddenly the thought came: 'You are not like that man; for he had faith even to command the sun to stand still, and it obeyed him; also, God was his Friend. But you have neither God nor faith; and living and dying without God, you will be lost for ever.' I saw myself for the first time among the number the apostle describes, where he says, 'At that time ye were without Christ, being aliens from the commonwealth of Israel, and strangers from the covenants of promise, having no hope, and without God in the world.' O what an emptiness I felt within me,

---

[1]  William Hatton (*c.* 1795–1865). Minister at Macclesfield, Accrington and Wolverhampton.

a vacuum which no mortal power could fill! I felt lost, as though I stood alone without a fellow, and realised Solomon's words: 'Two are better than one; because they have a good reward for their labour. For if they fall, the one will lift up his fellow; but woe to him that is alone when he falleth; for he hath not another to help him up.' Truly I felt alone.

"I closed the Book, and went out into an outhouse, where I dropped on my knees, and begged of God to have mercy on me and save me, and to be my God. I used all the arguments I could think of to persuade Him to be my God; for I saw how blessed was the state of that man, both in time and eternity, who had God, the God of Israel, for his God; and how awful was the state of that man who was without Him. This made me wrestle urgently with the Lord, and promise Him how good I would be, and how I would serve Him with all my heart, if He would but take me into His service. I got up from my knees with my mind fully bent on serving the Lord. I vowed I would watch my mouth, eyes, ears, hands and feet, lest I should sin with them against the Lord and so bring the wrath of God upon me; for I knew it was written: 'Let no man deceive you with vain words; for because of these things cometh the wrath of God upon the children of disobedience. Be not ye, therefore, partakers with them.'

"At this time, when I was first brought to know my lost estate, I was living with my parents at Macclesfield, Cheshire. I worked with a young man who had just turned Wesleyan, who had been very wild, but now had turned very grave, and I never saw him smile. This young man I took for my pattern of life. He would often reprove the rest of his shop-mates for their light conduct, but in this I could never come up with my pattern; for I could not keep my own inside clean, and I thought I must do so. Indeed, my conscience accused me for thoughts, looks and desires. I was always coming short myself; so that my mouth was shut in the reproving system and this proverb was continually sounding in my ears: 'Physician, heal thyself.' My conscience would not allow me to reprove others while I felt as bad as they before God; nay, worse, 'for I know better,' I thought, 'and have vowed to be good, and have broken my vows.' Yet I took it for granted that my friend was what he appeared to be, and resolved to try to be as good as he. For this purpose I engaged to read the law of God very carefully, that I might know and do the commandments; and I vowed to pray three times a day. This was to be my rule and work; and a hard rule I found it to be."

Mr. Hatton goes on to speak of hard bondage under the law.

"I resolved to try once more. I had no sooner begun than matters were made worse. In the midst of my legal striving, I dropped upon these words: 'They that sanctify themselves, and purify themselves in the gardens, behind one tree in the midst, eating swine's flesh and the abomination and the mouse, shall be consumed together, saith the Lord.' Although I had not committed all these abominations, yet I had some of them. And these words came upon the back of those: 'He that is guilty in one point is guilty of all'; and condemned me as if I had been guilty of the whole. I knew that I had tried to sanctify and purify myself; and more than that, I had eaten swine's flesh, and must be condemned for that one point, if there were no other. But I made up my mind to eat no more; for I verily thought if I did I should be damned.

"Not many days after this, there was some bacon for dinner; but I could not touch it. I trembled all over at the thought of such a thing. My parents asked me the reason I refused to eat it as usual, but I durst not say why; I was afraid to say what was the matter with me. Indeed, I could not open my mind to any one, but kept myself as close as possible. But eat swine's flesh I could not; for salvation or damnation seemed to hang on that piece of bacon. Thus I felt condemned and cursed in my eating and drinking, working and all that I put my hands unto.

"About this time I was very much tempted to work miracles. Sometimes I did try. I prayed that it might rain, to see if I had any faith in God, or whether God would hear me. I would catch at anything for a little hope. But when my prayer failed, I sank very low in my mind, being sure I was not like Joshua. Again, when it rained, I prayed for it to cease; but this did not answer. Then Satan would accuse me of sin, and ask me what I thought of my faith. I was wretched and miserable, feeling without God, breaking my vows every day, and committing sin, either in thought or deed. Sins I had long committed and forgotten came to my mind, and brought fresh guilt on my conscience. I began to think I should never have done with sin, sorrow, and misery. Yet I desired to be as holy as God is holy. I looked at some of the old saints, and wished I was like them. I thought they did better than I; they were not such sinners as I was, in my estimation. O how anxiously I looked forward to be like them, if it should please God to spare me and bless me! For a little hope sprang up now and then that God would have mercy on me, although I could not see how. Some might be ready to say, 'But did you not know that Christ must save you?' In answer I say that I was so much taken up with keeping the law that I could not see how I could come to Christ until I had made myself more acceptable.

"Somewhere about this time my father left Macclesfield and went to Accrington, Lancashire, the church at Accrington having given him a call to be their pastor. It was here that I was brought to have my mouth shut. I felt that I would have done anything or endured anything if God would only be my God. But instead of this, He appeared to be against me; therefore I looked upon Him as a hard God. One day, while thinking how hard God was not to have mercy on me, I felt anger rise in my breast towards Him; when suddenly such a solemn and awful feeling came over me that I trembled from head to foot. I saw something of the majesty, holiness and power of God, and myself a poor, sinful, black, polluted sinner. I felt something of what the prophet felt when he 'saw the Lord sitting upon a throne, high and lifted up, and His train filled the temple.' And the seraphims cried one to another, saying, 'Holy, holy, holy is the Lord of hosts; the whole earth is full of His glory.' A little of this holiness dropped into my soul, which made me cry out, with the prophet, 'Woe is me! for I am undone; because I am a man of unclean lips, and I dwell in the midst of a people of unclean lips; for mine eyes have seen the King, the Lord of hosts.' I felt that God would be just in sending me to hell; and I stood before Him trembling, with my mouth shut, with not a word to say for myself. God appeared so holy, just and good, and I so unholy, unjust and bad, that I was ready to cry out, and say to the mountains and rocks, 'Fall on me, and hide me from the face of Him that sitteth upon the throne and from the wrath of the Lamb; for the great day of His wrath is come, and who shall be able to stand?'

"At last I felt a cry spring up in my soul: 'O Lord, do save me, I beseech Thee. Do not banish me from Thy presence, and send me to hell, that place of misery, where they curse their king and their God, and look upward. I do not want to hate Thee and curse Thee. But O, let me love Thee, and serve Thee, and bless Thy name for ever and ever! Deliver me, I beseech Thee, from going down to the pit. Yet if I must go there, grant me this one request, that I may not join with Thy enemies in hating, cursing and blaspheming Thy holy Name. Let me love Thee even there.'

"Immediately these words came to my mind with power: 'How much more shall the blood of Christ, who through the eternal Spirit

offered Himself without spot to God, purge your conscience from
dead works to serve the living God?' This raised me to a good hope
that God would be my God. It brought me to the tip-toe of expectation of obtaining the coveted blessing—'This God is our God.' I also
felt some joy with it, and a little peace of conscience. I was not
delivered right out of my trouble and brought into gospel liberty; but
I now saw all my works as dead works and therefore polluted. This gave
a death-blow to my law-keeping and trying to please God upon law
terms. I saw also that it was impossible to serve God acceptably until I
was washed in the precious blood of the Lamb. This brought a different
scene of things. I began to wrestle earnestly with God to deliver me from
the law, and pleaded the name of Christ, and prayed for pardon, that I
might be made acceptable to God. I now understood what Peter said
(Acts 4. 12), and could see there was no name under heaven, given
among men, that could help me, but the name of Jesus Christ. By this
one passage about the blood of Christ, I learnt more of my need of Him
than by all I had heard or read before.

"But the words I could not find anywhere in the Bible. I searched
the Book of God from back to back; but nowhere could I see them.
Then Satan came in like a flood upon me: 'Ah! You are deceived; for
that portion is not in the Bible. So your hope, joy and love are all
wrong.' O how I sank in my feelings to think after all I was deceived!
My old burden returned and I began to labour afresh. But keep my
trouble any longer to myself I could not. I was obliged to inquire if
there was such a portion or not in the Bible; and soon I received
information that there was. O how pleased I felt to know that the
words were the same in the Book as had come to me without the Book!

"The person I inquired of wanted to know why I asked that
question. Now what I had tried to keep secret so long ran abroad. It
came up; and I told him all about it. This was the first time, I believe,
that I opened my mouth to any one about the things of eternity. Often
since I have wished I had never said a word about them. I have said, 'O
that I had kept my mouth shut; for if I am deceived, what an awful
thing it will be!' Then I would carry my burden to the Lord, and cry,
'Am I deceived? O Lord, if I am, do undeceive me.' What a dread of
being deceived has a child of God!

"It was a common practice with me to walk behind any that were
good people, to listen to their conversation; and when they dropped a
remark I understood in any measure, O how eagerly I caught it up!
But I shunned being drawn into conversation with them, and kept far

enough away, lest I should be asked anything about my state of mind or why I was so attentive to hear the word. Yet I have often been attracted by some expression, and forgotten myself, and crept a little closer, until I have been drawn into the talk and have been refreshed by it. Whenever this happened, I had to go by myself, and look at all I had said, to see if I had spoken of anything I had not tasted, handled and felt for myself; for my conscience was tender, and I knew that I must stand before God and not before man. And what advantage is it to be approved of men if we have not the approbation of God?

"As I have stated, this portion of truth produced a great result in my heart: 'How much more shall the blood of Christ, who through the eternal Spirit offered Himself without spot to God, purge your conscience from dead works to serve the living God?' It cut me off from all hope of satisfying the law of God; yet not experiencing a full deliverance from bondage into the liberty of the gospel, I soon fell into great trouble of soul. I saw no hope but that which comes through the blood of Christ; and this I felt sensibly I had not got. Hell was before me as a law-breaker; but not a glimpse of heaven could I obtain. I attempted to pray for it; and then the law worked wrath, wrath against God too, because He would not hear me and deliver me. Thus I experienced something of the nature of what eternal wrath effects in the bosoms of the lost.

"In this way I went on for about two years, when one day I was crossing a street in the town of Accrington, as miserable and as full of condemnation as any poor wretch could well bear, and as soon as I reached the opposite side, these words dropped into my soul: 'When Christ, who is our life, shall appear then shall ye also appear with Him in glory.' I was in glory instantly in my feelings; the guilt, sin and misery fled, and were removed out of sight; and in their stead sprang up love, joy, and peace in believing. I adored the Lord with all my heart, and fully believed I should do so to all eternity. I know, therefore, how God speaks the forgiveness of sins by His Word, and how effectual He makes it in a sinner's conscience, both in its power and effects.

"But at length the Lord withdrew; and one thing after another brought me to the verge of despair. For nine long years I walked in this dark path, until I gave up almost all idea of ever seeing the face of the Lord Jesus any more. These days of darkness can never be described.

"After this long, dreary season, the Lord commenced a second

conviction; but not like the first. This was a conviction of my utter
helplessness to serve God apart from His power. I was convinced that
sin could and would overcome the strongest, if suffered to do so. Here
I saw that power belongeth to God and to Him only. It appeared now
as though the very belly of hell was opened against everything that
was godly within me; and awful floods of blasphemy were poured into
my mind, so that I dared not read the Bible. Great fears of death
followed me night and day until I was afraid to move about, lest I
should meet with something to put an end to my useless life. In this
way I went on for some considerable time, when at length these words
were savingly applied: 'Whether we live therefore, or die, we are the
Lord's.' I now felt that I had not only passed through death in law in
my former soul trouble, and a deliverance from it, but that this
blessing had caused me to pass through death to all hope in self in a
gospel point of view, and that it was impossible to form vows,
resolutions, or even to think a good thought, apart from the entire
grace of God.

"Henceforth I have been made to depend on Him who is able to
save, which dependence has been tried again and again; and sore
conflicts have succeeded each other until desperation has called for
rebukes and stripes from God. Then He has sent His Word and healed
me."

After this second deliverance from long darkness, Mr. Hatton gave
up his business, and began to preach the Word. He seldom spoke of
his call to the ministry. He preached three times before the church at
Wolverhampton, of which his father was pastor, and was approved
and sent out by it. One of the senior members there went to hear his
first sermon with a determination to oppose him on account of his
youth, but the Lord was present with the preacher and blessed the
Word; so that the prejudiced hearer was among the first to go up to
him after the sermon and wish him God speed. He was almost
immediately placed over a poor, country people, where he spent the
most active years of his life in peaceable retirement and study, and
remained pastor until his death.

One of his early hearers has put down the following interesting
facts relating to his coming among them:

"Mr. Hatton first came to Outwood [close to Smallfield, Surrey]
about the year 1849, under an engagement to supply for three
months. At the end of that period the Word had the same effect as of
old. Some believed and others did not receive him; so that it was

concluded for him to discontinue his labours there. Accordingly he left them, but stayed in lodgings in the place with a Mr. Budgen. In the course of the same week the use of a barn was offered him by a man who had no care for religion; and as there were many who gladly heard the Word from him, he was induced to preach in it the next Sabbath. When the distant friends came to Outwood chapel on the Sabbath morning and found Mr. Hatton was not expected there, but would preach elsewhere, they left almost with one accord to go and hear him. There were about two hundred persons the first Sunday and in a little time a booth was added to accommodate the numbers that could not get inside the barn. This was continued during the summer months and as winter began, the people met in Mr. Budgen's house. The congregation meanwhile increased, until those who loved the truth deemed it right to try and build a chapel.

"However, here lay a great difficulty. Their hearts were warmed with the love of God; but their pockets were low. But it proved that the God who had opened their hearts to cry unto Him to make room for His servant also ruled over the hearts of those on whom He had bestowed the gold and silver. By this means a piece of freehold land was secured and the way was opened by one here being inclined to lend them a little money; another there to let them have bricks, timber, etc., and the farmers round carting all materials *gratis*. Our aged friend, the present senior deacon, being very active in the matter with the assistance of others, the present chapel at Smallfields was built, and opened in the year 1851.

"Mr. Hatton continued to labour among us until prevented by failing health, his ministry being blessed to the comfort of many of God's living family; and it may be truly said of many that this and that man were born there."

"*Horley*.                                          H. W. Batchellor"

In these early days the congregation was composed almost wholly of poor persons, but they loved their minister, and made many sacrifices for his comfort. In later years the chapel was well filled, and families were in the habit of driving many miles to attend his ministry. He became well known to the churches in London and other places, where he paid yearly visits, and was much esteemed for the grace of God that was in him and spiritual gifts as a minister of truth.

After a time of deeply sanctified affliction, being strong in faith, Mr. Hatton was enabled to speak with authority of the nature and power of faith, showing it is the substance of things hoped for, in possession in the soul. His ministry was plain and clear, penetrating to the bottom of his subject. In this it had a peculiar value. It contained a depth of thought and spiritual instruction which made it, by the blessing of God, as deep waters and a well of life to the tried and exercised of the Lord's family; and its extreme simplicity placed it within the understanding of all who were taught of God. "How forcible are right words!" His natural disposition was quiet and retiring; but when he opened his lips to preach, he set before the people the fullness of the gospel, that they might "suck of the abundance of the seas, and of treasures hid in the sand."

Before his second marriage, owing to repeated attacks of erysipelas, he removed from Smallfields to live at Red Hill[1], eight miles distant. This was in the year 1859. From that time until his illness in 1881 he continued to drive to Smallfields to preach twice on a Lord's day, returning home after the afternoon service. Having his Sunday evenings at liberty, after a time he was led to preach on these evenings and once in the week at a chapel in the Station Road, Red Hill. Here he felt increasingly his ministry was not accepted by several of the leading members, and therefore preached in bonds. Under these feelings he remained among them about fifteen years. Several of the Lord's children were gathered under him; and a lasting union was formed between himself and the poor and needy, who valued his ministry. Many are living who can testify to the life and power that accompanied the Word from his lips, during these years of oppression and trial.

At length a circumstance occurred which led to his leaving this chapel, and afterwards preaching to the few who cleaved to him for his work's sake in a chapel built for the purpose. A minister to whom he objected was placed in his pulpit in his absence, after he had expressed his disapproval to the church. On this account entirely Mr. Hatton resigned his pastorate in the Station Road. A church meeting was held after one morning service, without previous notice being given, and the few members who were present accepted his resignation. The time had come for him to be released from the burden under which he had laboured so long; and such was the relief he experienced that he has often compared it to a ton load being taken off his shoulders.

Several of the people and members left with him. They hired a room that he might continue to speak to them, and in a few months

---

[1] Now written as one word, Redhill

built a chapel at Shaw's Corner, in the same town. It was opened in May 1876. At this juncture the Lord manifestly put His seal on the word preached in a marked manner, sending it home to the hearts of the hearers. One man, who was a stranger to the truth, having heard various reports in the town of the minister and people, turned into the room from a feeling of curiosity, when service was being held, and was arrested by the Word. The living power which accompanied that first gospel sermon to his conscience convinced him that he was one of those described who were blind and could see no beauty in the gospel; and he has since been held fast to the truths which he heard so blessedly set forth by Mr. Hatton.

And now, when loaded with reproach and forsaken, according to his own feelings, by friends, the Lord remembered His servant, and gave him a most blessed manifestation of Himself while driving to Smallfields to preach one Sunday morning. He speaks of it in the following letter of May 21st, 1876, to the late Mr. Covell (Francis Covell of Croydon):

"I had a most lovely sight of the Redeemer's Person as I was driving to chapel on Lord's day, April 9th. O, I felt His gracious presence to such an overpowering degree that my very flesh quivered on my bones. I am not straining it. It was too big for me to strain; it was a big blessing. I tucked up my reins, and begged the dear Lord to let me come. O how easy it was then to die! I think it must have been something like what the martyrs felt; for I felt anything that would send me to Him would be a favour. I wept and begged of Him to let me come to Him; however, He did not see fit to let me have that as well. Nevertheless, the savour of it has not left me; neither do I think it ever will."

In the year 1872, Mr. Hatton took an active part in forming a plan which has since proved to be a means of much benefit among the Lord's poor people. He suggested to several ministers and friends that a general fund should be raised and invested for the relief of aged ministers and ministers' widows. He was supported by Mr. Covell and others, and the same year "The Gospel Standard Aid Society" was formed and a Committee appointed to carry out the proposed object. The usefulness of this Society has since been extended every year, as its funds have increased; and many poor servants of Christ are now receiving from it temporal supplies in their old age. Mr Hatton continued to be an active member of the Committee until his death.

His own narrative concludes with an account of a severe illness which he had in 1877, the year following the opening of his new chapel:

"A few months afterwards I was awaked with blood in my mouth, flowing rather freely. The thought struck me very forcibly: 'You may be in eternity in a few hours; how about your religion?' I appeared to be looking about for my religion, when it seemed to come up to the front, and say, 'I am from heaven, and to heaven I shall go.' 'Lord,' I exclaimed, 'I am ready and willing to die.' O how easy it was then to look death in the face, and long to die! Not a speck appeared in the heavens; all was clear and bright."

After this serious illness, Mr. Hatton returned to his labours, driving sixteen miles and preaching three times every Lord's day, as well as in the week; and has preached as often as ten times within eight days. In addition to his toil in the work of the ministry, in June 1881 he was constrained to undertake the office of editor of the *Gospel Standard*. By this means God has been pleased to preserve in a measure, by his pen, the gracious experience of a long, active life in the service of Christ. In the Reviews, Answers to Inquiries, and other of his writings during the short time of his editorship, some valuable thoughts on passages of Scripture and many points of doctrine have been given to the church. These bear witness that he possessed a deep understanding in the Word, and was a scribe of the law of the God of heaven above many.

In November, 1881 he went to Brighton to fulfil an engagement to preach for two Sabbaths. When there, on Monday evening, the 21st, he was seized with a slight stroke of paralysis while preaching and was obliged to return home the next day. His speech and sight were slightly affected for a few days and he was laid aside from the ministry for several months. This illness fell upon his people as a heavy blow and a token of a worse to come. His mind continued unimpaired; but he was never again restored to his natural strength of body and was therefore compelled to give up his journeys to Smallfields on Sundays and to decline all invitations to preach at any distance from home. In the autumn of 1882, he was so far recovered as to be able to preach twice on a Lord's day at Shaw's Corner, and once in the week; or occasionally to visit Smallfields or Croydon.

Mr. Hatton continued in his usual health, with slight variations, until his last illness, April 13th, 1884. He preached at Croydon on Sunday, the 6th instant, taking these words for his text: "Yet Thou in Thy manifold mercies forsookest them not in the wilderness; the pillar of the cloud departed not from them by day, to lead them in the way; neither the pillar of fire by night, to show them light and the way wherein they should go" (Neh. 9. 19). He gave a full description of passing through the "great and terrible wilderness."

In the evening he spoke of the death of the righteous, telling the people how easy it is to die when Jesus is sensibly with the soul. He referred to his own experience, as related in his letter to Mr. Covell, when he had such a sense of the Lord's sacred presence, while driving to Smallfields, that he felt nothing separated him from the Lord but the bridge of death and all his desire was to depart; when he placed the reins for the pony to go without his guidance, thinking it would only be his dead body that would reach the chapel.

After the service he administered the Lord's Supper, and spoke a few encouraging words to those present. He said that the worry and confusion which a child of God too often felt at such a time was not eating and drinking unworthily; but to partake unworthily was to eat and drink not looking by faith for salvation alone in Christ Jesus; that is, "not discerning the Lord's body." On Monday, before leaving Croydon, he remarked to a friend, "With me the bitterness of death is passed, whenever it comes."

On Tuesday, April 8th, he preached with evident liberty at Shaw's Corner. His subject was Eph. 3. 17: "That Christ may dwell in your hearts by faith." He said Christ had a home in the heart in the faith of His children, and always dwelt there, whether they could see Him or not, and sometimes would talk to them about it. That He dwells in the faith of His blood, that it cleanses from all sin, and nothing else can; and when the Holy Spirit takes of His blood, and shows its virtue, the soul cannot help believing. That He dwells in the faith of His almighty power to save, and sometimes talks to His people about it; and then they laugh at impossibilities, and say, "It shall be done." That He dwells in the faith of His justifying righteousness, that no other righteousness will justify a sinner before God, and that will; and where that is felt, it makes the sinner feel fit and ready to see God with open face, and be with Him. He is ready to enter the full, glorified presence of the Lord; no terror, no fear to dwell in it for ever; for he is innocent. Sometimes He will talk to His people about their innocence, and say "Thou art all fair, My love; there is no spot in thee"; and when He does, they cannot find a spot in themselves. That Christ dwells in the heart as God's finished salvation and sometimes shows

the sinner that the work was complete before he could receive anything from God; and when he sees that, he will say,

"Yes, I to the end shall endure
As sure as the earnest is given;
More happy, but not more secure,
The glorified spirits in heaven."

He addressed his people for the last time on Thursday evening, April
10th, at the prayer meeting. He read 1 Cor. 13; and commented
particularly on the last verse: "And now abideth faith, hope, and charity,
these three; but the greatest of these is charity." He dwelt on the
difference between false faith and real; how possible it is to have a faith in
the Lord as a God of providence, which He honours, yet which is not the
faith of God's elect; and went on to show what that faith is that will take a
soul to heaven. He spoke very sweetly, and some present that evening felt
that much power accompanied his words, and said it was a time never to
be forgotten by them. In taking up the last part of the subject, charity, he
said the child of God would very soon have done with faith and hope; and
then the greatest of the three, love, would really begin. What the
enjoyment of heaven would be he could not tell; he knew he had felt a
little of it; but words were lost to attempt to describe it. He spoke with
much confidence, and closed the meeting with earnest prayer that the
love of God might rest upon the people until the time, which would
shortly come, when they would not see through a glass darkly, but face to
face.

On Friday, the 11th, Mr. Hatton preached at Chelsea from Psalm
130. 7; and returned home on Saturday.

On Sunday morning, the 13th, he seemed as well as usual, but on
rising from his chair after breakfast he complained of a strange sensation
in his left side, and found he was unable to stand. His doctor was sent for
at once; but he was suffering from apoplexy, and in a few hours became
helpless. He remained sensible until about four o'clock the same afternoon, but unable to speak without difficulty. Then he sank into a state of
insensibility, and never again opened his eyes or moved. He had done
with all consciousness of the things of time and sense, and come to those
dying moments he used often to dwell upon in preaching, where, as he
expressed it, "No mortality can come between God and the soul; the way
to heaven is open. Jesus Christ is present to view, 'who hath abolished
death, and brought life and immortality to light through the gospel.'"

He gently ceased to breathe about 8.15 p.m., on Wednesday, April 16th, 1884, in the 64th year of his age.

He was buried on the following Wednesday in the graveyard behind his chapel at Smallfields. Mr. John Warburton of Southill and Mr. Eli Ashdown conducted the service. Numerous friends followed him to the grave, deeply mourning for the great and sudden loss that had fallen on themselves and the church of God.

See also:
*Memoir and Sermons of Joseph Hatton, 1884*

# JAMES DENNETT

## 1828–1900

*M*r. *Dennett's life is one of much interest and much mercy. As Enoch Feazey, when Editor of the* Gospel Standard, *wrote: "Who would have thought that that poor, motherless boy, stowed away in a canal boat in Oxfordshire and bound for Birmingham, after five days' hardship, would become in after life the great preacher of the 'mysteries of godliness' in Frederick Street Chapel in that vast city called 'the Midland metropolis'?"*

*As a preacher he was remarkably blessed. The cause at Birmingham was in a poor way when he began his pastorate as one of their own members, but he lived to see 200 church members and a regular congregation of about 400.*

*This account is extracted from a long obituary written by his children. We are favoured to have so much of it in his own words.*

The following brief account of his early days, call by grace, and exercises respecting the ministry, was found in our dear father's own handwriting after his death. It was written about the year 1858:

"I was born at Summertown, near Oxford, on October 22nd, 1828. My parents were poor. After my mother had borne four children, of whom I was the youngest, it pleased God to take her away by death, and thus I was bereft of my mother at the age of two years. My father then removed from Summertown to a small village seven miles from Oxford, named Bletchington, where his mother lived, and he placed us under her care and there left us while he went out seeking employment, he being by trade a plasterer. Sometimes he was away for three or four years at a time without seeing us. My grandmother, being left a widow soon after we were taken there, had to work very hard to support us by keeping a school and teaching children to knit stockings etc. She was at this time about seventy years of age. Often did she feel uneasy about us and thought her lot a hard one.

"At last, through the persuasion of my uncle, she determined to send us to Birmingham, as my father had not sent any money for a long time for our support and he was living in B. At first she resolved to send only my two brothers and keep me, as I was the youngest, but my uncle persuaded her to send me also, which she did. I think her reason for wanting to keep me was that she thought I should get into trouble, for I was very unruly. Many times have I heard her say I should come to some bad end and indeed, if God had not prevented, I should. I left my grandmother's altogether against my will and it was such a trial that I hardly knew how to bear it. I was broken-hearted, and my grandmother, who was very fond of me, was almost broken-hearted too. The mode of conveyance to Birmingham was a coal-boat on the canal and the journey occupied five days.

"We arrived in B. on Sunday, April 30th, 1839, where we found our father and a mother-in-law, having married again and not told his wife that he had a family. I was at this time about ten years of age. My mother-in-law behaved very cruelly to me and at once got me a place of work at 1s.(5p) per week wages; but in the course of a few weeks a fresh place was obtained for me at 2s. per week and shortly after my wages were raised to 2s. 6d. per week. Then my mother-in-law said I had better keep the money and support myself; but my father would not agree to it. Soon after this I was out of employment for a week and my mother-in-law would not let me have anything to eat, so I had to do as well as I could. However, I got a place to go to the next week at 4s. 6d., and then I lived in lodgings and supported myself. My lodgings cost me 1s. per week, so I had 3s. 6d. to find me in food and clothes.

"About this time my father and mother-in-law left Birmingham and did not tell me they were going away. I did not see them again for some years. Thus was I left exposed to all the temptations that youth is frequently ensnared with. I shall not at the present time give all the particulars of my life up to the time that the Lord called me by His grace; but O the many evils God preserved me from! Many hardships had I to endure before I was thoroughly able by my earnings to provide the necessary comforts of life. I was now about fourteen years of age and I got into company that did me no good and practised many things of which I am now ashamed.

"Thus I went on till I was about twenty years of age when I took to me a wife and resolved to give up all company and forsake my evil ways; but I can bear witness to the truth of God's word where it says, 'The heart of the sons of men is fully set in them to do evil', and that 'God is not in all their thoughts,' unless it is when their conscience tells them they are doing wrong; then they may think of Him, but it is with thoughts of hatred. O the lengths of sin into which I was permitted to run and the evils I practised, so much so that I have often felt astonished God did not cut me off in my sins and appoint me a portion with the damned in hell! Thus I went on adding sin to sin. Many times have I cursed and sworn until I have been almost black in the face, and uttered most solemn oaths and awful lies and then called God to witness that I was speaking the truth. In fact I now shudder at the recollection of many of the things I then practised. O the long suffering mercy of God! But even at this time I was not without checks of conscience, and since God has called me by His grace I can remember feeling at times checks of conscience almost from my infancy.

"But the time was drawing near when I was to feel something more powerful than natural conscience; for in the year 1854, when the cholera was raging violently in London where my eldest brother was living, it pleased God to snatch him away in a few hours by that fearful disease, and on the 15th of August I received the intelligence of his death. When I opened the letter and found he was no more I felt as though an arrow had pierced my soul, and in a moment my eyes were opened to see that if it had been me instead of my brother I should have been in hell. O the horror of mind that I felt, and the terrors of hell how they did afflict my soul! Now, for the first time in my life I *felt* what it was to be a sinner in the sight of a holy God, and my sins stared me in the face. God was a terror to me; my own shadow seemed to affright me; the world appeared a horrible wilderness; hell stared me in the face, and I saw no way of escape. Thus I continued for some weeks, and my flesh wasted from my body.

"I went about from church to church with scarcely a gleam of hope, and every time I went to church this was sounded in my ears, 'Do and live'; but the only language I could feelingly utter was, 'Lord, have mercy upon me!' Still I struggled to do what they said I was to do; but, alas, I found that 'the more I strove against sin's power, I sinned and stumbled but the more'—not outwardly, for I was now so altered that I became a mystery to many and they could not think what was the matter with me, and I was a mystery to my wife. [He here refers to his first wife. He was married to our dear mother on Feb. 20th, 1858.] And instead of practising the evils I formerly had done, I began to read the Bible and would go upstairs and fall on my knees and sigh and groan to the Lord. Pray I knew not how, or at least I thought so at the time; but I believe my groans were the language of a broken heart and contrite spirit. I longed to be away from the cares of business, for I scarcely knew what I was doing. The spiritual requirements of God's holy law seemed to pierce my soul through and through, and how to escape the righteous judgments of God I knew not. Like David, I felt the terrors of hell and the snares of death. I tried to put away the thoughts of death and eternity, but I could not. In this state of soul I went on for some weeks. One day I took up the Bible and began to read in the Acts of the Apostles, and these words struck my mind so forcibly that they made my heart to leap for joy and caused hope to spring up in my soul, where the jailor cried out, 'Sirs, what must I do to be saved?' and the answer was, 'Believe on the Lord Jesus Christ and thou shalt be saved.' At this moment there seemed to be something run through my veins, which made the hair of my head almost stand upright. It was not a feeling of terror, but something that imparted joy to my soul and animation to my body; for I had such a view of Christ as the Saviour of the lost.

"About this time I was induced by a friend to go to a place (Frederick Street Chapel, Birmingham) where he said election was preached. Although I hated the thoughts of such a doctrine, yet I reluctantly complied; but I could not bear the thought of God choosing some and leaving others. However I went and heard these words spoken from: 'Surely goodness and mercy shall follow me all the days of my life,' etc. and while the minister was speaking of David and how the Lord preserved him whithersoever he went and at last took him home to glory, and that at times the Lord so anointed him with the oil of divine grace that his cup ran over, such joy and peace flowed into my soul that my cup ran over. It was indeed a feast of fat things to me, and I feelingly exclaimed with Ruth, 'This people shall be my people, and their God my God.'

"Thus I went on for quite twelve months enjoying the blessings of gospel peace. One time in particular I could triumph in redeeming love whilst hearing Mr. Tiptaft from Psalm 116. In closing his discourse he said anyone who knew the 116th Psalm from experience was assuredly a child of God, and I then felt I did know it for myself. But after a time darkness came over me and I could not hear with such comfort as I had formerly done. One Sunday morning after this, one of my old companions called for me and asked me to go for a walk with him and I thought within myself, 'Well, as I believe God has saved me with an everlasting salvation, it will not matter about me going to chapel so regularly; I will go out with him this time.' So I consented; but O the misery I felt all the day after, so much so that I thought if God would but forgive me, I would never do so again; and I must say, to the honour of preserving grace, that the devil has never got me into that trap again.

"In the year 1857 I joined the church at Frederick Street, and in 1858 I was chosen as deacon at their quarterly meeting. This was very unexpected, as I had not even thought of such a thing when I went to the meeting or should, I believe, have stopped away; but I do hope and trust it was according to divine appointment. I felt it a solemn office to hold in the church of God and feel it to be so at the present moment. About this time thoughts were often coming into my mind about preaching and I was continually striving to put them away from me, but I found I could not. Sometimes these thoughts would leave me for a day or two and then return again. This caused me to cry to the Lord, that if it were not of Him, He would keep these thoughts away; but they still kept following me and a desire sprang up in my soul that if it was the will of God I should preach His Word, He would increase my anxiety about it, and I found my anxiety did increase. O what deep exercise of mind it cost me to know whether the matter was of God or not; but still I could not feel any positive assurance that the Lord was the Author of it. Sometimes such words as these have dropped into my mind, 'Be still and know that I am God,' and 'My grace is sufficient for thee'; but this did not seem enough to assure me that it was of the Lord. At this time my body was very weak and my mind very dark, so that I thought, 'How can it be possible for me to preach?'

"Still I kept crying to the Lord that He would make it plain, and in this way I went on until the 25th of October, when, after my wife had got up and gone downstairs to do something for the children, I remained in bed until between eight and nine o'clock when I got up and washed and dressed, and just as I was about to go down stairs something seemed to prompt me to kneel down and pray, which I did, and in so doing felt unusual liberty in telling the Lord about the exercise of mind I was passing through, and asking Him to lead me into the unsearchable riches of Christ. I entreated that if this exercise of mind respecting preaching His Word were of Him He would give me a sign and assure my soul that He was preparing me for the ministry. When I got downstairs I was about to do something, but I felt constrained to take up the Bible, and opened it upon these words, 'And this shall be a sign unto thee, Ye shall eat this year such as groweth of itself; and the second year that which springeth of the same; and in the third year sow ye, and reap, and plant vineyards, and eat the fruit thereof'. As I read them such a sweet feeling came into my soul that I scarcely knew where I was and it quite melted me down.

"Then these words followed, 'Fear thou not, for I am with thee; be not dismayed, for I am thy God; I will strengthen thee; yea, I will help thee; yea, I will uphold thee with the right hand of My right-eousness.' About an hour after this, as I was sitting by the fire-side, thinking I should perhaps have to leave my abode and endure hard-ships, while I sat thinking upon these things and the comforts I was surrounded with on every hand, these words dropped into my mind, 'He that forsaketh not wife and children, father and mother, houses and lands for My sake and the gospel's is not worthy of Me.' This so strengthened me that I could say, 'The will of the Lord be done.'"

During the year 1859 one of the members, and one or two of the ministers, asked Mr. Dennett if he was not exercised about the ministry, and he had to confess that this was the case; and in

September he received a letter from a friend, asking him to go and speak at Winslow in Bucks., where a few people met for worship. This he felt led to do, and was feelingly helped to speak to them three times on Lord's Day, October 2nd and again in the following two months. On April 12, 1860, he related his call to the ministry before the Church at Frederick Street, and received the sanction of the majority. Following this he preached at Salem on April 25th, and other calls followed in various places.

Of these days he wrote:

"August 9th, 1859.—Have been humbled and astonished at another minister telling me that some words which fell from my lips had quite broken his heart, and although it occurred two days before, he was much affected in telling me of it. In the afternoon, as we were in conversation together, he asked me if I was not exercised about the ministry. I evaded the question and left the room, but on returning he would have an answer, when I had to confess that I was exercised about it. He gave me an invitation to go to his chapel nearly 100 miles away, where I should be a stranger, and he said I might there try the gifts which I might think I had. I however declined."

"Sept. 8th.—This day my mind has been relieved by Mr. Thornher, of Bedford, having put the question to me if I were not exercised about the ministry, when I told him I was. We then had some conversation together which was profitable and instructive, and I felt assured God was answering my prayers, as I had begged of Him thousands of times to impress it upon the minds of His people, and I thought it would sure to be some of the people with whom I met for worship; but how different are the ways of God to our finite apprehensions!

"Sept. 21st.—I received a letter from a friend asking me to go and speak at Winslow, in Buckinghamshire, where a few friends meet for worship, to which I consented. I was to go on Oct. 2nd; but although I had been praying to God to open a way, I had reason to hope this was of Him, yet I felt afraid of going for fear I should be running when God had not bidden me.

"Sept. 30th.—O what a week have I passed! The weight and solemnity of going to speak in the name of the Lord has quite bowed me down and I feel that I have no strength to lift up myself. At times I have felt a blessed hope spring up that all was of the Lord and that He would be with me, and at other times I have felt quite full, passages of Scripture flowing into my mind which caused a burning desire within to tell to the Lord's people what I felt; for while I mused the fire burned, and then I was ready to speak with my tongue.

"Oct. 1st.—Contemplating upon the coming day with sorrow and joy, but did not feel uncomfortable in my mind. Reached Winslow about 6 o'clock. I enquired for the friend I wanted to see and soon found him and had some conversation with him, when I felt he was more fit to preach than I was, and I thought, 'O that man will soon discover that I am not fit to preach.' This cast me down very much. I went to bed about 9 o'clock, but I do not think I slept more than two hours all night. I arose early in the morning to search the word and to call upon the name of the Lord.

"Oct. 2nd.—This is the day I thought I should be made manifest. O the workings of my mind I cannot describe, neither can anyone enter into the feelings of a minister unless they have been in the same position. Went to chapel, read and prayed and took my text from Isa. 51. 1, and felt pretty comfortable. In the afternoon I read these words for a text: 'For the gifts and calling of God are without repentance' (Rom. 11. 29). Felt liberty in speaking and very comfortable in my mind. After service I was met by some who told me with tears in their eyes how God had blessed the Word to their souls. I made inquiries about them and was satisfied that they were people well taught of God who knew the power of true religion for themselves. At night I read these words for a text: 'Blessed are they which do hunger and thirst after righteousness; for they shall be filled' (Matt. 5. 6). At the close of the day I was compelled to acknowledge that God had helped me. Before leaving the people the deacons wanted to know when I could come again. I told them I did not know that I should ever come again. They, however, wanted me to engage to come once a quarter, but I refused, being determined to watch the hand of God in making ways and opening doors for me to speak, as I felt sure He would if He had anything for me to do. They were not at all aware that I had not been out to speak before.

"Oct. 5th.—I have this day received an invitation to speak in a large chapel on Oct. 30th; but I refused.

"Oct. 12th.—Received a note from a minister asking me to go and speak in his pulpit. This I declined; but I went and saw another minister and asked him to go, which he promised to do.

"Nov. 1st.—I have been in some measure humbled and broken down in hearing from the friends at Winslow, through Mr. Thornber, they sending me an invitation to go again, and telling him that he was not to leave me without a promise that I would go again to speak to them, to which I consented, naming Nov. 13th.

"April 12th, 1860.—By the request of the church at Frederick Street I have been before them to give in my experience relative to my call to the ministry, when I had the sanction of the majority, but was opposed by some who have opposed everything that is right in church matters. I would here state that I had a dream a few months previous to this, and in my dream I saw in the vestry between the two doors several persons assembled together and they were whispering one to another against me. I said, 'You are trying to overthrow me, but I tell you in the language of Luther when the messengers met him on his way to Worms and said if he went to Worms he would not return alive, his reply was, If there were as many devils in Worms as there are tiles upon the housetops, yet in the name of the Lord will I go to Worms; and I tell you, In the name of the Lord will I go through all your opposition.' These persons that I saw in my dream were the very persons who so opposed me. I believe they went to the meeting in bitterness of spirit determined to oppose anything that might be received by others. Indeed their envy seems quite outrageous, and the devil is stirring up all the spleen of hell and sending it forth in volumes against me, which is a great evidence that the matter is of God, although my poor soul is cast down and I scarcely know where I am.

"April 25th.—Have spoken at Frederick Street from Psa. 8. 4: 'What is man, that Thou art mindful of him? and the son of man, that Thou visitest him.' After the service some of the people said they wished me God-speed and several said they had been blessed, while others, I believe, were sorely vexed. May the Lord enable me to wield the sword of the Spirit and to leave all my enemies in His hands.

"April 27th.—Been very much tried and bowed down. Tempted to believe that I had no religion, mourning the absence of God, and tried in providence. Tomorrow will be Saturday and I want £150 to pay my way with, but do not know where it is to come from and, although God hath helped in times past, my staggering faith gives way to doubt and I seem driven to the ends of the earth. O Lord, undertake for me; for I am oppressed!

"April 28th.—After passing through a day of trouble yesterday, groaning and crying to God, at night I felt a sweetness break in upon my soul and a sweet dependence upon God which has not yet left me, but it has been greatly increased this morning, I having seen the good hand of the Lord towards me in supplying my wants. One business house in London has sent me £84 which they owed me, and another firm has sent me £132, and another person has paid me this day £116, so that I have enough to pay my way and sufficient to buy £200 worth of articles which I greatly needed. I feel full of the blessings of the Lord and have truly felt this day what it is to praise His holy name for all His goodness to a worthless worm. 'Bless the Lord, O my soul, and all that is within me bless His holy name.'"

On December 28th, 1875, he resigned the pastorate of the church at Frederick Street, after having preached to them for more than fourteen years, during which time uninterrupted love and union existed between him and the church. He then became pastor of the church at Galeed Chapel, Brighton, but after a few months was compelled to resign owing to ill-health. His going to Brighton was a great trial and also a mystery to his old flock; but undoubtedly it was of the Lord, as appears from a letter written from Brighton by our father to Mr. Savage, the senior deacon at Frederick Street, in which he informs him that some souls at Brighton had been blessed under the Word from his lips, one dear woman in particular being delivered from the burden of her sins and brought into the glorious liberty of the children of God, who had been a seeker for thirty years, and others quickened into divine life under his short ministry there. [Mr. Savage was chosen deacon before our father took to the pastorate of the Church at Frederick Street, and has held that office until now. He was always a faithful friend and a staunch supporter to him. He is now in his 87th year.]

On July 26th, 1876, it was decided by the church at Frederick Street to invite him to become their pastor again, which he accepted, and entered upon in January 1877. In the year 1881 a severe family affliction came upon us, in the illness and death of our sister Agnes.

In August 1884, after much exercise of mind respecting the matter, he complied with the unanimous request of the trustees and committee of the Aid and Poor Relief Societies, and took the editorship of the *Gospel Standard*, which office he held for over seven years, at the end of which time, owing to the delicate state of his health he felt compelled to resign. In his Farewell Address he wrote as follows:—"The best reward we have had in the work is the power and sweetness that we have felt in conducting the magazine, and the assurance that the pieces we have written have been owned and blessed to the strengthening and comforting of many gracious souls, and especially our 'Thoughts on the Book of Ruth,' every line of which we can truly say was neither feigned nor forged, borrowed nor stolen; but was written, we trust, under the sacred teachings and readings of the Holy Spirit who is the infallible Teacher in all doctrine that is holy, sacred and precious to the souls of God's elect."

In April 1897, our father had a most serious illness and we all feared his end was near. In this affliction he was much favoured in his soul, so much so that he told two of his deacons who visited him after that he scarcely knew whether he was in the body or out of the body, Psalm 103 being the language of his heart. In referring to this when again able to stand up in the Lord's name he said, "God did indeed bless my soul, and I blessed Him in return."

On June 28th, 1898, to his great surprise, not having had the least intimation of what was going on, he was presented with a purse containing £116 10s., as a token of love and esteem from his church and congregation. On Lord's day, October 15th, 1899, he preached at Gower Street Chapel, London, for the last time, and although unable to speak but for a very short time, many testified that the word was accompanied with much power and sweetness to their souls. On the morning of October 22nd (which was his 71st birthday) he went into his pulpit for the last time and preached a solemn and impressive sermon from Isa. 52. 7; "How beautiful upon the mountains," etc. After this he was laid aside for five Lord's days, during which time the Lord sweetly indulged him with His gracious presence; but it was a great trial to him to be laid aside from the work he so much delighted in, his one desire to live being to preach the everlasting gospel to perishing sinners, and to extol a precious Christ.

On December 3rd he was again able to administer the Lord's supper to his flock. From this time, even until the Sunday before he died he delivered a short discourse every Sabbath evening (with one exception) sitting in a chair in the chapel. His last text was Heb. 12. 16, 17, spoken from on February 25th, 1900. It was then evident to all present that the end was drawing near.

During the following week he became much weaker, and on the day before he died there was a decided change for the worse. His deacons were communicated with and two of them came to see him; but he was too weak to converse much with them though he was able to tell them he was resting on the faithfulness of God. He gradually sank, and on Sunday morning, March 4th, at 9.30, peacefully and quietly entered into the joy of his Lord aged 71 years.

If any should feel disappointed that our dear father did not have what is commonly called a triumphant death, we refer them to a letter written by him on December 15th, 1899, to the Editor of the *G.S.* and published in the February number of that magazine, in which he speaks of how much he had been favoured in his affliction, and it may well be called his dying testimony.

On the following Wednesday he was interred in the General Cemetery, Key Hill, by Mr. Feazey, his body being first taken into the chapel where he had for so many years loved to proclaim the gospel of his Lord and Saviour Jesus Christ. Hymn 466 was sung. Mr. Feazey read Psa. 39 and part of 1 Cor. 15. and gave a short address, after which he offered up a prayer on behalf of the bereaved widow and family and the church. He was then borne by his deacons to his last resting-place, followed by his widow and family and sorrowing church and people.

# ALFRED COUGHTREY

## 1826–1911

We have very little information about Mr. Coughtrey (pronounced *"Cawtry"*). He was appointed Editor on the resignation of Mr. Dennett at the end of 1890, but owing to illness could only write the Annual Address. However, by July 1891 he was well enough to continue, laying down the burden owing to increasing age and infirmities at the end of 1898. For a long time before his death he was unable to preach.

The following account is written by his successor at Nottingham, Mr H. T.

*Stonelake (1860–1933), who buried him in the Nottingham General Cemetery. It is supplemented by one paragraph from* Further History of the Gospel Standard Baptists.

On June 11th, 1911, Alfred Coughtrey died aged 85 years. He was for many years pastor of the Strict Baptist church meeting at Chaucer Street, Nottingham, and for some time the Editor of the *Gospel Standard*.

It is to be regretted that he left no written record of his call by grace. He related a few years ago some particulars of the Lord's gracious dealings with him to the present pastor of the same church. He then said that in his early days he attended the Church of England, and being a moral young man, was what the world would call a Christian. He knew nothing, however, of what a sinner he was before a just and holy God until the Lord cut him down with a stroke of His rod. This took place during a violent thunderstorm.

The solemn awe he felt produced such an effect on his mind that all his supposed goodness and profession of religion were brought to nothing. The holiness, justice and righteousness of the law of God were opened up to him in such an awful manner that he could see no way of escape from the wrath to come, nor how it was possible for him to be saved; and he came to the conclusion that hell would be his portion.

Soon after this Mrs. Coughtrey was laid upon a bed of affliction, and her life quite despaired of; which was the means of bringing her into concern about her soul, and added to Mr. Coughtrey's distress. Satan tempted him sorely, so that he did not dare to bend his knees to pray; for he feared it would be an act of presumption, and only add to his condemnation. With much fear and trembling he at last resolved to make an attempt to pray for his poor wife, that it would please the Lord to restore her to health and have mercy upon her never-dying soul; and finding access in prayer, he was encouraged to plead with the Lord for himself. The Holy Ghost helped his infirmities, and enabled him to pour out his heart with strong cries and tears for mercy. Hope arose in his breast that his groans would be regarded, and in answer to their united cries, Mrs. Coughtrey was restored to health and strength.

Mr. Coughtrey was then led by the Holy Spirit's teaching to see God's plan of salvation, that He could be just and yet justify the ungodly. Many great and precious promises were applied with power to his wounded spirit, and he was eventually brought to know and feel that his sins were pardoned, and to enter into the glorious liberty of the sons of God.

He was baptized at Chesham (Bucks.) and soon after began to proclaim to others the things which he had tasted, handled and felt.

In the early days of his ministry he laboured at Eaton Bray (near Dunstable, Beds.), many being added to the church there; afterwards he ministered at Waddesdon Hill (Bucks.), and later at Over (Cambs.). He commenced his stated labours at Nottingham in the year 1878, over the cause founded by Lady Lucy Smith; and soon after, he formed it into a Strict Baptist church. In the year 1881 the present chapel at Chaucer Street was built, and within two years was free from debt.

Mr. Coughtrey was, by the help of the Holy Spirit, enabled to proclaim a full and free salvation by Christ Jesus to needy sinners; and I believe many can testify of the power and unction attending the word before his mental powers began to decline.

The church was favoured with considerable prosperity for several years, both spiritually and temporally, and speaking of one occasion when ten persons were baptized, Mr. Coughtrey said: "The Lord be praised for His loving-kindness and tender mercies to us. . . . We were greatly encouraged and refreshed to hear so many speak of the love of Christ constraining them to put Him on by a public profession. We pray the dear Lord, whose goodness to us is so great, to preserve them, and bless them, and make them a blessing." The following extracts from his letters were written previously to his coming to live at Nottingham:

"At times we feel as though Christ and heaven and all that is pure would fetch our very souls out of us; and O, what utter hatred to sin! How extremely loathsome the sight and stench of sin is in every form! And soon after this we seem to be over-run again with troops of evils." "He is so immensely good He has filled me with gratitude. When the Son of God will come and walk through fire and flood with us, we feel both honoured and humbled." "It must be an endless wonder to us that God should so regard such base things and things that are not. I belong to that tribe—'things that are not.'"

"Poor base things like me may and do forget His goodness; and if we are so base as that, how much more likely are we to be guilty of ingratitude—and neglect towards one another? Ah, here is our mercy—He hath not dealt with us as our sins deserve. If we are blessed of God, He will have us know that it comes sovereignly. The cause is in Himself, not because we are either black or white, rich or poor, sweeps or kings. He finds us all on the dung-hill, filthy beggars, clad in rags. Can we boast of our high pedigree? Our mouths are for ever shut here, and bless the Lord for closing them. If we sing, it must be of grace.

'Grace all the work shall crown.'

"I was very glad of spiritual sympathy just then [referring to a time of affliction]. My pains of body had given me a rare shaking, which left me in my feelings poor, helpless and needy, and grateful for a crumb. The Lord seems to be so kind in everything; everything seems to endear Christ. He was indeed worth something last week. How unwilling we are to lose the savour of His presence! You cannot know the delight it affords, without saying, 'Master, it is good to be here!' O may He grant us many earnests of His eternal favour! Nothing kills sin like a sense of His love and blood; and poor, guilty creatures (who are) so prone to wander from the God they love, need a little to keep their heads above water."

With advancing age Mr. Coughtrey's health began to decline; and after having two strokes he was heavily afflicted, which greatly enfeebled him in both mind and body. His infirmities increasing, he was in the year 1900 obliged to discontinue his ministerial labours. This was a very sore trial to him and some considerable time elapsed before he seemed to be reconciled to the mind and will of the Lord in this matter. As time advanced, however, he appeared to be much more submissive and on several occasions, when I visited him during the last few years, he said that while he had much to say against himself, yet he had not a single word to say against the dear Lord Jesus Christ.

Notwithstanding his enfeebled condition, in divine things he remained sound and clear to the last. The day previous to his death he repeated with fervour the following lines:

"And lest the shadow of a spot
Should on my soul be found,
He took the robe the Saviour wrought,
And cast it all around."

Hymn 747 was a great favourite with him, portions of which he often repeated:

"How hard and rugged is the way,"

I saw him shortly before he passed away, but he was then unconscious. When he breathed his last, those about him scarcely knew his spirit had fled. I believe it can be truly said.

"He's gone in endless bliss to dwell,"

# ENOCH FEAZEY

## 1836–1905

*M*r. Feazey has proved the most elusive of all the Editors. Though a number of present day Strict Baptists can trace their relationship with him, yet very little seems to be known of him.

Even more strange is the fact that nothing at all is known of the place where he preached in Leamington, Warwickshire. The older people at nearby Coventry (who were adults when Mr. Feazey died) had no knowledge of any chapel there.

*In the old magazines there are sermons, letters and a photograph, but we can trace no biographical details, except the following (in a letter dated: Leamington, December 1884):*

"It is now more than thirty years since it pleased the God of all grace to call me out of darkness into His marvellous light, and I distinctly remember the peculiar sensations wrought in my soul at the time by God's good Spirit. I did not then know what was the matter with me, except that I knew I was a vile sinner standing as it were before a holy God. I remained in this solemn frame of mind for some considerable time.

"It pleased God to put it into the heart of a godly person, now in glory, to lend me the works of the late Mr. Gadsby, for which from that day to this I have had to bless the Lord. No one could conceive the vast amount of spiritual good my poor, sin-sick soul received from those blessed writings. Having all through life had to toil hard for the bread that perisheth, I could not get time to read these precious books in the day time, so turned night into day, and also read them on Sundays. Thirty years ago, this Christmas, I read the Memoir of this good man, and it had such a wonderful effect upon my mind that I wept like a child. How I wished I had known the dear man, and had the pleasure of hearing him preach. I mentioned these things to my dear, godly father, and was delighted to hear him say that he knew Mr. G., and had heard him preach once in his life-time. He told me he had not lost the savour of that blessed sermon to this day."

*His obituary in the* Gospel Standard *was as follows*:

With deep sorrow I have to inform the readers of the *Gospel Standard* that my beloved father, Mr. Enoch Feazey—who for the last six years has been the Editor of the *G.S.*—has passed away. He had been unwell for some considerable time, in fact he never thoroughly recovered from the serious illness that attacked him three years ago, but that did not prevent him continuing his labours. On Sunday, May 7th, he preached at Southport, and returned to his home the following day. On Tuesday and Wednesday he was engaged in his editorial work, and on the evening of the latter day he went for a short walk. After a light supper he retired to rest, very weak and tired, at 10.30. At midnight I was called by my dear mother, and on entering their room I found my father lying on the floor. I fetched the doctor, who pronounced the case to be very serious, but everything was done that was possible. He became very restless, and I had to call in the assistance of a neighbour to help me lift him.

At a few minutes before seven a.m. he spoke—though very indistinctly—of his work in connection with the G.S., saying that the proofs must be sent that morning. I offered him a little refreshment, but he was unable to take it. He gradually became unconscious, and at 7.30 on the morning of Thursday, May 11th, he ceased to breathe. The medical certificate stated, as the cause of death, degeneration and hemaplegia (paralysis).

Thus at the age of 69 has passed away a devoted, loving husband and father, a man of a strong religious nature, and one who set forth his religion not only in the pulpit and by his pen, but in every act of the daily routine of his life.

He was laid to rest in Leamington cemetery on Monday, May 15th, his esteemed friend, Mr. Picknell, of Redhill, conducting the funeral service. On behalf of my dear invalid mother, who is bearing her great loss fairly well, and myself, I would venture to take this opportunity of most sincerely thanking the many friends for the very kind letters of most encouraging sympathy that we have received from them.—W. HERMAN FEAZEY.

The following account of the funeral of Mr. Feazey was sent by a friend who was present:

The funeral of our late dear friend took place on Monday, the 15th, at Leamington cemetery, leaving the residence of the departed about half-past two, and followed by his only son and his five brothers, Mr. Picknell, Mr. Shillingford, and other members of the Committee of our societies, feeling we were following a brother beloved.

The service was conducted by Mr. Picknell, who read a few verses from the seventh chapter of Job, making comments thereon, showing that our dear friend was one in spirit with Job, longing and desiring for the selfsame help, deliverance and rest; also a few verses of the latter part of the fourth chapter of James, that our life is but a vapour, a shadow, and that the suddenness of the departure of our friend was an instance of it; that his toils and labours were now over, his many and long journeys far and wide to preach the everlasting gospel of the grace of God were now completed, and the labourer had entered into rest, for he was truly a labourer in the Lord's vineyard, many times with an afflicted body, but love to Zion and the poor and needy, and the outcasts of Israel, made his willing feet move with sweet and heavenly delight, to the comfort of many; for be it known that many dear lovers of God are still scattered abroad as to the bounds of their habitation, but yet the Lord still cares for His scattered few, and raises up those that love and care for them too, and our dear departed friend was especially endowed, and we may say anointed and appointed for this work.

Mr. Picknell then read from the seventh chapter of Revelations as to the certainty, and reality, and blessedness that our dear friend was now one of the great multitude before the throne, clothed with white robes, and palms of victory in their hands. Blissful thought for those of us who are still struggling on in tribulation's thorny path!

> "My soul anticipates the day,
>     Would stretch her wings and soar away
> To aid the song, a palm to bear,
>     And bow the chief of sinners there."

O, what a prospect! At times it seems too good to be true; yet it is the desire and expectation of the poor, and the word still remains, "The needy shall not always be forgotten, and the expectation of the poor shall not perish for ever." "Cheer up, ye travelling souls," etc.

Mr. Picknell then addressed the family and friends, and spoke of our friend as being, with all the human race, born in sin and shapen in iniquity, and went from the womb speaking lies, but in accordance with the immutable counsels of Jehovah,

> "The appointed time came on apace,
>     Not to propose, but call by grace:
> To change the heart, renew the will,
>     And turn the feet to Zion's hill."

And thus our dear friend was made a real traveller, a poor and needy man, a real broken-hearted sinner, and the Lord, having put His holy fear in his soul, made him an upright man, set apart the godly for Himself, and made him so poor, and helpless, and destitute that he was a real object for the Lord to bestow on him His rich mercy and grace, for "none but the wounded patient knows the comfort of his cure." The free, full, finished and unmerited mercy and gospel of the grace of God being made so precious to his soul, made him a suitable preacher to poor, hobbling, fearing souls, who often fear they are out of the secret. And so our brother commenced to speak in the name of the Lord about thirty years ago, and although he had not the ability of some, yet he had grace and love, and many can bear witness to the life and savour that attended his ministry; many little causes of truth, where but few now gather together. All honour to such godly, gracious men, who care for the poor, walking in their Master's footsteps. O, what a truth, Jesus *will relieve* the poor!

Our brother's name was Enoch, and, like his namesake of old, "he walked with God," and as an Editor of our magazine, when such was needed some six years ago, we believe the Lord fitted him to fill that post, though oft with fears, but the Lord was his all-sufficient Friend, and bestowed on him that grace and ability to keep its pages clean and free from error, maintaining its purity and the intentions of the godly men who commenced that periodical; and though he was not Mr. Gadsby, Mr. M'Kenzie, Mr. Philpot, or Mr. Dennett, he was himself and what the Lord made him, and his kindly spirit, and love to the welfare of Zion, endeared him to thousands.

As a husband and father he was most kind and affectionate. May the Lord bless and sustain the widow and son. Our friend had a warm heart towards those who had but a little of this world's goods, going miles to take them a few shillings and speak a kindly cheering word; many a poor widow's heart has rejoiced at his coming, and how his heart was gladdened when any friend gave him something for his charity purse, as he called it, so that he and the giver and the receiver had the sweet feeling that all these things are *from Him*, for blessed is he that considereth the poor. May the Lord raise up more to go and do likewise, and as one of our dear friends used to say, "The little that thy hand findeth to do, do it with thy might." Brethren, the time is short.

Mr. Picknell then engaged in prayer committing the bereaved into the hands of the Lord, and thanking Him for that grace that had been bestowed.

The body was then committed to the earth, and we may say with dear Tiptaft, "well laid in the grave." Mr. Picknell then read a few verses of the fourth chapter of the first Thessalonians, and repeated that sweet verse of dear Hart's:

"Now the grave's a downy bed,
    Embroidered round with blood;

> Say not the believer's dead,
>     He only rests with God,"

and spoke of the certainty of death, and that soon those around the grave would fall under its mighty scythe, with the hope that the hearers might, by the grace of God, be ready for that great change. Our departed brother was as ready for the grave as the open grave was ready for his coffin. Let me die the death of the righteous, and may my last end be like his.

There were present at the cemetery friends from Birmingham and other places, who, with some feeling, expressed that they had lost a real friend. O, what a gap the removal of a man of God makes! May the great Head of the Church—the living God—that still rules and reigns in Zion, raise up more such humble followers of the Lamb with a willing heart to the comfort of His church in these cold dark days; for Zion's ways do mourn; the hearts of the godly are often sad. Dear Berridge said, over one hundred years ago:

> "Send help, O Lord, we pray,
>     And Thy own gospel bless;
> For godly men decay,
>     And faithful pastors cease:
> The righteous are removed home,
>     And scorners rise up in their room."

What would he say now? Arise, Lord, for the help of Thy poor distressed Zion, and may we hear Thy sweet voice of invitation, "Come, My people," etc. Amen.

# JAMES KIDWELL POPHAM

## 1847–1937

*There are many still alive today who with love and affection remember the ministry of Mr. J. K. Popham, a sacred, Christ-exalting ministry. He was pastor for a short period at Liverpool, and then for 55 years at Galeed Chapel, Brighton.*

*A popular London minister paid him this tribute in 1934:*

*"I worshipped not long ago in a chapel in Brighton, as plain a chapel as you could imagine, but the minister of that chapel was a pulpit genius. He has occupied that pulpit for more than fifty years, and is as fresh as ever, although he is eighty-five years of age. . . . That chapel holds one of the largest congregations in that watering-place. There are no attractions, no side-shows, but worship, Bible-teaching, prayer and hymn-singing. The secret is a spiritual secret."*

*It was the weight, savour, authority and power of his preaching that attracted and held such a large congregation for over half a century. His delight was to preach Christ crucified—as he so often exclaimed:*

> *"The blood of Christ, a precious blood!*
> *Cleanses from all sin, doubt it not,*
> *And reconciles the soul to God,*
> *From every folly, every fault."*

*In many ways this has been the hardest "life" to compile because of the wealth of material. So much had to be left out. It is extracted from* Further History of the Gospel Standard Baptists, *based on J. H. Gosden's* Memoir and Letters.

James Kidwell Popham was born at Lancaster in 1847, and brought up in the worldly atmosphere in which his parents lived, although it appears that his mother was convinced of her sins while in a theatre in Nottingham, and afterwards lived a different life and attended a Mission in the town. This led to her son James becoming a student in theology at the Congregational Institute, where he was brought up under Arminian teaching, which he found suitable to his nature. But the purposes of God were that he should be taught and led of the Holy Spirit, and this made a marked change in his life. He gives the following account of the way in which he was arrested and called by grace:

"As I was walking along a road the word, 'Blessed are the pure in heart, for they shall see God,' was borne in upon my heart with an amazing power and penetrating light. The view of divine holiness then given me filled me with consternation and alarm, and I stood still at that spot near the Market in Nottingham and inwardly said, 'Where that God is, I shall never be.' It laid fast hold of me, for in that awesome sight of divine holiness I saw the uncleanness of my heart; then His divine justice flashed into my conscience, and I saw my sins;

the sorrows of death and the pains of hell took powerful hold on me. I tried to keep the law, as who would not, being ignorant of the gospel? I was miserable, tried to get happiness but failed, and grew constantly worse. I flew to more strenuous working, but my soul was filled with a sense of the nature of God, and His fire burned up all my works. Thus my meat and drink were my futile efforts, unavailing tears, black failures and shameful defeats. From that time I was called out of the world."

In this way he was brought to realize the impossibility of obtaining salvation by his own works, and wandered about feelingly lost and as a stranger on the earth. One day he saw a handcuffed prisoner being taken into Nottingham gaol, and the thought that it might have been himself brought a softness of heart before the Lord, so that he was unable to restrain his emotions. His father, noticing this, asked what was the cause and James in simplicity related the circumstance, and what he had felt. But this called forth his father's proud anger, to think that his son should feel he might have been like the criminal whom he had seen taken to prison. "You bear my name," he said, "and dare to compare yourself with a criminal? I forbid you ever to mention religion again in my presence." Nor could he again mention anything of religion to his father until after his mother's death. He learned that he must forsake father and mother and all for Christ, and was brought so to walk.

One doctrine his proud nature could not receive was election. So bitter was his enmity when it was first mentioned to him, that he uttered the fearful words: "If the God you speak of is the God of heaven, I neither want to know Him, nor to be where He is." But his pride and enmity had to be brought down with hard labour, for he "became filled with the terrors of the Almighty," so that he dare not pray for some weeks. He envied the cattle, and thought there could be no forgiveness for such a sinner as he felt to be; until one day, the Lord spoke that word in his heart: "All manner of sin and blasphemy shall be forgiven unto men." This brought a sweet gleam of hope, and enabled him to go on praying again.

About this time, he set out one evening to visit a friend, but on his way he found a sudden impulse to go in the opposite direction to see another friend. This apparently small influence affected the whole of his future, for at the house where he eventually went, he met a gentleman connected with the Congregational Institute, who invited him to preach the next Lord's day at Lubenham. His objections were of no avail, and he was involved so far as to be compelled to go and attempt to preach. Speaking of it afterwards, he says, "I just felt Christ was very precious, and spoke as I felt."

However his preaching was too Calvinistic for the hearers, which was a means of his coming amongst the Strict Baptists; for a fortnight later he was asked to preach at Clipston, about four miles from Lubenham. The service was held in an upper room, and several Strict Baptists from Lutterworth attended. Through this connection, Mr. Popham was brought to attend the ministry of Mr. de Fraine at the Strict Baptist chapel in Lutterworth [the village where John Wycliffe preached] under which it pleased the Lord to instruct his soul in the truth. Speaking of this period, he says:

"By the mouth of His servant, de Fraine of Lutterworth, God counselled me and instructed me in the doctrines of free grace. Whereas I was trying to stand on works, which never afforded me standing room, He showed me the standing of a sinner, when good, was in grace. Dear room in Thurland Street, Nottingham, where I heard Mr. de Fraine! His text was: 'By whom also we have access by faith into this grace wherein we stand, and rejoice in hope of the glory of God.' Never can I forget or give up the life, light, and power accompanying that sermon. It was God's counsel in my soul to seek free grace. In that room too I heard Mr. Searle quote two lines of Hart:

'Sinners are high in His esteem,
And sinners highly value Him.'

It was a revelation of God to me, for I was a sinner called to repentance, and was sure that where the God of infinite justice was, I could never be."

Mr Popham joined the church at Lutterworth, and was baptized by Mr. de Fraine on the 6th September, 1868. Under this ministry he was instructed in the truth, and brought more and more to despair of hope in himself, being directed by the Spirit to seek the mercy of God in Christ. The way in which this was obtained, he thus relates:

"I went to my room one night with a fearful sense of despair. As I locked my door, I felt my heart moved to pray, and soon found a peculiar liberty in confessing my sin and all my sins. How I justified God, should He carry out His severest sentence! While I was thus engaged, Paul's word concerning the mercy of God to himself fell on my soul with power, life, and light: 'But I obtained mercy because I did it ignorantly in unbelief.' By the power of that marvellous word, my soul was filled with a gracious energy in prayer for the same mercy. Soon it came; it seemed almost immediately, I could not quite tell. But the mercy, the full pardon of my sin, of *all* my sins, was conveyed by the word of Peter: 'Forasmuch as ye know that ye were not redeemed with corruptible things, as silver and gold . . . but with the precious blood of Christ, as of a lamb without blemish and without spot.' My conscience was filled with peace and comfort, and as I laid my head on my pillow that night, I said, 'Now it would be as easy for me to die as it is for me to put my head on this pillow.' "

Although Mr. Popham had preached on a few occasions, he had not felt he was truly sent to the work until just before he had the blessing mentioned above. His health had failed so much, that it was thought he could not live. But one day the Lord spoke to him the words: "Depart ye, depart ye, go ye out from thence, touch not the unclean thing; go ye out of the midst of her; be ye clean, that bear the vessels of the Lord. For ye shall not go out with haste, nor go by flight; for the Lord will go before you, and the God of Israel will by your rereward." With this word came the persuasion that he would have to preach, and so strong was it that he told the Lutterworth friends that he was satisfied it would be so, and his pastor was able to receive this testimony. He preached at Walgrave Strict Baptist chapel and other places round, and also frequently at Clipston in a room. While still residing at the latter place, he was married to Harriett Adcock in 1869, and moved to Wigston Magna in Leicestershire, where he preached regularly for about three years.

He received invitations to preach at Langton in Dorset, and on one occasion had to baptize two persons in the open sea at Swanage Bay. Although his eldest daughter was very ill, and it was feared that she might die, he was shown that he must attend to the work to which the Lord had called him, and was given power to commit his child into the Lord's hands. It was at this baptism that he was given a view of the glory of God in the ordinance, as he thus relates:

"On the following morning early, my mind was completely taken from my circumstances, and a view given me of the glory of God in the ordinance of baptism from Matt. 3. 16, 17: 'And Jesus, when He was baptized, went up straightway out of the water; and lo, the heavens were opened unto Him, and He saw the Spirit of God descending like a dove and lighting upon Him; and lo a voice from heaven saying, This is My beloved Son, in whom I am well pleased.' I saw the Father acknowledging the Son as He came up out of the water, and the Spirit descending upon Him; which filled me with a sense of His glory and love revealed in that ordinance. I had felt a love to it when I was myself baptized, but not as I did then. The fear of baptizing in the open sea, lest I should be carried off my feet, was quite taken away, and my mind continued calm during the service. I felt the presence of Christ with us."

In 1871, Mr. Popham was invited to preach at Shaw Street Chapel in Liverpool, and two years later he received a call to become their pastor, which he felt led to accept. Recognition services were held on the 17th May, 1874, when his old pastor, Mr. de Fraine, preached morning and evening. But his pastorate at Liverpool was no easy path; he was subjected to much trial and persecution, and at one time felt he must run away from it all, and even went so far as to try to get a house in Leicestershire. It was not the Lord's time, and proved to be a futile attempt. The time drew near however, when it should please the Lord to move His servant to Brighton, which brings us to his coming to preach at Galeed.

Some friends of his at Wigston Magna, Mr. and Mrs. Levesley, had a grandson in Brighton, and through him they became acquainted with Mr. and Mrs. Marshall at Galeed. A letter written by Mr. Popham to Mrs. Levesley in her illness, was sent on to Mr. Marshall, and he took it to the next deacons' meeting and read it. This resulted in an invitation to supply at Galeed on two Lord's days, June 12th and 19th, 1881. Mr. Popham was at that time feeling that his ministry at Liverpool was drying up, and with this there was a powerful temptation that he had not been called to preach. He relates how he came to supply at Galeed under these heavy fears, and the wonderful deliverance that was given him:

"On the morning of the 12th, I was arrested by the clock striking ten. In weakness and fear, and crushed by sorrow, I said: 'Lord, one hour more and the people expect me; I cannot go like this, and I will not.' In infinite mercy and compassion, He immediately spoke to me. He said: 'I will help thee.' I knew the voice, felt the power of it, and falling on my knees, I adoringly said: 'Lord, I believe it.' Now, though physically weak, I longed to go to the pulpit. Often since then I have said 'If I am in my right place, I was put in it that morning.' O blessed day! Rather, blessed be God, who so graciously delivered a poor captive from the mighty lion-like enemy and oppressor."

An invitation to supply for three months at Brighton with a view to the pastorate was given. This was in January, 1882. In the meantime, however, the deacons at West Street Chapel, Croydon, asked him if he was free to leave Liverpool. He replied that he was free, but not to come to Croydon. In spite of this reply the church at Croydon gave him an invitation to become their pastor. This was received a month before the call from Galeed. Here then was a dilemma for the good man, which put him under a great deal of exercise until the following March. Providentially he was engaged to supply at Croydon on a Wednesday evening, and at Galeed on the following Friday evening. Writing of this anxious time, he says:

"At Croydon I had liberty, as on some former occasions, but nothing more. At Galeed, I had not spoken long, before my soul was filled with the peculiar love which I believe a pastor has to the people over whom the Lord places him; and when I sat down in the pulpit, I said in my heart: 'This is the place.' Thus I was settled. After the people had left that evening, one of the deacons said to me, 'I almost told the people you are our pastor.' I said, 'But you have no authority.' He replied, 'I *know* you are our pastor, for I have such a hold of you in prayer, I *know* you are.'"

On December, 15th, the new Pastor called the church together, and delivered an address on the occasion of his acceptance of their invitation. He said:

"Last week when the exercise was exceedingly severe, and I was saying, 'If the people ask me, I dare not come, I cannot stand before them, I am so weak,' the Lord graciously dropped these two Scriptures on my spirit: 'We have this treasure in earthen vessels, that the excellency of the power may be of God, and not of us'; and, 'That your faith should not stand in the wisdom of men, but in the power of God.' They were very seasonable and precious to me, and enabled me to be content to be a weak, foolish creature if God would but glorify Himself thereby. I have also had some feeling from this Scripture: 'We preach not ourselves, but Christ Jesus the Lord; and ourselves your servants for Jesus' sake.' And many times when I have been before the Lord about this matter, I have found these words sweetly following me—I do not say they have dropped with that power and unction I like to feel, but they have been whispered quietly on my soul: 'Certainly I will be with thee,' and O the help it has been!"

In the early days there were one or two defections, yet the church grew and prospered under the ministry of their pastor, and almost every church meeting records the proposal and acceptance of fresh candidates for membership. In July 1891, Mr. Popham was taken ill and had to be absent from his pulpit for seven weeks. After the first week of being laid aside, he says:

"The Lord came. I had found the bottom—that I deserved the affliction for my sins. When ice was brought to me, I felt: 'They gave Him vinegar to drink.' Feeling so weak, I was on the point of falling into self-pity at being reduced so low as to need to be fed. Then my most merciful, pitiful, glorious Redeemer came near and spoke to me. If anyone had told me the Lord would have come in the way He did, I could hardly have believed it. He spoke these words: 'Blessed is he that considereth the poor; the Lord will deliver him in the time of trouble. The Lord will strengthen him on the bed of languishing. Thou wilt make all his bed in his sickness.' I said, 'Lord, I have never done it, I have not had the opportunity; mine has been *receiving*.' I took the word literally. Then He showed me He had seen every desire and cry I had put up for *His poor*; that I had considered them in my heart, and He accepted it, and would be with me in trouble; and I could hardly bear it, and wept as He spoke to me. He talked with me and made me believe His astonishing words, showed me His Person, and poured in His everlasting love. Then I began to confess my sins, my utter unworthiness; told Him I was not fit for Him to look on and love; not worth all the trouble He was taking with me. But the more I confessed, the more He seemed determined not to notice what I said. Day after day I lay in unutterable peace."

In 1897, on the occasion of his fiftieth birthday, December 20th, the church and congregation at Galeed presented him with a clock and a purse of money, together with an affectionate address.

Towards the close of the year 1899, Mr Popham was laid aside for several weeks, during which time he was very favoured in his soul, as he told his friends at Galeed when he was able to return to his pulpit on December 10th, and preach from the words: "Herein is love, not that we loved God, but that He loved us, and sent His Son to be the propitiation for our sins." "This was the first word," he said, "that touched my poor, prayerless, hard heart, after some days of illness. It pulled prayer through all my death and bondage and I learnt that if the Holy Ghost only gives a wretch a sight, a hint even, of the free, eternal love of God, it will pull prayer up through all things. It did in my case. I know, if I were to live fifty years hence, and preach constantly all that time, and felt every time of preaching the love of God in my heart, I could never describe half the drawing, attracting influence of a sight and sense of the free eternal love of God."

Again in the following September, he was laid aside for three months, and had an operation performed on his throat. "By prayer," he says, "I put the hand of the surgeon into the Lord's hand, as the instrument was put down my throat. It was wonderful to me, the sharp pain was made bearable. I still feel the Lord is not far from me. This affliction now has no anger in it. I see no frown of God in my painful silence. My weeks of anguish, black as night and the shadow of death, are turned into the morning of His favour."

In 1905, Mr. Popham's labours as the pastor of Galeed, were added to by his appointment as the Editor of *The Gospel Standard*, in which he was wonderfully helped and sustained for a period of thirty years.

At the twenty-fifth anniversary of his pastorate, Mr. Popham was presented with two hundred guineas, his beloved wife with forty pounds, and a suitable address.

In September 1914, a heavy bereavement fell upon the pastor, in the loss of his beloved wife. Mrs. Popham in her early days had been a hearer of Mr. A. J. Baxter, when he was in Nottingham, but after his removal to Eastbourne, she attended services held in a large room in Thurland Street, opened by Lady Lucy Smith. Her early convictions made her dead to the law as a means of life, but she received helps under Mr. Baxter, and eventually a deliverance from bondage when he preached from the words: "O Naphtali! satisfied with favour, and full with the blessing of the Lord; possess thou the west and the south." A strong opposition to baptism, which may have gained a hold upon her in following Mr. Baxter, was sweetly overcome, and she was led to join the church at Galeed in answer to the pastor's prayers.

In September 1916, Mr. Popham was married to Elizabeth Ashley Keen, of Cambridge, who proved to be of much help to him in his declining years. Although she suffered with spinal weakness, she did not spare her strength in endeavouring to help the needy, and also assisted the Pastor in his editorial work, which in 1919 was increased by the addition of *The Friendly Companion* to his charge.

In October of 1922, the 40th anniversary of his pastorate at Galeed was commemorated by the presentation of a cheque for £201. Again in December 1927, on his eightieth birthday, he was presented by the church and congregation with £200. In an address afterwards, Mr. Popham said: "You have borne with me; you have been extremely kind to me. Great changes of course I have seen, as you can realize. I have practically buried all the chapel-full of people I came to in 1882."

When the pastor's Jubilee at Galeed was reached, the event was signalized by special services, which were attended by about 1,500 people from all over the country. These were held on October 5th, 1932, at the Countess of Huntingdon's Chapel in Brighton. Mr. J. H. Gosden preached in the afternoon from Romans 6. 17; and Mr. Popham in the evening from Romans 1. 16, 17. Mr. J. Banfield was able to choose the hymns for the two services, but passed away before they were held.

Part of the address from Galeed read:

"Many now in heaven, together with many now on earth, have abundant cause to bless the great Head of the church that it pleased Him to place you over us, a pastor after His own heart to feed us with knowledge and understanding, seeing that your ministry has been blessed of God to the quickening of their souls into divine life, to their being turned from darkness unto light, and translated from the kingdom of Satan into the kingdom of God's dear Son. Many such seals has the Lord given you to your ministry, confirming the word with signs following, and thereby testifying abundantly that it has been His work to establish you over us.

"In your ministry, you have not shunned to declare the whole counsel of God, and have sought to know nothing among us save Jesus Christ and Him crucified, labouring day and night in your prayers to God for us; and the fruits of your labours are manifest, not only in our midst, but also up and down the land where, in the providence of God, you have been enabled to speak in His name. As your concern has been that we might be established in the truth, so also you have not ceased to oppose and warn against the errors and heresies that have lifted up their heads.

"Besides your labours in the study and in the pulpit, your pastoral visits to those who have been in trouble or sickness have been owned and blessed of the Lord.

"The promise with which the Lord graciously started you in your ministry at Galeed, saying, 'I will help thee,' He has abundantly fulfilled; so that you may say, 'By the help of God I have continued unto this day.' Times of sickness, times of trouble, times of opposition within and without, times of darkness and calamity in the nation, have called for an exercise of that divine help which was surely promised, and which has been as surely afforded as occasion required.

"May we this day give glory to the Lord for these His mercies, praying that they may be continued to us, and that you may yet be spared to labour in our midst for some while to come."

Previous to the evening service, Mr. Popham made the following reference to the occasion:

"I deeply feel my position today. I thank my friends who have come from various distances to show their kindly feeling to me—from Scotland, Blackpool, Bristol, Bath, Canterbury, and many other places. I speak the truth when I say, I am conscious of not deserving such a demonstration of kind feeling as the congregations today manifest. I ask myself, 'What have I done?' I am a plain man, and a plain, much-tried preacher, and it is difficult for me to realize that I am known outside my own small congregation, or at most perhaps occasionally thought of by the readers of the magazines which I endeavour to conduct. If now I may just fade away from your view, and God will kindly make Himself 'Alpha and Omega' in this service, it will be an answer to many prayers. May He grant that answer."

But further trials and losses awaited the Galeed pastor. About a year after the Jubilee Services, his wife was taken ill, and after many months of suffering, passed away on December 17th, 1934. Writing of this he said, "In shortening tribulation's day for my dear wife, the Lord has made me desolate, and I would continually submit to His most holy, wise, and good will."

During the year 1936, Mr. Popham's strength seemed to be revived for a time, and he was able to undertake a preaching tour among the Northern churches, and also for the last time to preach at the Annual Meeting of the Gospel Standard Societies. But this appeared to be just a flicker of the mortal flame before the end, which was then approaching. In the evening of October 25th, 1936, he came to the service at Galeed under much physical weakness, but very favoured in his soul, as he thus related to the friends gathered together:

"When I reached home from the service this morning, I was so exhausted, I mentally said, 'I shall go out no more today.' Instantly, powerfully, sweetly, this great word dropped into my heart: 'My grace is sufficient for thee.' It melted me into a wonderful happiness, and I said, 'Lord, I can go on that word.' And I am here. He knows my physical condition, of which I do not wish to speak; but I do want to honour Him. His goodness once or twice this afternoon was so powerful that I could only just bear it. A verse of a hymn often sings in my heart. I do not sing it; it sings in my heart. It did so this afternoon:

'Thou shalt see My glory soon,
    When the work of grace is done;
Partner of My throne shalt be;
    Say, poor sinner, lovest thou Me?'

The word 'soon,' as I measure it, may not be God's measure. He may spare me longer than I think He may. But O the glory, the wonder of grace! And it is greater to me than to any of you, than it can be to any of you, because of my unusual sinfulness and sins; and I say again and again, 'But Lord, my life, my sinful life, my unprofitable life!' But He will not listen to me. He just, as it were, covers it all. The infinite merit of Jesus Christ is sufficient. On that I live, on that I shall die. And I thought one thing that I would say to you this evening was this: 'If I do not speak much more, this is my testimony, that what I have preached to you these many years, I am now living on. I am supported by those precious doctrines which I have known and preached very feebly, and I believe the day is not very distant when I shall be with Him.''

Early in 1937, he had to take to his bed and developed a distressing cough. Although unable to be present at the services for some time, he frequently sent messages for the deacons to read to the assembled congregation when there was no minister.

As the warmer weather approached, Mr. Popham was able to get up again, and with the help of a carrying chair was conveyed up and down stairs. He now anticipated getting to Galeed to preach once more, but was confronted with the difficulty of mounting the stairs to his vestry, from which access is gained to the pulpit. So great was his desire to be in the pulpit again, where the Lord had so often been with him in years past, that he made enquiries as to the cost of installing a small lift at the chapel to take him up to the vestry. This however proved to be too expensive for the little use that he could have made of it. Hence on May 2nd, 1937, when he was able again to be taken to Galeed, he spoke from the reading-desk for about half an hour. On May 16th he ventured again, but to the surprise of his deacons, who were waiting to help him again into the desk, he began to mount the vestry stairs. This he was able to do, and was then assisted by them into his pulpit chair, which he had been in the habit of using for some years. He was more at home in his pulpit, and was enabled to preach both morning and evening.

Again he preached on May 23rd, and for the last time on May 30th, when his text was: "Elect according to the foreknowledge of God the

Father, through sanctification of the Spirit, unto obedience and sprinkling of the blood of Jesus Christ; grace unto you, and peace, be multiplied."

This his last sermon was a wonderful testimony and a fitting conclusion to his long ministry, emphasizing those doctrines which had been blessed to his own soul and which he had so loved to preach. But it was with great difficulty that he was helped into the pulpit, and his extremely ill appearance, while showing that his time here was short, seemed to add greater weight to every utterance. The following week he remained in bed, but on June 3rd he was enabled to sit in the garden for a short while, conversing with the oldest member at Galeed, Miss Davey, who had called to see him on her 105th birthday.

A few days later he was taken much worse, and had incessant pain. On June 12th he said, "I cannot express how happy I am. Tell my dear Galeed people, with my deep, deep, deep love, that my black, black, black sins, as black as the confines of hell, are *all* forgiven. Luther said, 'Seas, rivers, oceans of black sins'; and *my* black, black sins are all washed away in the precious blood of Christ. 'Jesus, lover of my soul, Let me to Thy bosom fly.' O how I love Him! And now I shall soon be with Him, who has loved me from all eternity. I am dying, am I not?. . . . O Galeed! precious Galeed! Give my love to my dear, dear friends there (naming several). They have been in my heart in life, and they are in my heart now. Tell them I am dying on the truths I have preached, am blessedly supported by them."

To the deacons he said: "How glad I was when the doctor told me the end was near. Happy day! The sting of death is removed. . . . I am going to see the 'Rose of Sharon and the Lily of the Valleys.' The burden of the church will fall upon you. You will come to say, 'The burden of the church is a heavy burden.' But the Lord will be with you. He has been at Galeed, and He is still at Galeed, and He will be with you. Do not forget that the church was commenced by seven men on their knees. They had not prayed before in public, but they met for prayer in each other's houses. Perhaps there is hardly another church that was commenced just like that."

On the last day of consciousness, June 14th, he was able to converse with about twenty friends who called to see him; but on the following day he became unconscious, and passed away on Thursday, June 17th, 1937.

On the following Lord's day, Mr. J. H. Gosden of Maidstone

occupied the pulpit at Galeed, and preached twice from the words in Heb. 13. 7, 8: "Remember them which have the rule over you, who have spoken unto you the Word of God; whose faith follow." On the following day, Mr Gosden also conducted the funeral service at Galeed, and then the interment in the Brighton and Preston Cemetery, after which Mr. J. Delves of Clapham engaged in prayer at the graveside. It was a fitting conclusion that the mortal body should be thus committed to its mother earth by the two ministers who had been sent out by him from the church at Galeed into the solemn work of the ministry.

See also:
*Memoir and Letters of James Kidwell Popham, 1938*

# JOHN HERVEY GOSDEN

## 1882–1964

*M*r. *Gosden was highly esteemed as a faithful minister of Christ. The pastor at Maidstone for over 35 years, his emphasis was on the glory of Christ in His Person, offices and work. He delighted to speak from the Epistle to the Hebrews.*

*On one occasion, at the Annual Meetings at Manchester, he gave a beautiful summary of vital godliness. He said something like this: "Real religion is very simple, and very solemn. It consists in the knowledge of self and*

*the knowledge of God: the knowledge of self as a sinner, and the knowledge of
God in Christ as a Saviour."*

*Though outwardly somewhat austere, Mr. Gosden had a tender, loving
heart and sympathy for all God's people, especially those in affliction.*

*The following account is extracted from* Memorial of John Hervey
Gosden.

John Hervey Gosden was born in Brighton on September 17th,
1882, and was brought up to attend with his parents at Galeed Strict
Baptist Chapel in that town. His mother had, with her father,
attended the chapel since it was opened in 1868.

We have no record of John's schooldays in Brighton, but doubtless
he was diligent in his studies, as he was in everything he entered
upon. Before he left school at the age of fourteen he gained a
scholarship, and the headmaster, Mr. Lethbridge, seeing his ability
wanted him to continue his studies; but to use his own words, he said:
"I would rather leave school and work like father." Viewing the case
naturally, it would seem that if the headmaster's advice had been
followed, John would have found the further knowledge he might
have attained very useful to him in the work to which he was
eventually called. But this future was unknown to him, although not
to the Holy Spirit who called him to it and gave him that grace and
inward teaching, without which he could not have been the good
minister of Christ that he was. Moreover, we feel that this lack of
higher education at school was largely made up by his own industry in
private study and reading.

His commencement in a business career seems to have taken place
at Worthing, probably at Mr. Fenner's shop, as he speaks in one of his
Letters of leaving Worthing after completing his apprenticeship in
1898/9. Later on he was employed at Frederick Gorringe's, the large
stores in Buckingham Palace Road, London.

Of his early spiritual impressions he himself writes: "I remember
when God was first made real to me. I lived in religion more or less
from the cradle, and did not disbelieve in God; but the time came
when I was brought to *know* there was a God." Mr. J. K. Popham
commenced his pastorate at Galeed on the first Lord's day of October,
1882, and the first child for whose safe birth he gave thanks to God
from that pulpit was John Hervey Gosden, then only a fortnight old.
Doubtless this humble token of thankfulness from the parents was
accompanied by the earnest prayers and good wishes of the new pastor

for the child's future; but this future was hidden, and the good man could hardly have conceived how much his own influence and minis- try would be instrumental in shaping the child's career in years to come, and bringing to pass the purposes of God concerning one who was to be His servant, also in the ministry of the gospel.

The work of grace was commenced in John's heart in early life: "I hope my first sense of God's omniscient eye upon me was while at Worthing in my teens. . . . It was at Mr. Fenner's (my wife's father) funeral in 1898 that Mr. Popham quoted Romans 5. 20"—a word which was made special to him in raising up a hope in the Lord's mercy and grace. He further mentions in one of his sermons "that from a very early age the Word of God was made effectual to his soul." It would seem however to have been some few years after he left Worthing before he became more fully established in the truth so as to receive it in the love of it.

We can, however, gather a definite year when he came under a law- work while in London, and obtained his first glimpse of hope in the gospel. This was in 1903, as the following statement indicates:

"When I was under the law —what a dreadful life it was in this metropolis for months together—my heart was as hard, my soul was as dark, my spirit was as full of self-pity, as it could hold. Fear, and dread, and trembling took hold of me; and yet now as I look back I believe there was a feeling after mercy, but no sensible praying; that is, no access to God, no laying hold of, no hope in the gospel. But when the Holy Spirit revealed this Door, this opened Way where a sinner deserving hell might entertain warrantably the hope of salva- tion, who can express the blessedness of it? And how precious Christ is in this as He is the Hope of Israel! I could never tell you how wonderful the smallest hope in God's mercy through Christ was made in my soul one day when walking in Kensington Gardens (London), now nearly thirty-five years ago (preached in 1938), after a period of almost blank despair."

His teaching under the law was evidently severe and deep, and he related on one occasion how he first had a conviction of the Being of God, and the solemn effect it had upon him:

"If our religion came from God it began with the new birth, with the discovery of God and the discovery of ourselves. We believed there was a God, a holy, heart-searching, almighty, omniscient, eternal God. I have looked back myself countless times to a spot—I think I could put my foot pretty near the spot of ground— where first

I felt God's presence, first saw Him gazing with those holy eyes into my black heart and upon my crooked life. O how solemn it is!"

Another glimpse of his solemn feelings under the law, but of a measure of relief from it, he gives us thus:

"Speaking for myself, I can say that when I thought I was going to hell and walked about under the law in great distress of mind, I said to Him on one occasion, 'Lord, if I must go to hell, where I deserve to be, I must love Thee there.' It was produced in my heart; I *had* to say it, and I felt it; and that was the beginning of liberty, the beginning of the lessening of the rigour of the law, and the beginning of a hope in the mercy of God."

It was this teaching, this sight of the majesty and holiness of God, and of his own sinfulness, that made the things of God and eternity so great and solemn to him; and like that of his early pastor at Galeed, his ministry was correspondingly weighty and searching.

Another interesting account he gave of one of his first hopes in the mercy of God, was the following:

"I remember as a young man, deeply convicted of my sinnership and high-crying guilt, and could see no way of escape (I had been cradled in Strict Baptist things, but notion is of no use when the reality of sin and guilt is felt in the heart; you must have power). I was bemoaning myself and was tempted to give up all in a kind of sullen silent despair. . . . But I believe the Lord gave me a sacred glimpse of the truth of the gospel in that word in the Romans: 'Where sin abounded, grace did much more abound.' That verse gave me such instruction that I saw for the first time, vitally and under a sense of the need of it, how a sinner could be saved, and my heart was after that salvation, after that fulness of grace. Sin was mighty in me, and heaven-high it seemed to be in its crying guilt; but I think I got a sight of the illimitable ocean of the merit of Christ and His grace. Now that was the beginning, as far as I can remember, of a hope, a turning round from that sullen despair; and there was some love in it, a little love to Him, the Lord God of all grace."

How long he continued to be employed in London we do not know, but it would have been but a few years, as by the year 1907 we find him stationed at Guildford, where he worked in the establishment of Williamsons, and often had to spend whole days in London doing business for them.

Soon after 1909 he gave up the occupation of travelling. It would appear that he was not very successful at the work, and in some ways unfitted for it. Perhaps he was too honest in submitting goods for sale, for we feel sure he would not price things above their worth. We must remember also that the Lord had other work in store for him, for which he was being trained in a far different school. This change of life brought him to be employed at the business of Fenners in Worthing. He did not take over the business, but was only employed there. Mr. Fenner had been successful in raising up this business at Worthing, and also used to hold meetings for divine worship in a chapel which he built next to the shop, called Hope Chapel, several of our ministers preaching there when their services could be obtained. Hope Chapel was closed in 1905 however, and after that the meetings were held in various rooms in Worthing until Mr. Fenner's sons were instrumental in building the existing Ebenezer Chapel in Portland Road, and the present Strict Baptist church was constituted. This would be before Mr. Gosden went to the business, which was of course no longer used for the services. It was during this period that he became friendly with Mr. Fenner's eldest daughter, Rhoda, and they were eventually married by Mr. Popham on October 19th, 1910. The day previous he had received a special blessing when his pastor preached from Rev. 19. 9, and was so favoured in soul that he said, if asked to choose whether to be married or taken to heaven, he would have chosen the latter.

But the time came when it pleased the Lord to set his soul at liberty by a gracious gospel deliverance and the knowledge of forgiveness; and we must now give an account of this as gathered from his own occasional references to it in the course of his ministry.

On one of these occasions he said: "I believe the Lord forgave my sins, pressed into my poor, but then happy heart, a sense of His redeeming love, many years ago. It was sweet. It was sacred. It did make the Lord Jesus everything to me. It made me feel I would never have another sin against Him. O it made me feel rich for time and eternity!"

In another sermon also he mentions this effect of forgiveness in creating the earnest wish never to sin again: "You feel when you have Christ you have everything; there is nothing more you want except to be for ever with Him, and to be like Him, and to be without sin. I remember when this was first my experience I had but one petition—it mingled with my sweet worship, and my weeping over sin, and my love and my satisfaction; it came out— 'Lord, do not let me live to sin against Thee.'"

From another such reminiscence we get the actual word by which the sweet sense of forgiveness was conveyed to his heart: "I hope never to forget while I have my memory what that word was once made to me, where the Lord Jesus said in the prophet: 'I have blotted out as a thick cloud thy transgressions, and as a cloud thy sins.' It will never be undone."

The sovereign manner in which the blessing came, he related on another occasion as follows: "When, as I trust, the blessed Lord Jesus Christ came and brought this sweet forgiveness into my poor heart, I was not just then so earnestly seeking it, though looking for it. There was not at that time such terror and awful agony of soul as previously; for I had been brought to feel a sweet hope from time to time. But the blessing came so sovereignly; it was too great, too rich, too free, for one so poor and unworthy to receive. Yet O how gladly and thankfully it was received! Rather how gladly was *He* received who brought the blessing with Him, Jesus Christ, and who had died for it."

On the morning after receiving this sweet sense of pardoning mercy, the blessing was confirmed to him by the application of a further word, as he thus tells us in another sermon: "That morning after I got the blessing of the atonement in my conscience overnight, I was suddenly awakened as it were with a strange sense of liberty and light, and wondered what it was. Long had I been burdened and darkened in my mind, but now had lost all my darkness and all my burden; and then as an explanation that word dropped into my heart: 'In those days and in that time, saith the Lord, the iniquity of Israel shall be sought for, and there shall be none; and the sins of Judah, and they shall not be found; for I will pardon them whom I reserve.'"

As might be expected, this experience of gospel liberty awakened a desire to testify of the Lord's goodness to His people, and to put Him on by an open profession of His name; and in due course we find him coming before the church at Galeed. His testimony being accepted, he was baptized on July 1st, 1912, by Mr. J. K. Popham, who preached on that occasion from the words: "Is there not a cause?"

Now that he was married and both he and his wife members at Galeed, they might have looked for a smoother path; but whether so or no, this outward peace was soon to be disturbed by the outbreak of the First World War in 1914. Mr. Gosden, feeling he must do his part in endeavouring to help the country in this great calamity, and not wishing to be engaged in the actual fighting, joined what was then called the Royal Army Medical Corps, so that he could assist in tending the wounded, either in the battlefield or in the War hospitals. This led to a period of training in the North of England, and we have a record of one of his spiritual blessings received there in the midst of such trying circumstances. It occurs in a sermon which he preached on justification, and referring to this experience he says: "O it is a sweet experience! I shall never forget, I hope, when walking across the parade ground in the North of England on the eve of proceeding to France during the First World War, feeling an inkling of that word in the midst of chaos and trouble: 'Therefore being justified by faith, we have peace with God through our Lord Jesus Christ.'"

During his period of service in France he was awarded the Military Medal for bravery on the battlefield, when under heavy gun-fire he went out alone to attend a young soldier who had been left on the field badly wounded, and as a consequence was wounded himself. There is no doubt he used every opportunity of speaking to the wounded and dying soldiers.

Out of this mysterious providence of serving with the forces in time of war, there came the unfolding of the Lord's purposes concerning him in his being sent out into the solemn work of the ministry, which we must now relate. After being wounded in France as already mentioned, he was sent home to this country in 1918 to the Bradford War Hospital, Yorkshire. After his recovery he was then stationed for a time at Blackpool, and while attending the chapel there on one occasion when the minister was absent, he was asked to take a prayermeeting and to expound on the chapter which he might be led to read—a practice which is not unusual for deacons in some of the Northern chapels when taking prayermeetings. Notice of this came to Mr. Popham's ears, and he immediately summoned a church meeting at Galeed for Mr. Gosden to speak of his exercises concerning the ministry, and to preach before the church. But as we are favoured to have a record of what he said at this meeting, it will be best to let him tell us in his own words, which are as follows:

"The first time I remember feeling anything respecting the ministry was in 1908, when this scripture was spoken upon my heart: 'I the Lord have called thee in righteousness, and will hold thy hand, and will keep thee, and give thee for a covenant of the people, for a light of the Gentiles.' I was quite aware that this scripture in the first instance related to Christ, but I also felt that it spoke to me and told me that

He would make me a minister of His Gentile people. This made much exercise for a time; but then my ignorance, my peculiar ignorance and darkness came up before me so that it seemed an impossibility, and I was glad to dismiss the matter from my mind as far as I possibly could. After this, when our pastor preached from that text, 'How great is His beauty!' I was so favoured in my own soul, and felt so full of love to the Lord Jesus, that I really longed to speak of Him to others, and earnestly asked Him to make me a minister of His gospel; and I did hope that the exercise might not prove abortive, but that it might be brought to a good issue. But after a time the sweetness that I had felt abated, and this self—the vile, black, polluted self came up, and my ignorance, my terrible ignorance and darkness of mind, together with the greatness of the work, so came before me that I was ready to call myself a thousand fools for ever having entertained such a thought, and really felt it would be absurd for me to think of doing so.

"Well, the exercise died down for a time, though there were not many months went by without my thinking about it. I suppose about three years after this, when I was in great darkness of mind and felt to want to know the real cause of my darkness, the scripture arrested me: 'Hear ye, and give ear; be not proud, for the Lord hath spoken. Give glory to the Lord your God, before He cause darkness, and before your feet stumble upon the dark mountains, and while ye look for light He turn it into the shadow of death and make it gross darkness. But if ye will not hear it, my soul shall weep in secret places for your pride, and mine eye shall weep sore and run down with tears, because the Lord's flock is carried away captive.' I thought that this showed me the reason of my darkness; but again the exercise, though very keen for a time, died down, and I was glad to put it from me as far as possible and get a little peace.

"There was another scripture; this also related to my soul's exercises. I had been very much tried for some time on the point of election, though I believe it had been previously cleared up to me; but I was strongly tempted upon the point and felt that no word from anyone would be sufficient for me, but that I must have a word from God. And this was it: 'Ye have not chosen Me, but I have chosen you and ordained you, that ye should go and bring forth fruit, and that your fruit should remain.' This scripture affected my heart in two ways. The point of election, I felt, was nicely cleared up to me, and also it affected me with respect to the call to the ministry: 'I have chosen you and ordained you, that ye should go and bring forth fruit.'

"A little while after this Mr. Dickens was coming to preach, and I felt to go before the Lord like this: 'Lord, he doesn't know anything about my case, but do cause him to speak to it.' And during the course of his sermon he quoted the text I have just mentioned, 'Ye have not chosen Me,' etc. and it had a considerable effect upon me. There was another time before I left Worthing. We were experiencing a good deal of difficulty in the business, and certain things transpired with respect to some goods which seemed only to annoy me. I felt very much annoyed with the whole thing; and just then I thought of our pastor here, and this was the thought that I had: 'He has wares to sell which are always perfect'; and the desire came up again about the ministry, and I felt I should like to be made a dealer in those wares.

"I cannot remember anything else particular until a little more than a year ago, when our pastor sent for me and asked me if I had any exercise about preaching. I then told him what I have now told you; but I said this to him: 'Now let it remain that no one shall know what I have said to you, but let us seek the Lord in the matter.' Then followed on this some very keen exercise, and I felt what a solemn thing I had done even to suggest that I should pray about so great a matter. After a time the keenness of the exercise died down again, though at times I could not rid myself of it.

"As you know a while ago—about two months it is, I left here to go to the Depot at Blackpool. On my arrival there I felt desolation in my soul, and to have come to a very desolate place. On the next Sunday after my arrival, in the evening I found out the little room where our people meet there. I did not feel much in what was said, but I felt glad to be there to hear the Scriptures read, and the hymns were good; and it was good to turn in there out of the levity of the place, for Blackpool is an awful town. During the week following I was approached by the deacon with the request that I should read and speak at their next meeting. In the North, reading seems to include making a few comments upon what is read. Well, a time was appointed for me to decide and let him know my decision, and such a sense of my ignorance and lack of love came before me (and this lack of love has tried me much lately), that I felt it would be absurd to attempt it. I was a good deal tossed after refusing, and that former word came up again: 'Give glory to the Lord before He cause darkness'; and when I was feeling much exercised as to what was the right thing for me to do, this Scripture was spoken on my heart: 'We preach *not ourselves*, but Christ Jesus the Lord.' I felt, 'No not ourselves,' and it worked in me such a desire to say a little about the gospel to poor sinners that I thought if they ask me again, I cannot refuse.

"The Sunday following I was asked to conduct a prayer meeting. The minister for that day had failed them, and the deacon told me he should be away from home, and he wished me to conduct a prayer meeting. I said to him, 'Why not have a read sermon?'; and he replied, 'We don't like read sermons; the people would much prefer a prayer meeting.' Well, when I arrived at the chapel there were no members present that I knew. Usually there were several R.A.M.C. men there, members at some of our other causes, but this particular morning none of them were present; and I gathered from a lady member that the males who were there were not members, so that there seemed nothing left for me to do but to conduct an ordinary service. The scripture that I spoke to them from was this: 'He hath made Him to be sin for us who knew no sin, that we might be made the righteousness of God in Him'; and I believe I felt some liberty in doing so, and at the end I felt to be on the Rock. This over, I thought there must be an end of it, and nothing more was said about it; but I found that my wife, without my knowledge, had written and told our pastor about it. His reply gave me to understand that he considered I had acted irregularly; his letter was kind, but to the effect that it was not as he would have wished, and that I must explain myself.

"During the week that has passed I have been very keenly exercised; in fact, I have felt nearly torn to pieces, so much at times as to feel I could sustain no more. The devil suggested to me—I believe it was the devil—that I should not look into the Scriptures for direction; but thousands and thousands of times, I may say, day and night did I wrestle with the Lord to know His will in the matter. Upon my arrival here on Saturday evening I felt it my duty to see our Pastor, and he told me that I must relate to the church my exercises upon the matter, and also exercise the gift before you; and that you should decide whether you believed me to be sent to preach or not. This seemed just an impossibility. Then our Pastor said: 'Well, leave it for tonight, and let me know before chapel in the morning.' Needless to say I got but little rest, and I felt that I must have an overpowering word from the Lord to decide the matter for me. Well, this overpowering word did not come. I feel I want to be perfectly candid with you, dear friends, and to be saved from the deceit which is in my heart. This overpowering word did not come, but some scriptures did come and they spoke to me. One was that former word: 'Give glory to the Lord before He cause darkness'; and it had that effect upon me to make me feel I dare not refuse. And just as I was crossing the road to go to see our pastor, I did feel to want to be doubly sure if it were possible, and that word came upon my heart: 'Ye have not chosen Me, but I have chosen you, and ordained you that ye should go and bring forth fruit.' And so I am here, and I do hope that no feeling of union and friendship (which I would be thankful to believe does exist), but that no such feeling may influence your decision. And may the Lord give you discernment in the matter, so that you may be able to discern whether the thing is of God or of the devil."

Mr. Gosden then preached from Romans 5. 1, and the church was unanimous in accepting his testimony and preaching, so as to send him out into the ministry. This was on January 15th, 1918. From that time calls to preach came quickly from the various Gospel Standard causes, and he soon was felt to be a most acceptable supply. Whenever he was free from military duties he was able to fulfil these engagements, although of course preaching in uniform until demobilisation came about in November of the same year. During the latter months of his army service he was stationed in the Military Hospital in Brighton, which then occupied the new Grammar School which had only just been built, so that he was in his home town and able to attend Galeed Chapel when free to do so. Occasionally he would occupy the pulpit in Mr. Popham's absence, while at the prayer meetings his public prayers were much appreciated and gave further evidence of the ministerial gifts which had been bestowed upon him.

While serving in this Hospital he was very attracted to a young New Zealand soldier who was very ill. He found this young man in deep concern of soul, and whenever opportunity came he would read and pray with him; but he had to endure persecution for this, and was forbidden to do it and given all menial tasks. On one occasion a spirit of rebellion rose up in his heart when told to clean an officer's boots; but in a moment that hymn dropped into his heart: "When I survey the wondrous cross," especially the lines:

> "My richest gain I count but loss
> And pour contempt on all my pride."

His heart was broken and filled with love to the Lord Jesus and his menial duty willingly taken up.

When Mr. Gosden was sent out into the ministry, Mr. Popham had the oversight of the Church at Priory Chapel, Maidstone, and also preached there once or twice a month. Doubtless in course of time he would recommend his son in the faith to the Maidstone friends as a suitable supply minister for them to invite, and we accordingly find Mr. Gosden preaching there on the 22nd February, 1920, and several other times later in the same year. Towards the end of the same year also, at a church meeting at Maidstone held on October 5th, the deacons, Mr. Wakefield and Mr. Harnett, put forward a resolution to the effect that Mr. J. H. Gosden be invited to supply for the first three months in 1922 with a view to the pastorate. Eventually he was called to the pastorate, commencing in January 1925.

From his commencement in the ministry Mr. Gosden's preaching was of a searching and discriminating character, and this feature was maintained throughout his long and useful ministerial life. That it was so at Maidstone the following extract from one of his sermons there will show: "My friends, while I have breath to speak and am permitted to speak to you, as it pleases God to maintain me, I will resist the clamour for widening the way of life, and by God's merciful help will declare unceasingly that there is no way to heaven but by Jesus Christ, and no getting to heaven but by the knowledge of Jesus Christ—Christ not merely in the Scriptures, but Christ in the heart by the teaching of the Holy Ghost."

Mr. Gosden's early usefulness on the Committee of the Gospel Standard Societies, to which he was elected in 1924, is manifest by his having been chosen in those days to serve on the Sub-Committees, both for revising the Rules for admitting ministers to the Gospel Standard List, and for producing a new edition of Gadsby's Hymns. But the time was now arriving when his gracious abilities were to be put to use in a wider and more important sphere. Mr. Popham, who had been Editor of *The Gospel Standard* for thirty years, and of *The Friendly Companion* for the latter half of that period, now felt that he must relinquish this exacting work owing to failing health and advancing years, he having well entered into his eighty-seventh year. At the Annual Meeting of the Societies, in April 1935, it was announced that Mr. Popham had felt compelled to resign his editorship of both magazines, and that the Trustees of the magazines had unanimously appointed Mr. J. H. Gosden to succeed him after the issue of the June number. Referring to this later in the meeting, Mr. Gosden said: "When I consented to assume the responsibility of the magazines, I did so with considerable reluctance, solemnly feeling my unfitness. In agreeing to undertake the matter for the time being, as the Lord may help, I do bespeak your prayers that I may be enabled to sustain that position becomingly with a view to God's glory and the good of the Lord's people and the denomination. Of course it will be exceedingly difficult for me, especially following our aged friend's most able editorship, and I only depend upon the help and grace of God and the prayers of His people."

In the year 1939 the church and congregation at Priory Chapel, Maidstone, presented their Pastor with a cheque to signalize his fifteen years' pastorate, together with an album containing the signatures of the subscribers and an illuminated inscription.

Ten years later a similar presentation to commemorate the conclusion of twenty-five years as Pastor, was accompanied with the following affectionate message: "Our beloved Pastor,—We, the church and congregation over which God has placed you in His holy providence as our pastor and minister for twenty-five years, desire to acknowledge the longsuffering of a covenant-keeping God in maintaining you in our midst, making and keeping you faithful to the charge committed to your trust; also in strengthening and enabling you to reprove and exhort us and feed our souls with the Bread and Water of eternal life."

Yet another testimonial was presented to him on his attaining his seventieth birthday on September 17th, 1952.

Mr. Gosden's further usefulness on the Committee of the Gospel Standard Societies may be seen by his serving on other Sub-committees, such as the War Damage Committee and the Watch Committee, and for some years also on the Bethesda Committee, although he felt it necessary to relinquish the last-mentioned activity in order to confine his time and strength more exclusively to the ministry. After Mr. Raven's death in 1953, he was elected to succeed as the Chairman of the Societies, which position he held until the end. As a recognition of this useful work on the Societies, as well as of his extensive and able labours in the ministry and with the denominational magazines, he was presented at the Annual Meeting of the Societies in 1954 with a testimonial which had subscribers from Gospel Standard Churches all over the country and amounted to £1,131, together with an album of signatures.

Besides the Committee work there was the constant editorial labour with the magazines, from which there was no respite, as month by month the "copy" for the printers had to be sent off promptly to get each issue out at the appropriate time. As Mr. Philpot used to say, the press is always crying, "Give, give," and calls for its monthly quota whatever else may occupy the attention of the Editor. From 1935 until 1950 Mr. Gosden had the management of both denominational magazines, but at the end of 1950 he relinquished *The Friendly Companion*. Even so, the work was onerous, especially as he was approaching the threescore years and ten, and much correspondence was entailed in the editorial labours. Often we believe there would be a pile of letters on his desk awaiting a reply, as his aim always was not to let these extra duties interfere with his pulpit labours, which often necessitated an absence from home for two or three days at a time. Among his other literary publications the *Memoir and Letters of J. K. Popham* was of course his outstanding work, recording as it does the valuable life and labours of his dear old friend and pastor. This was published in 1938 and has received general approval among the lovers of truth, especially in our own denomination. Previously to this he had written papers occasionally for the Sovereign Grace Union, of which *Bunyan; His Doctrine* was published in 1929, and *Faith's Reward* in 1933, both in pamphlet form. Added to these there was the pamphlet on *Believers' Baptism and the Lord's Supper*, which was issued in 1953 and is still obtainable from the Gospel Standard Publications. In 1936 he wrote several articles in the Gospel Standard on *The Church of God*, and from 1938 to 1944 a series of *Comments on the Gospel Standard Articles*, and at one time he considered republishing these together with the *Historical Sketch of the Gospel Standard Baptists;* but this fell through, and eventually the historical work alone was published.

But as we have already remarked all other work had to give way to what he rightly considered of paramount importance, namely the work of the ministry. This solemn occupation of standing between God and men to declare His truth, whether men would hear or forbear, to show to men their fallen and sinful condition, and to preach the gospel as the great and only remedy, was we believe from the outset the one absorbing labour of his ministerial life. After his settlement at Maidstone his chief concern was of course for the little flock there under his charge, and the greater part of his sermons were delivered from the pulpit at Priory Chapel; but on the other hand it may be regarded as a centre from which he travelled far and wide throughout the country preaching in many of our pulpits, both regular services and also at many anniversary and thanksgiving services year after year, as long as his strength would admit. Added to these there were his sermons at the Annual Meetings of the Gospel Standard Societies in April from 1937 until 1964, and also at the Manchester Meetings in September from 1951 until 1956, when he felt the journey too much for his failing strength. Mr. J. K. Popham at his end asked him to help at Galeed Chapel, Brighton, as much as he could, and to this charge he was faithful all through the twenty years of a pastorless state, supplying each year on six Lord's days, as well as on several week evenings.

Nor were his sermons delivered without due preparation, but on the other hand there was a gracious labour beforehand, in his study when at home, or as he could obtain quiet and solitude when away from home; in searching the Scriptures with meditation and prayer to be guided and instructed by the Holy Spirit into the truth. Instrumentally we believe it was due to this previous labour in secret that his sermons were so full of gracious and unctuous matter. A friend in a recent letter gave us an instance of this, when relating what happened on one of the occasional calls which he had to make at Mr. Gosden's house. Being asked into the study, Mr. Gosden said: "Well, Mr.—, you have caught me in my study. Now I will show you something. Some, I know, make it their criterion that they do not know their text until the second hymn is given out, but I do a little preparing beforehand." "Then," the friend continues, "he showed me his rough outline. My impression was that there was a seed of thought, and others arising from it"; by which we understand that the "outline" would be enlarged upon in the pulpit as the Spirit gave utterance and opened up the truth. In this we believe he followed his own pastor, Mr. J. K. Popham, who sometimes jotted down the headings which came into his mind during this preparatory labour, of which also he writes: "The dependence on the Spirit, who separates men for the work whereunto He has called them, in no way militates against a *diligent, prayerful study* of the subject a minister is to handle in the pulpit. He is, as a labourer, to compare scripture with scripture, to store his mind with such matter as he may deem necessary and suitable to his congregation."

Added to his extensive labours, both with the pen and in the pulpit, not to mention denominational and committee matters and the care of the churches, Mr. Gosden suffered a good deal with painful bodily infirmities, especially in these later years. He rarely spoke of his sufferings in this direction, but occasional remarks which appear in his letters, and the nature of his trouble as it came to light in his last days, show that he must have endured a good deal of bodily pain and physical discomfort in addition to his spiritual exercises and labours. In 1950 he was seized with severe pains in the head arising from sinus trouble, which at times seemed so unbearable that he feared he would lose his reason; but he was gradually restored from this sharp affliction and enabled to continue his many activities, except that he felt he must then relinquish the editing of *The Friendly Companion,* which he did at the commencement of 1951 as already mentioned. From about 1953 onwards also, when his wife's health became impaired, he had the added anxiety of her failing condition, which often meant disturbed nights, and he watched her at times with the fear that every breath would be the last. Often for this reason he would make the return journey home after preaching away, instead of staying the night, arriving home frequently in the middle of the night. All these things were a means of wearing down the strength of nature and evidently told upon him with advancing years.

Yet it is little wonder that after the loss of his wife on April 18th, 1962, Mr. Gosden should feel exceedingly disconsolate, himself now approaching the fourscore years. Yet he looked to a higher source for his consolation, as he wrote to a friend at this time: "My life seems sorely and strangely dislocated, but the one thing I want is the abiding presence of the Lord, and to win Him and be found in Him at last." But nature is weak, and the sense of loss, together with a serious report from the doctor as to his own physical condition, brought him very low in body and mind; and the great cruel tempter of the saints took advantage of this weakness by suggesting that after all he was mistaken and would prove to be but a hypocrite. This assailed his dearest hopes and for a time he was brought into great distress of soul, so as to be unable to resume his ministerial labours. But in due season the Lord restored him again and enabled him once more to take up both the ministry and the work of editing *The Gospel Standard.*

He was able to take up some engagements to preach away from home, as well as to his dear flock at Priory, and once more to preach the sermon at the Annual Meeting of the Gospel Standard Societies in April, 1964, although this proved to be the last time. On June 4th, 1964, he preached at the anniversary at Irthlingborough, but returned home and had to take to his bed, suffering much pain. On Tuesday, June 16th, the doctor said he must go into hospital for an operation, and when he was told this he said: "The will of the Lord be done. I can go anywhere and bear anything if I have the Lord's presence." This he had been favoured with, entering into the words of the 31st Psalm: "Into Thine hand I commit my spirit," and "My times are in Thy hand." After asking his brother Frank to read this Psalm, he himself spoke a little in prayer, and then calmly addressed himself to the ordeal before him, insisting on walking downstairs and to the front gate, although with help and much difficulty. His agonizing pain continued until the operation was performed on Friday, June 19th, after which he was somewhat relieved of pain, but very weak. On the following day nature began to sink under the strain, and on the Lord's day morning, June 21st, 1964, he passed away into an eternal Sabbath and entered into rest from his labours, to be for ever with the Lord, in his 82nd year.

The funeral of Mr. Gosden took place on Friday, June 26th, a service being held first at Priory Chapel, Maidstone, and then afterwards the interment in the Brighton and Preston Cemetery in the grave alongside that of his parents, and in which the body of his late dear wife had already been laid. By request of the departed the services were conducted by his friend and fellow-labourer, Mr. Jesse Delves, pastor at Ebenezer Chapel, Clapham, who had also been sent out into the ministry from the church at Galeed, Brighton.

On Saturday, June 20th, the day before he died, he had dictated in the evening the following message to be read to his congregation the next day:

"This is a pass we must all be at (1 Cor. 15. 56, 57). But for the infinite merit of Christ's obedience and death, there could be no hope for eternity. 'The sting of death is sin, and the strength of sin is the law,' and that would send us to hell if left to our own merit; 'but thanks be to God, which giveth us the victory through our Lord Jesus Christ.' The conflict is unspeakably severe, but the Captain of our salvation has gained the victory and entered upon it before His Father's throne. Here we must, by the Holy Spirit's help, plead for it in our own souls as the given victory. Thanks be to God if we gain that victory through our Lord Jesus Christ.

"I cannot write or speak or think, but these are a few thoughts. O may the Lord subdue every enemy, internal, infernal, external! May it be ours indeed to lay hold by faith of the Lord Jesus Christ as our Saviour, Refuge, Righteousness, Sanctification and All in all.

"With love to those who love our Lord Jesus Christ in sincerity. Brethren, pray for us, and may He enrich us each in the truths of the

gospel, and when heart and flesh fail, be the strength of our hearts and
our Portion for ever."

See also:
*Memorial of John Hervey Gosden, 1965*

# SYDNEY FRANK PAUL

## 1883–1971

*T*he following account, written by Mr. Paul's daughter, Mrs. Ruby
Poole, appeared in the Gospel Standard following his death.
   Apart from his Editorship he wrote various books for children, Bible
Animals, Bible People, Bible Prophecies, etc. and several histories of our

*churches. He remembered John Gadsby in his old age—so there was a link with the originator of the* Gospel Standard *in 1835.*

*He and John Gadsby were the only two Editors who were not also preachers. In fact, Mr. Paul never appeared on the platform at the Annual Meetings in connection with the* Gospel Standard.

*Slightly built, very quiet, dignified, gracious, a gentleman of the old stamp, Mr. Paul is lovingly remembered.*

Sydney Frank Paul, a deacon at Galeed Chapel, Brighton, for 40 years, Editor of the *Friendly Companion* 1951–1964, and of the *Gospel Standard* 1964–1970, died on September 30th, 1971, aged 88 years.

He was brought up by godly parents and taken to Galeed Chapel from infancy, but seems to have had no concern for his soul until 1901, when he was 18 years of age. At that time he wrote to a brother, who in reply reproved him for an inconsistent remark in his letter. He writes, "As I read his reproof, there was a conviction in me that something was wrong, and from that time there arose a concern in my soul, which has never really left me to this day." His prayers before that time had been only for temporal things, "but now prayer seemed to spring up from desires and fears felt within."

He now became attentive to the things spoken in the house of God, and, whenever he could do so unobserved, he searched the Scriptures and read the works of good men, with an anxious desire to know the truth. Mr Popham's pamphlet on *Divine Sovereignty* was made a great help to him at this time, and seemed the means of opening to his understanding for the first time the whole truth concerning the fall of man and the great plan of salvation. He also read the lives of godly men, convinced that they were the people of God, and with a desire to find the same teaching with which they had been favoured. Of this time he writes: "There was not the deep conviction and burden of guilt that many have; and O how often has the thought of this been a grievous trouble, making me to doubt whether there had yet been any right beginning—but it was a sense of being short and lacking the knowledge of salvation, with a desire to be made right with God, and to know His teaching and the fear of His name."

When he was appointed Examiner at the Patent Office in London, he had to work with two other men, who were tainted with infidelity—also one of them would break out into oaths and curses at the least provocation. This was a heavy trouble to him, especially as he felt he had not the courage to say anything against them. Continuing about this, he says, "I foolishly said before the Lord that I would rather have the heaviest soul trouble which I could bear in secret before Him than have this trouble which seemed to bring guilt for not speaking openly against wickedness. Shortly after this, the Lord remarkably removed the outward trouble by giving me quieter colleagues, but at the same time left me to fall into great distress of soul. I had taken a room in Croydon to live alone so as to be able to read my books. But my continual loneliness, together with the remembrance of my past sins, was made a means of bringing me extremely low in mind, so that in looking back I have often thought it would be right to say of that time, 'Then had the proud waters gone over my soul, if it had not been the Lord who was on my side.'"

In this despondent state, he was helped in reading a sermon by Mr. Covell, and also by hymn 761:

> "Show pity, Lord; O Lord, forgive;
>   Let a repenting rebel live."

On another occasion, when feeling the hopelessness of his case, these lines from hymn 893 were a comfort:

> "Still follow with thy feeble cries
>   For mercy will prevail."

He appeared to be passing through a trying time spiritually, but was encouraged from time to time—on one occasion by the words in Isaiah 54. 11, together with the whole of the following chapter. Through reading Owen on Sanctification and Augustine's *Confessions*, he was enabled to seek the Lord again with more hope of finding mercy.

At another time, feeling his darkness so much, he prayed, "Lord, show me the way of life, the way of faith." Opening his Bible, his eyes immediately rested on the words in Jeremiah 21. 8, 9: "Thus saith the LORD, Behold, I set before you the way of life, and the way of death. He that abideth in this city shall die by the sword, and by the famine, and by the pestilence, but he that goeth out, and falleth to the Chaldeans that besiege you, he shall live, and his life shall be unto him for a prey." These words seemed a direct answer to his prayer and showed that to abide in the "City of Destruction" was death but to go out of the City (the world) and learn one's own painful captivity, this was the way of life.

Writing further, he says, "In 1906, a way was made for me to come home to Brighton every day, so that I was now favoured to sit constantly under the ministry of Mr. Popham, and at the same time found the journeys to afford opportunity for reading and seeking the Lord. The ministry I found often to be searching, and it was a means of showing me that although the Lord would carry on His work where begun, and would display His sovereignty in the time and manner of blessing those who sought after Him, yet there may be much in ourselves to cause Him to withhold the blessing. I found there was much slothfulness and love of ease, and many things pursued in heart in such a way as to be rivals to Him, and that these things were hindrances to obtaining assurance. How I was again and again distressed with the carnality of my affection, and with the conviction that there was so much in me which preferred the pursuit of natural things, and so little, if any, real love to spiritual things. Fears of death and eternal misery seemed to underlie one's seeking after the Lord, rather than real love for the things of God. Many times there was a struggling to prevail to obtain the blessing, but the heart so much hungered (like Lot in Sodom) after some earthly good or happiness. Fears of being left to utter despair were sometimes heavy, and caused many cries to the Lord to be kept waiting on Him.

"Now and then, helps would seem to be obtained to keep me seeking. One Sunday evening before the service, feeling very carnal and hard, I sat down in a despairing way, and said before the Lord: 'It is no use to go to chapel like this; my heart is as cold and hard as a stone.' Immediately those words came into my mind: 'I say unto you, that God is able *out of these stones* to raise up children unto Abraham.' How timely and encouraging they were, and enabled me to go up eagerly to the house of God, believing that He was able to work a change in me, and to make me a true child of Abraham! At another time, after crying to the Lord over my sad case, the words came gently into my mind: 'I have heard thy prayer, I have seen thy tears'; also the words in Exodus 3. 8: 'I am come down to deliver.' How suitable this seemed to my case! Did He not cause me to light on this sweet promise in His Word?"

During the years following his marriage in 1912 and the birth of his children, he was made to prove what an idolatrous heart he possessed. One thing after another, although lawful in themselves, were pursued after with unlawful affections, thereby hindering him from following the Lord more fully. He felt the only hope of deliverance from this bondage of the affections was by a revelation of the Saviour in his heart, constraining him by His love to live to Him.

In the summer of 1926, while his son was seriously ill, he felt constrained in prayer to vow before God, that if recovery were granted, he would follow Him in His appointed way. This prayer was answered in a remarkable manner, and in consequence he was enabled to go before the church at Galeed, and was baptized in October of that year. In 1930, a few years before the death of Mr. Popham, he was appointed deacon.

Retiring from the Patent Office in 1943, he devoted much time to literary work on behalf of the denomination and served as a member of the Gospel Standard Committee. In 1970 he resigned from the Editorship of the *Gospel Standard*, and began gradually to fail in health. Always very reticent, he said very little about himself, but it appears that for some months he had been under great temptation, but obtained relief on reading 1 Corinthians 10. 13, especially the words: "God is faithful." Also the words found in Amos 5. 9 were a great help and comfort to him. After being able to attend most services until the last two weeks of his life, he failed somewhat rapidly and passed away to be forever with the Lord.

The interment was in the Brighton and Preston Cemetery on the 5th October.

*Note by his pastor, Mr. F. L. Gosden:*
The lamentable but blessed death of our beloved friend, Sydney Frank Paul, is a serious loss to the denomination and especially to the church at Galeed, Brighton.

During the six years as Editor of the *Gospel Standard*, he maintained that spiritual standard which from its inception has imbued its pages with heavenly doctrine and experimental truth. His many volumes of denominational history will have enriched our bookshelves with interesting reading for the young, and spiritually edifying to others. The Committee mourns a gracious colleague whose sound judgment was a support and of great value in resolving difficult matters.

All his natural gifts and qualifications were tempered with the fear and grace of God. He was a man of unusual self control, and was enabled to maintain the tranquility of faith in the midst of deep sorrows and severe conflicts. These gracious qualities made him a pillar in the church at Galeed where he used the office well.

Personally I have lost a loyal and affectionate friend. Although a man of few words, there was an influence even in his silence. He felt things inwardly, things both natural and spiritual. He was never demonstrative, but by dignified sobriety magnified his office. The spirit of such a character is diffusive, and has left behind a gracious savour.